Legal and Ethical Concerns in Treating Kidney Failure

LEGAL AND ETHICAL CONCERNS IN TREATING KIDNEY FAILURE

Case Study Workbook

Edited by

Eli A. Friedman

State University of New York,
Health Science Center at Brooklyn, NY, U.S.A.

SPRINGER-SCIENCE+BUSINESS MEDIA, B.V.

A C.I.P. Catalogue record for this book is available from the Library of Congress.

ISBN 978-94-010-5875-9 ISBN 978-94-011-4355-4 (eBook)
DOI 10.1007/978-94-011-4355-4

Printed on acid-free paper

Originally published by Kluwer Academic Publishers in 2000
Softcover reprint of the hardcover 1st edition 2000

Dedication

Mildred (Barry) Friedman, my wife of forty years, was the stimulus for often troubled thinking that conceived, nurtured, and ultimately gave birth to this book. Barry's innate morality combined with exceptional insight into those forces, virtuous and dark, that drive us to do what we do, unmasked behavior patterns that I might have denied existed. Barry, a diabetic kidney transplant recipient, devoted her energy and considerable writing ability to improving the welfare and life quality of kidney patients. Reading her comments on Cases 1 through 22 is unnerving as it is as if Barry is in the room sharing her wisdom with ease, as was her habit. Barry died before submitting her analyses of Cases 23 and 24 though I have learned so much from her that I can almost hear what she intended to say and incorporated these inferences into my comments.

Table of Contents

CONTRIBUTORS

John D. Bower, M.D.
Professor of Medicine
Chief, Division of Nephrology and Hypertension
University of Mississippi Medical Center
Jackson, Mississippi

Judith E. Columbo*
Secretary, Renal Disease Division
State University of New York
Health Science Center at Brooklyn
Treasurer, Mildred (Barry) Friedman Chapter
American Association of Kidney Patients

Amy L. Friedman, M.D.
Assistant Professor of Surgery
Department of Surgery
Yale University, College of Medicine
New Haven, Connecticut

Eli A. Friedman, M.D.
Chairman, Medical Advisory Board
American Association of Kidney Patients
Distinguished Teaching Professor
Department of Medicine
State University of New York
Health Science Center at Brooklyn
Brooklyn, New York

Mildred (Barry) Friedman (Deceased)*
President, Diabetic Kidney Transplant Self-Help Group
Columnist, Renal Family
American Association of Kidney Patients
Brooklyn, New York

Carl M. Kjellstrand M.D., Ph.D.
Adjunct Professor State University of New York Health Science Center at Brooklyn and University of Alberta, Clinical Professor Loyola University Medical School
Vice President Medical Affairs
AKSYS Corporation
Lincolnshire, Illinois

Monique Janelle London, J.D.*
Board of Directors
American Association of Kidney Patients
Patient Affairs Committee
United Network for Organ Sharing
Consumer Action Committee
ESRD Network 17
San Francisco, California

Robert J. Pristave, B.A., J.D.
Chairman, Health Care Department
Senior Partner
Ross & Hardies
Counsel, Renal Physicians Association
Chicago, Illinois

Katie L. Watson, B.A., J.D.
Associate, Health Care Department
Ross & Hardies
Senior Fellow
University of Chicago/Pritzker School of Medicine
MacLean Center for Clinical Medical Ethics
Board Member, Chicago Clinical Ethics Programs
Chicago, Illinois

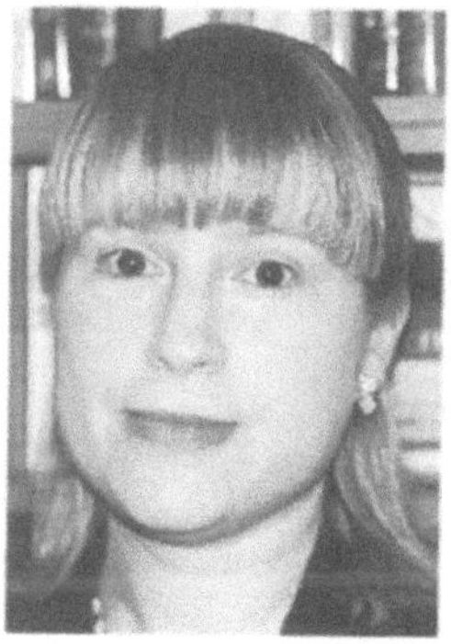

Connie Zuckerman, J.D.
Formerly, Assistant Professor Of Humanities in
Medicine and Family Medicine
Coordinator of Legal Studies
Division of Humanities in Medicine
State University of New York
Health Science Center at Brooklyn
Brooklyn, New York
Bioethics Consultant
White Plains, New York

---

* Kidney transplant recipient

PREFACE
Eli A. Friedman, M.D.

Attendance at our Renal Disease Division's Morning Report almost immediately illustrates the pervasive intermixing of medicine, law, and ethics comprising the everyday practice of nephrology. Situated in the inner-city, we manage more than 250 newly presented patients in end-stage renal disease (ESRD) annually. Throughout the 1960s, we gradually appreciated the impact of Belding Scribner's formulation of a regimen for life prolongation after kidney failure. Estimates of the number of Americans who might benefit from ESRD therapy suggested a top limit of about 50,000 patients. To be accepted by a dialysis program one had to be between age 18 and 45, employed or a full time student, have renal disease and no other serious disorder, and be a US citizen. Obvious, in retrospect, the majority of suitable *candidates* for life extension after onset of kidney failure were never referred to the few kidney centers and of those evaluated, a selection process chose those who were considered most suitable while the remainder died.

As program after program confirmed Scribner's report, the number of treated ESRD patients began to rise sharply a growth stimulated by the incredible passage of legislation to include renal failure as a Medicare funded therapy. Removing any arbitrary upper restriction on the number of treated dialysis patients prompted a remarkable expansion in the number of facilities and the intrusion of established and new corporations as dialysis providers. By the 1980s, ESRD was big business with some entrepreneurs able to generate tens of millions of profit dollars as total Medicare expenditures passed $2 billion.

Throughout the last decade of the 20th Century, ESRD therapy continued to increase at an annual rate of about 9%. Incident patients were of progressively older age and were likely to be afflicted by diabetes and geriatric disorders. Advances in immunosuppression made the transplant experience attractive with a first-year cadaver functional graft rate above 90%. Peritoneal dialysis, encouraged by many nephrologists was viewed as a satisfactory - if not preferred - modality for many ESRD patients. Thus, nor only availability of any ESRD treatment but application of the preferred modality became concerns for the renal team. With universal acceptance for ESRD therapy, the obverse issue of who would be best untreated emerged. Were there rational criteria for denying treatment in cancer, old age, or extreme debility? Should the expense of ESRD therapy be restricted to citizens?

Are parents able to consent to removal (donation) of a child's kidneys? These and other bothersome challenges stimulated my preparation of the present volume. After knocking on doors of consultants including the hospital counsel, ethics committee, and multi-denominational clergy, I was left dissatisfied with the failure to provide lucid and understandable guidance. I came to respect the term psychobabble. Lessons learned while substituting for one vital organ might- at least in large part - be transposed to other organ systems. Examination of the legal and ethical ramifications of renal replacement therapy offers insight into what is to be expected in the near future when liver, heart, and lung substitution become routine medicine.

The 24 "hypothetical" cases submitted for your analysis derive from my actual practice of nephrology. Details have been modified to emphasize a single issue in most instances. By resort to lawyers, medical doctors, and articulate patient advocates each an expert with a record of excellence, it is my intent to assemble the best answers that might be synthesized. The reader is encouraged to study each case and write an opinion before seeing the resolutions of others. If in the process you are stimulated to think about what was otherwise routine, I will have succeeded.substitution become routine medicine.

The 24 "hypothetical" cases submitted for your analysis derive from my actual practice of nephrology. Details have been modified to emphasize a single issue in most instances. By resort to lawyers, medical doctors, and articulate patient advocates each an expert with a record of excellence, it is my intent to assemble the best answers that might be synthesized. The reader is encouraged to study each case and write an opinion before seeing the resolutions of others. If in the process you are stimulated to think about what was otherwise routine, I will have succeeded.

Editor's Note

John Bower is a personal friend. As he confronted the threat to his program's integrity and function posed by what amounted to an assault by a hostile patient, I watched from a safe distance. With dismay I observed abandonment by the judiciary, condemnation by external critics, and the absence of constructive advice from any source. A decade later, my dialysis unit was forced to cope with a similar attack on reason and rationality by an angry noncompliant patient. The genesis of the concept of this book includes a seed sown by Bower in distress.

When I was unable to find an epilogue to his patient's course, who while discharged, had to be retained, I became intrigued with the extensive substitution of Orwellian *doublethink* for common sense. I then pleaded with Bower to recount the subsequent events and any "truths" that he was able to extract from the experience.

FOREWORD

Brown Versus Bower - The Rest of the Story

Everybody thinks the answer is at the courthouse. Don't count on it!

On December 21, 1987 in Civil Action No. 086-0759 (B) in the United States District Court, Southern District of Mississippi, Jackson, Mississippi, Judge William H. Barbour, J.D. ruled that Dr. John Bower, Kidney Care, Inc., B.F. Simmons of the Division of Medicaid, and Dr. Thomas Brittain of the Department of Welfare were dismissed from any obligation with prejudice.[Endnote 1] The University Medical Center was ordered to continue providing Michael Brown chronic hemodialysis treatment as long as he was a resident of the service area of the University Medical Center on the condition that Michael Brown shall be accompanied by some member of his family during the time that he is receiving treatment and shall not engage in abusive speech or conduct while receiving treatment and shall conform to a reasonable regimen or self treatment and diet prescribed by the treating physician. The justification for this decision against the Medical Center was based upon the community service assurance required by the Hill-Burton Act to provide treatment for patients in the area of the hospital receiving these funds. The litigation actually lasted over eighteen months channeling through many federal and state regulations including The Civil Rights Act, The Americans With Disabilities Act, the ESRD regulations, Medicare regulations, and several others. The defendant in the case relied upon the 13th Amendment to the Constitution of the United States stating that we could not be forced into involuntary servitude. The lawyer defending the Medical Center called the Hill-Burton Act to the attention of the judge; not a real wise move.

In an act of desperation, the judge forced the Medical Center to perform these treatments for Michael Brown under the Hill-Burton Act. Dr. Bower, as the Medical Director of the University Medical Center's Dialysis Program, was therefore required to treat Michael Brown. We won the litigation which was extremely important because no physician should be forced into accepting a patient against his will. Had we not won this lawsuit, physicians could be forced into accepting patients against their will. In summary, we won, but we lost.

Michael Brown continued to completely ignore the court order. He remained extremely noncompliant. His family disowned him. He continued to miss dialysis treatments, show up frequently in the Emergency Room in pulmonary edema under the influence of drugs, and remained in complete violation of the court order. When confronted with this disruptive reality, the judge simply stated that there was nothing else that he could do. Michael Brown continued with his antisocial behavior. Finally one night in a "borrowed car" when he was trying to outrun the police, he was unable to navigate a turn at over 100 mph, missed the turn, was thrown from the car, and crushed by the car rolling over him. He came to the Emergency Room at the University Medical Center alive but seriously injured. His brain apparently intact. He sustained severe chest injuries. The attending physician in the Emergency Room notified me. Since the Emergency Room staff knew Mr. Brown too well, the question arose as to how aggressive should they be at resuscitative efforts. The attending physician was told to do everything possible including open chest massage. Despite comprehensive and rapid therapy, he died. Again, we lost.

The reason for the reluctance on the part of the physician to accept this patient was based upon a ten year track record of misconduct. The patient had two kidney transplants and rejected both when he refused to take the provided immunosuppressive medicines. He had two attempts with peritoneal dialysis with multiple episodes of peritonitis. Hemodialysis in a limited care facility was a constant verifiable challenge. One day the patient did not show up for dialysis, and two weeks later we were called from a dialysis facility about 300 miles away stating that he was there and they were trying to get rid of him. Under a court order in that community, the facility was forced to dialyze him against his will including if necessary gagging and binding as indicated. When he requested to return to Jackson, Mississippi, I refused to accept him. My refusal to accept him was due to the fact that after ten years of trying, I was unable to manage this patient. It was my feeling that the patient needed more guidance and discipline than I could provide, and I knew that the management would be virtually impossible. This was not an issue of rejecting a noncompliant patient as much as it was an issue of refusing to establish a doctor-patient relationship. Again, we won on the 13th Amendment of the Constitution of the United States, but we lost because we ended up with Michael. The trial was interesting. The physician was basically alone with many adversaries.

In November, 1988 in the American Kidney Fund's Nephrology Letter, an article appeared entitled The Yangtze Syndrome.[Endnote 2] The Yangtze Syndrome is based upon a Chinese philosopher who described 3,000 years ago a concept foreign to our current culture. The Chinese proverb stated "Pull man from Yangtze, responsible for man's life". This is the position that the physician is in with the delivery of dialysis services. If we save a person's life with our technologies specifically dialysis and transplantation, we find ourselves responsible for that man's life. Withdrawal after the initiation of dialysis treatment becomes virtually impossible in our society. This concept of life long responsibility is being played out now in the dialysis and transplant community. The reason is that our treatment is very powerful. It can completely change the course of an otherwise 100% fatal disease.[Endnote 3]

For the first time in history, we can replace the function of a vital organ system. With this power responsibility shifts. The ethics community juggling beneficence, non-maleficence, and autonomy invariably came up with a simple solution; the physician is responsible. Psychiatry actually filed an amicus curiae on the behalf of the plaintiff stating that no physician has a right to refuse to accept a patient or refuse to establish a doctor-patient relationship if the patient is in need of the physician's services. This was somewhat paradoxical coming from the subspecialty of medicine that refuses more patients than any other field of medicine. The members of the clergy in our community felt that it was the Christian thing to do for the physician to treat any person in need. No help here either. A famous bishop once stated "that for $30.00 and in 30 minutes, he could find a verse of scripture to justify anything".

In the absence of any support from ethicists, psychiatrists, or clergy, we turned to the judiciary. In the judiciary, we won, but we lost.

The Yangtze Syndrome is very much alive in dialysis. The moral and ethical problems that we have precipitated by the nature of our therapy have not been approached comprehensively. Our technology is many years ahead of the social sciences and religion that might be used for addressing such problems. Neither the clergy, the ethicists, psychiatrists, or the judiciary proved to be of any benefit.

As it stands in the present state of the art, there appears to be only one solution to these dilemmas. We will find this solution in the most sacred part of our profession. This is the doctor-patient relationship. The nephrologists as the primary care physician must shoulder this responsibility as the Brown Versus Bower case so typically exemplified. The physician must approach these problems with what is in the best interest of the patient as his primary goal. The physician then must rely on his support team derived from all sources available to him including ethics, judiciary, psychiatry, and social services. The physician then must decide not based upon economics or any other factor but doing what is best for the patient. The buck stops here.

This book edited by Dr. Eli A. Friedman of Downstate Medical Center in Brooklyn attempts to address these major burning issues confronted by the nephrologists in practice. None of us have the answer, but this book does take a bold step forward in identifying these issues in a clear and concise manner with the hope that we can find solutions to these dilemmas that we have created with our technology. I strongly recommend this book for every nephrologist providing therapy for end-stage renal disease as well as for those members of the renal team who may be forced into contact with difficult kidney patients.

FOREWORD
Robert J. Pristave, J.D.

I have been involved as an attorney representing clients providing dialysis services to patients since the inception of the End-Stage Renal Disease Program in 1973. In the early years, the provision of services to dialysis patients was accomplished by teams of nephrologists, nurses, technicians and social workers utilizing primarily hospital-based dialysis units. Since that time, the delivery of care has evolved so it is now provided by a range of providers including physician-owned dialysis facilities, hospitals and large chain providers. Further, there is not a region of the United States that does not have dialysis care available to its population.

Along with the business and technological evolution of dialysis, there has also been an evolution of ethical and legal issues generated by complex factual circumstances that are faced by the dialysis team. Eli A. Friedman, as general editor of this book has provided a very valuable resource for, not only the health care professionals involved in dialysis care, but for also attorneys and ethicists. The chapters in this book are designed to be problem-solving scenarios that allow the reader to stretch his or her mind and become immersed in the methodology of legal and ethical dilemmas. These problem-solving scenarios will be rewarding for those who work through them and also provide useful guidance for real life problems.

HOW TO USE THIS WORKBOOK

Medical ethics was a silent subject for me in medical school and housestaff training. I did not require formal instruction to understand that patients had dignity and that every aspect of their treatment was based on their trust and belief that their welfare must be my primary concern. This simple construct was blown away in 1963 with the success of our first federally funded hemodialysis unit which was the only recourse east of the Mississippi for patients in renal failure. Suddenly, I had the terrible power - by selection or exclusion for dialysis - to determine "Who Shall Live?" Like the Seattle pioneers in uremia therapy, we established a committee to evaluate each potential dialysis candidate and attempted to chose worthy from less worthy individuals for salvage. After attending these meetings, listening to reports from social workers, psychiatrists, and clergy purporting to supply data that would permit rating one person over another, I felt demeaned and depressed. In fact, the induced angst was a beginning awareness that forces other than my opinion must determine what is the "correct thing" for me to do.

Then came the lawyers. Cunning and thorough, these professionals inflicted a new dimension to medical practice. No longer could physicians drive their actions solely by an inner morality. The concept of defensive medicine was born, meaning that a paper trail must be in place to "defend" every substantive service. Finally, governmental regulators and health maintenance organizations (HMOs) defined and now micromanage every aspect of healthcare delivery. Physicians lost freedom and independence. To an old timer, medicine in the 21st century can be frightening and dehumanizing. Medicine, however, has always been a calling in tumult, with the pace of evolutionary change constantly accelerating. Just as the profession was able to cope with Flexner's three reports, in 1910, that forced closure of half the medical schools because of poor performance[Endnote 4], it will prevail and indeed flourish despite monitoring, law suits, and constraints of HMOs. Accordingly, with optimism that there will still be doctors treating patients for the foreseeable future, I thought it worthwhile to collect and dissect what we know about the obligations - legal and ethical - that impact on the treatment of patients in renal failure.

Toward this end, I collected these 24 patient summaries, each presenting ethical questions arising in delivery of treatment for end-stage kidney disease (ESRD). Given the exceptional cost ($70,000 annually for maintenance hemodialysis in US), high mortality (23% first year loss on dialysis in US), and current rationing (variable by nation and other criteria), exclusion of some uremic patients is widely practiced. Kidney transplantation is more cost effective over several years and has a lower mortality but strong physician bias directs who in the "pool" of dialysis patients will be referred (waitlisted) for a cadaver donor organ.

Each of the study cases is drawn from clinical experience at a large inner city municipal kidney program. After thinking through your reaction to the issues generated by the specific patient, take the time to write your answers to the exercise questions. Read the opinion of skilled and outstanding attorneys conversant with nephrology's stresses. Then note reactions of a transplant surgeon, a senior nephrologist, and two articulate kidney patients. Finally, compare your conclusions with that of the Editor and concur or disagree. Physician's comments and references appear as endnotes while those by attorneys are listed as footnotes. Consult the references for further study. For some stressful exceptionally difficult questions (Such as "Should a child a kidney donor,?" there is no correct answer though forcefully stated opinions and a dedicated chapter are proffered.

Your comments as to the morality and correctness of proposed resolutions may concur or be at variance with those included. Criticism and suggestions are solicited and will be welcome as a resource for constructing subsequent editions of this workbook.

Editor's Note

Whether in morning report for our renal service or informal polling of colleagues, few issues provoke as much heated discussion as the question of organ removal (?donation) by children or mentally unaware adults. Upon completion of the analysis of contributors remarks about the study cases, I realized that a more extensive analysis was needed for this subject. Fortunately, through friendship, I was able to entice Robert J. Pristave, who together with his associate Katie L. Watson, both established authorities in the broad field of kidney law, to tackle two vexing aspects of the discipline with the charge to produce a neutral critique. The essay that follows is both scholarly and complete while still disturbing. Ultimately, even though permitted by the court, each of us will have to decide for our self whether to countenance the purportedly *safe* and *non-life-threatening* surgery for these two special cohorts. Bear in mind that these are otherwise healthy individuals about to be subjected to surgical "assault" who depend on the law and our morality for their protection.

KIDNEY DONATION BY CHILDREN AND THE MENTALLY HANDICAPPED: EVOLUTION OF PRECEDENT

Robert J. Pristave, J.D. and Katie L. Watson, J.D.

A working knowledge of law and ethics is indispensable to every nephrologist's daily practice. Therefore, this casebook offers a practical guide to the legal and ethical issues raised by twenty five different scenarios common to kidney failure. Each of the casebook's twenty five scenarios is followed by a legal response which thoroughly discusses the relevant court cases and statutes.

The goal of this chapter is to clarify some of the legal concepts a non-lawyer must understand in order to comprehend the detailed legal analysis that follows each scenario. These legal concepts will be highlighted through a review of cases concerning kidney donation by children and by mentally handicapped persons ("incompetents"). These pivotal cases provide an excellent illustration of how courts construct legal standards in response to new technologies, and the relationship between law and nephrology. Comprehension of the evolution of these precedents will assist the non-lawyer in comprehending other areas of health law as well.

Because this chapter focuses exclusively on law, a word about the relationship between law and ethics is in order. In medicine, the law should be considered a floor. The fact that a particular action is legal says nothing about whether that action is good, desirable or "the right thing to do." The answers to those questions are the province of medical ethics. Simply put, law defines what physicians *may* do, and ethics addresses what physicians *should* do. One reason disparate outcomes between legal and ethical analyses sometimes occur is that American law is based on principles of individual rights. In contrast, though most ethical frameworks include an autonomy principle, they balance that autonomy principle with considerations of beneficence, nonmaleficence and justice between interested parties.[Footnote 1]

When Boston's Peter Bent Brigham Hospital ("the Brigham") performed the first successful kidney transplant from a living donor in 1954, it established kidney transplant as unique among organ transplant surgeries. The involvement of a living donor created an unprecedented situation: removal of a healthy organ from a healthy individual for the benefit of another.[Footnote 2] Though both medically and culturally radical, transplants between competent adult donors and recipients did not present a legal challenge. The patient's informed consent transforms what would otherwise be a battery into a permissible procedure, and a legal system based on individual rights will allow a competent adult to consent to almost any procedure she or he wants. Conversely, a legal system based on individual rights will not balance the risk to the donor with the benefit to the recipient. Courts will not force a competent adult to donate an organ, even if donation would be the altruistic and ethical choice.

When the potential donor is not competent, either by reason of age or mental status, concepts of individual rights are not as clear. Incompetents cannot offer informed consent. Parents and guardians has authorization to consent to medical treatment on behalf of an incompetent, but removal of a healthy organ is not medical treatment for that individual. Therefore, when the first kidney transplant between children was proposed in 1956, courts were required to answer the unique questions the procedure raised: Does anyone have authority to consent to removal of an incompetent's healthy kidney? Who? Is altruism sometimes in an incompetent's "best interest"? When?

Before we embark on this case study, a word about the structure of the American legal system is in order. The maddening "maybe" of lawyers is often a product of the American judiciary's system of precedent. In some cases, a statute or a court decision from your jurisdiction will provide a direct answer to your legal question. More often, definitive sources of law will not provide an answer. In those situations, your lawyer is making an educated guess based on analogous judicial opinions. Judicial opinions are collectively called "common law," or "case law." Case law can be generated by the federal court system, or it can be generated by any one of the fifty state court systems, each of which has three or more layers of review. For example, the cases involving incompetent kidney donors span six different states, and they arise from courts ranging from probate court (one of the lowest) to state supreme courts (the highest). Lawyers use existing case law to project outcomes in similar cases. For example, a court in your jurisdiction may have resolved a similar legal issue in a different factual context, and the principles in that opinion apply to your legal issue. Alternatively, a court in a different state may have resolved the precise legal issue you confront. The courts of your state are not bound to follow this decision, but they may consider its logic and conclusions when they confront the same type

[1] E.g., Jonsen, Siegler & Winslade, *Clinical Ethics* (McGraw-Hill 1998, 4th Ed.); Beauchamp & Childress, *Principles of Biomedical Ethics* (Oxford University Press 1994, 4th Ed.).

[2] Bone marrow donation involves living donors, but it does not remove an organ or require major surgery. Removal of a liver lobe from living donors may provide a parallel to kidney donation, but to date, it only involves adult donors and has not been the subject of litigation.

of case.

At first glance this system sounds like pure chaos, and of course, sometimes it is. But we encourage you to think of the development of common law, as illustrated by the incompetent kidney donor cases, as analogous to the development of new medical therapies. There is always a period of trial-and-error before a protocol is established. The outcomes of the first cases are watched closely and the approach is adjusted accordingly. In law, and perhaps in medicine as well, the relevant concept is "percolation." Issues bubble up across the country and lower courts resolve them in different ways. Though this creates inconsistencies, it also allows the issue to be considered from many angles. Ideally, this period of "experimentation" either leads to consensus in the courts, or it informs legislatures when they attempt to resolve the issue definitively.

The Legal History of Kidney Donation by Children and Incompetent Donors

Courts only have jurisdiction over cases which present an actual controversy, and the scope of the opinion they write can only extend to the facts of the case before them. (Any language addressing issues outside those fact is called "dicta," and is not a binding part of the decision.) Therefore, unlike a legislature, courts cannot be pro-active and anticipate issues. This results in an inevitable delay between the development of new technology and resolution of the legal issues the technology raises. Therefore, the first legal cases concerning child kidney donors arose only when the first medical cases arose, and the Massachusetts courts and the Brigham tackled the issues together.

In 1954, the Brigham performed the first successful kidney transplant. The donor and recipient were adult identical male twins. In 1956, parents of three sets of minor identical twins asked the Brigham to perform kidney transplants between each twin set. One potential donor, Leonard Madsen, was 19 years old (the age of majority at the time was 21) and two potential donors, Carl Foster and Ms. Huskey, were 14 years old. In 1957, the Brigham asked the Massachusetts courts for a declaratory ruling authorizing the transplants. Declaratory judgment is a procedural mechanism that allows parties that have no conflict between them to go to court and receive a ruling on whether what they propose to do is legal. Hospitals seek judicial approval of kidney donation by an incompetent because without it, the donor could potentially sue the hospital later for removing a kidney without proper informed consent. Therefore, although judicial approval of kidney donation by incompetents is essentially a mechanism to protect hospitals from liability, the practical fact is that both parental, hospital and judicial permission is required before an incompetent can donate a kidney.

The 1957 minor twin cases required Massachusetts' lower courts to apply existing law concerning incompetents to an endeavor which the law had never before contemplated, the new technology of transplant.[Footnote 3] The potential donors

[3] *Madsen v. Harrison,* No. 68651 Eq., Mass. Sup. Jud. Ct., June 12, 1957; *Huskey v. Harrison,* No. 68666 Eq., Mass. Sup. Jud. Ct., August 30, 1957; *Foster v. Harrison,* No. 68674 Eq., Mass Sup. Jud. Ct., November 20, 1957. These unpublished opinions are quoted and discussed in William J. Curran, *A Problem of Consent: Kidney Transplantation in Minors,* 34 N.Y.U. Law Rev. 891 (1959).

were not competent adults, so existing law on informed consent did not apply. Because the potential donors were children, existing law authorized their parents to make decisions concerning their medical treatment. But removing a healthy organ does not constitute medical treatment for the donor, so consent to kidney donation was outside of what parents could legally authorize. Therefore, the Massachusetts courts were required to either apply a traditional standard (such as the "best interest," "substituted judgment" or "mature minor" standards) to resolve the question of who can authorize a surgery with no medical benefit to the incompetent and when it can be authorized, or the courts could create a new standard that was unique to the facts.

Each of the three Massachusetts trial courts that considered the 1957 cases floundered. All three judges allowed the healthy children to donate, but each judge failed to develop a clear standard by which hospitals could evaluate future cases. The decisions do not turn exclusively on a "mature minor" standard, although each decision noted the "assent" offered by the nineteen and fourteen year old donors, stating that the children were mature enough to weigh the risks and benefits of the procedure. The decisions do not turn exclusively on a best interest standard, but they do accept psychiatric testimony that donation will benefit the children psychologically. This may be the most important contribution of the Massachusetts cases - they take the leap of considering psychological benefit to be as significant as physical benefit in a traditional evaluation of a child's medical "best interests."[Footnote 4] But ultimately, the Massachusetts courts review the facts of each case and punt. It's as if each judge decided that psychological benefit plus the minor's assent put the donation back in the realm of "medical treatment" because it was a physical invasion in the minor's best interest, and therefore back in the realm of parental decision making. This might be a reasonable standard, but it is not explicitly spelled out as such. Because both the hospital and the parents wanted the transplants to go forward, there was no "loser" to appeal the cases to a higher court for clarification.

Interestingly, the Massachusetts courts chose not to publish the three cases of minor identical twins decided in 1957. Similarly, the Massachusetts courts continued to decide cases concerning incompetent kidney donors after 1957[Footnote 5], but every single one of these cases is unavailable for review, either because they are not published or, in some cases, because the court impounded the record at the request of plaintiff Massachusetts General Hospital.[Footnote 6] Courts refuse to publish opinions when they don't want them to be used as precedent for future cases. That is decision is surprising in the cases of incompetent kidney donors,

[4] The introduction of social science evidence like the testimony of psychiatrists was still novel in 1957. The introduction of social science evidence was pioneered in 1954 in *Brown v. Board of Education*, 347 U.S. 483 (1954), when the Supreme Court relied on psychological testimony regarding the effects of segregation on African-American school children.
[5] For example, between 1970 and 1973, the Massachusetts courts decided more than seven additional cases of incompetent kidney donors in unpublished opinions. See, Charles H. Baron et. al, *Live Organ and Tissue Transplants from Minor Donors in Massachusetts*, 55 Boston U. Law Rev. 159 (1975).
[6] *Id.*

given their novelty, general interest and importance. One interpretation of the Massachusetts courts' unwillingness to publish is that the courts did not have confidence in their reasoning and/or outcome, and did not want to influence other courts' ability to come up with alternate approaches. Medicine was tussling with kidney transplants alongside the Massachusetts courts. Dolores Husky and Clyde Foster, the fourteen year old kidney recipients, died a few months after their transplants. Though their donor siblings had the psychological benefit of having tried everything they could, they did not reap the benefit of a living sibling (or, alternatively, avoid the detriment of the death of a sibling).

Because the cases that arose in Massachusetts in the fifteen year period after 1957 are all unpublished, a 1972 case involving a living donor transplant from a seven year old in Connecticut has the distinction of being the first and only published opinion concerning kidney donation from a mentally competent child. In *Hart v. Brown*, 289 A.2d 386 (Conn. Super.Ct. 1972), the parents of seven year old twins sought the court's approval for a kidney donation from Margaret to Katheleen. Katheleen was expected to die unless she received a transplant soon, and Margaret was the best match. The parents had offered their own kidneys, but use of a parent's kidney would require Katheleen to begin an immunosuppressive regimen with significant side effects, and would have only a fifty percent chance of success after five years. The Connecticut court concluded that Margaret strongly identified with her sister and would be saddened by her death, and that it would be better for Margaret to grow up in a happy family rather than one distressed by the loss of a child. Margaret's guardian ad litem agreed with these conclusions, and seven year old Margaret offered her assent to the procedure. The Connecticut court permitted the donation. It did not offer a clear standard, but instead stated that it was legal, under these facts, for parents to balance the interests of one child against the other and to consent to both operations as they saw fit. The court essentially reviewed the pros and cons of the procedure in relation to the entire family unit, found that the decision to transplant was reasonable, and therefore gave the decision back to the parents as within the realm of traditional parental medical decision making.

In addition to its status as a published opinion, *Hart* is distinguished from the Massachusetts cases by the fact that the court appointed a guardian ad litem ("GAL") to represent the donor's interests exclusively. The American court system is an adversarial one, premised on a passive judge which must rely on each of two sides to present the best competing arguments. In actions for declaratory judgment, both the hospital and the parents agree that the child should donate a kidney. Therefore, unless a GAL is appointed to argue on behalf of the child's interest in *not* donating, a court cannot provide the rigorous examination of competing interests that is required. In addition, resolution of two conflicting arguments requires courts to articulate standards for their decisions. Arguably, the presences of a GAL on behalf of the donor would have helped the Massachusetts courts develop a clearer standard in the 1957 cases. Therefore, although a declaratory judgment action requires families to go to court at particular difficult times, the potential donor deserves and requires the appointment of a GAL to represent his or her individual interests. It is natural for both parents and the recipient's physician to balance interess across the family. The GAL is the only voice that speaks for the incompetent as an individual.

Kidney Donation by Mentally Handicapped Persons

The approaches used for child kidney donors cannot be applied to mentally handicapped donors without some modification. For example, some of the psychological benefit of kidney donation may accrue to a child in the future, when she or he is old enough to truly comprehend the gift she or he made and its consequences for the recipient. The same growth potential is not available to most mentally handicapped persons. As a result, the psychological benefit of kidney donation to a six year old donor and a donor with a mental age of six may differ. In addition, courts have a heightened concern with protecting the mentally handicapped from exploitation. The four published cases which consider mentally handicapped potential donors employ two different standards, the substituted judgment standard and the best interest standard. Two of the cases approve the donation and two refuse it.

Strunk v. Strunk, 445 S.W.2d 145 (Ky.Ct.App. 1969) was the first adjudicated case regarding living kidney donation from a mentally handicapped person, and it is one of two opinions on incompetent donors to come from a state supreme court. The case of Tom Strunk, an institutionalized 27 year old retarded man with a mental age of 6 whose parents wanted him to donate a kidney to his 28 year old brother Tom, was heard in a County Court, a Circuit Court, the Court of Appeals before it ended up in the Kentucky Supreme Court in 1969. In each case, the court allowed the donation, and Tom's GAL appealed the decision, arguing that the state never has the power to authorize the removal of an organ from the body of an incompetent who is a ward of the state. Finally, the Kentucky Supreme Court allowed the donation by a vote of 4-3. The thorough review this case received, and the well-articulated and closely won opinion it produced, was arguably a result of Tom's GAL's vigorous advocacy.
The Kentucky Supreme Court asserted that it was applying the doctrine of "substituted judgement," which asks what the incompetent would do if she or he were competent. Tom was the only family member who matched his brother Jerry, and Jerry would die if Tom did not donate a kidney. The court concluded that Tom would miss Jerry's visits if he died, and speculated that Jerry might take care of Tom after their parents died. In this exercise, the court found that because of the close relationship between the brothers, the loss of a brother would be worse for Tom than the loss of a kidney. The three justices that dissented from the majority opinion disagreed with the majority's assessment of the psychological impact Jerry's death would have on Tom, arguing that a six year old does not grieve the death of a loved one for long. In addition, the dissenters raised the specter of Nazi experimentation in explaining why they could not bring themselves to grant the state power to remove organs from incompetents unless significant benefit to the incompetent was proven. The benefit in this case did not rise to the level the dissent would term "significant."

The *Strunk* court's use of the "substituted judgment" standard is problematic, because two factors prevent the application of a true substituted judgment for incompetent kidney donors. First, it is impossible to ascertain what a never-competent patient, such as a child or a mentally handicapped person, would have done if competent. Unlike an elderly patient with dementia, there is no competent life history to evaluate in order to determine what a retarded person or a child "would have" done if they were not retarded or six. The court can only guess what a hypothetical person might do, or what it thinks the potential donor ought to do. That is not truly "substituted judgment." Second, courts presume that human beings act in their own best interests. Therefore, when a court asks what the incompetent potential donor "might have done if competent," the invariable hypothesis is that the incompetent would do that which is in the incompetent's best interest. Then the court must proceed to determine what that is. As a result, a "substituted judgment" analysis for the never-competent quickly becomes a best interest analysis. Similarly, the "mature minor" doctrine from which the 1957 Massachusetts cases borrow easily collapses into a best interest analysis as well. In practice, when a minor's decision corresponds with adults' assessment's of the child's best interests, courts call the minor "mature" and they weigh the minor's "assent" (as opposed to "consent," which a minor is legally incapable of offering). But when a minor's decision conflicts with adult assessment of the child's best interest, courts readily deem the minor "immature" and discount the minor's opinion. Therefore, evaluation of whether a minor is "mature" or not typically involves an independent best interest analysis as well. For some of these reasons, the in the 1970s the following three cases shifted the jurisprudence of incompetent kidney donors to an explicit best interests analysis.

In 1973, three Louisiana courts refused to allow the parents of a mentally retarded boy to consent to his kidney donation to his 32 year old sister. First, a Civil District Court and a Court of Appeal held that neither parents nor the courts could authorize surgical intrusion on a retarded person for the benefit of another. Then, in *In re Richardson,* 284 So.2d 185 (La.Ct.App., 1973), the Louisiana Court of Appeals held that although such permission was not inconceivable, it would not be granted in this case. Roy Richardson was 17 year old with a mental age of 3 or 4, and a life expectancy of 25 years of age as a result of his Down's Syndrome. The court found that although Roy's sister Beverly's quality of life would improve with a transplant, she could survive on dialysis. In addition, although Roy was the best match in the family, other siblings were not precluded from donating -- there was a 4-5% chance of rejection of Roy's kidney, and a 20-30% chance of rejection of the other siblings' kidneys. The *Richardson* court stated that cases of kidney donation by incompetents must be resolved under a strict best interest standard. Then, without any discussion, the court summarily concluded that donation would not be in Roy's best interest. The concurring opinion in *Richardson* suggests that Louisiana courts should not even consider the best interests of the incompetent until it is established that there is an urgent need for the donation and there are no reasonable alternatives.

In 1975, the Wisconsin Supreme Court also applied a best interest standard and refused to allow Richard, a 39 year old mentally handicapped man, donate a kidney to his sister Elaine. *In re Guardianship of Pescinski,* 226 N.W.2d 180 (Wis.Sup.Ct. 1975). Richard Pescinski had been hospitalized for the previous 17 years with a diagnosis of chronic catatonic schizophrenia, and his mental age was estimated at 12 years old. Richard's guardian, his sister Janice, wanted

Richard to donate a kidney to their sister Elaine, who had been on dialysis for five years. Elaine's parents and her sister Janice were not candidates -- the parents were considered to old to donate and Janice had diabetes. The final sibling, Elaine's brother Ralph, refused to donate. In his testimony, he explained that as a dairy farmer with ten children it was not in his family's interest for him to donate. Finally, the nephrologist testified that his own "moral conviction" prevented him from considering Elaine's six minor children as potential donors.

In *Pescinski* the Wisconsin Supreme Court openly rejected the "substituted judgment" doctrine that the Kentucky Supreme Court relied on in *Strunk*. Instead, the *Pescinski* court determined that Wisconsin would use a best interest standard. Like the Louisiana court in *Richardson*, the *Pescinski* court decided that donation was not in Richard's best interests without offering much analysis of the issue. However, the court implied that Richard was incapable of benefitting psychologically from donation when it emphasized that part of Richard's catatonic schizophrenia was his emotional withdrawal from the world.

The *Pescinski* dissent argued that if Richard was competent, "in all probability he would be willing to consent to the transplant to save his sister's life." However, this speculation is undermined by Ralph Pescinki's unwillingness to donate! The difference between the Pescinski family members' willingness to donate highlights an underlying fear in cases concerning the mentally handicapped. Courts must insure that the lives and health of the mentally handicapped are not valued less than the lives and health of other family members, and that families are not permitted to turn to their most vulnerable members first, demanding sacrifices that other family members are not willing to make and that these vulnerable persons cannot refuse. This is likely the fear that triggered the *Strunk* dissenters' reference to Nazi experimentation on human beings the Nazis viewed as having low social worth for the future benefit of those they viewed as having high social worth. Though polemic, the comparison deserves careful consideration.

In the final published case concerning kidney donation by incompetents, in 1979 a Texas court approved a kidney donation from Anne Little, a fourteen year old girl with Down's Syndrome, to her brother Steven. In *Little v. Little*, 576 S.W.2d 493 (Tex.Civ.App. 1979), a probate court approved the donation and Anne's GAL made one appeal to the Texas Court of Appeals. The Court of Appeals found that Anne was the only acceptable match for her brother, and Steven was expected to deteriorate without a transplant. The court employed an explicit best interests test, and stated that the facts were similar to those in Kentucky case of *Strunk*. The testimony showed that Anne and Steven were close, that Anne missed him and was unhappy at his absence when he left home for dialysis, and that Anne was aware of Steven's plight and had offered her assent. The court concluded that Anne would receive a substantial psychological benefit by donating. The court went on to balance Anne and Steven's interests, noting that a minimal risk to Anne would result in a large benefit to Steven. Finally, the court noted that the presence of a guardian ad litem had insured that Anne's interests were fully and fairly examined, notwithstanding the fact that the guardian ad litem disagreed with the court's conclusion. (Anne's guardian ad litem argued that the government never has the power to authorize donation by an incompetent.) Therefore, the court permitted the donation.

Conclusion

Generally stated, the current state of the law is that kidney donation by incompetents can be authorized by courts when the donation is in the incompetent's best interest. Because children and mentally handicapped persons exist in a family system, courts recognize that the incompetent's best interest will include the fates of other family members, and therefore the analysis of the best interests of the potential donor actually subsumes some balancing of interests within the family. In summary, a court of any state is likely to approve kidney donation by an incompetent when the following six criteria are met:

1) The recipient cannot live on dialysis and will die without this donation;
2) The incompetent is the only suitable donor;
3) The parents or guardian of the incompetent consent;
4) The incompetent donor assents;
5) The incompetent donor has the capacity for psychological benefit (either presently or, through maturation of a child, in the very near future); and
6) A close relationship between donor and recipient exists which will create true psychological benefit to the donor from donation.

Every case of a potential incompetent donor which meets all six factors should be brought before a court for review, and a GAL should be appointed for the potential donor. If a nephrologist thinks a case merits consideration even though it lacks one of these six factors, the authors recommend that the case be evaluated by a formal ethics consultation or review by an institutional ethics committee. If the case passes internal ethical review, it should be brought for judicial review and a GAL should be appointed for the potential donor. However, cases which lack one or more of these factors are not likely to receive legal approval.

The law in the area of incompetent kidney donors will continue to unfold. For example, no published case addresses the scenarios of a child donating to a parent[Footnote 7], donation in the light of parent/child disagreement (e.g. an assenting child whose parents refuse consent, or a dissenting child whose parents consent), and donation from a child whose parents hold joint custody and who disagree with each other. This is not to say such conflicts have not arisen, or even that they have never found their way into a court -- only that if they were in fact litigated, they left no written trace.

---

[7] In *Pescinski* the court notes that the ailing sister has six minor children, but the doctor says that he will not consider the children as donors as a matter of his "own moral conviction." The age of the children is not reported, but it is interesting to note that this physician found donation by a child to save his or her parent's life more troubling than donation by a resident of a mental institution suffering from catatonic schizophrenia.

Case 1

WITHDRAWAL FROM DIALYTIC THERAPY

An 84 year old blind, widowed housekeeper who is unable to walk or care for herself because of a series of increasingly severe strokes has been undergoing maintenance hemodialysis for two years. Progressive deafness - now profound - prevents the patient's use of talking books or even the radio. Distressed over worsening urinary and bowel incontinence, the patient requests that dialysis treatments be discontinued. She states that her decision is the result of months of thought and a discussion with her minister. The patient's only living relative, a married daughter, rejects the concept of not continuing dialytic therapy until "the last spark of life is gone." She threatens a law suit against the hospital and attending physician if any action toward stopping dialysis is taken. ***The hospital director orders the responsible nephrologist to continue dialysis indefinitely.***

Study Questions

1. Who determines the application of a life sustaining therapy (patient, family, physician)?
2. Does a patient have the right to refuse a life sustaining therapy?
3. Once life sustaining therapy is begun, does a patient have the right to order it discontinued?
4. Can a family override a patient's wish regarding life sustaining therapy?
5. Is a physician obligated to initiate a therapy requested by a patient if it is judged inappropriate for any reason?
6. When family conflict is brought to a hospital administrator's attention, does the resolution shift from patient and physician to the administrator?
7. Do legal considerations (threatened law suit) override ethical issues in patient care?

Monique Janelle London, J.D.

Generally, the law requires that a competent patient's decision to discontinue lifesaving medical treatment (including dialysis) be honored, even over objections from a relative. A limited exception exists when state interests outweigh the patient's interest in self-determination. That exception probably would not apply to the present hypothetical. If the patient is currently incompetent to make the decision to discontinue lifesaving medical treatment, and she has left no advance directive or living will, and her daughter is her surrogate, and the daughter's decision to continue medical treatment is accepted by a court as being in the best interests of the patient or what the patient would want if she were competent, then the daughter's decision may carry legal weight. However, those elements do not appear to be present in Case 1.

Patient Right to Privacy and Self-Determination:

In Case 1, assuming the patient was competent when she made the decision to discontinue dialysis treatments, the hospital director probably would be subject to liability if he ordered continuation of the treatments. The U.S. Supreme Court has acknowledged that a competent, non-terminally ill person has a liberty interest under the Due Process Clause of the 14th Amendment in refusing unwanted medical treatment - even if it means the person will die as a result. *See Cruzan v. Director, Missouri Department of Health ("Cruzan")*, 497 U.S. 261, 264 (1990). In her concurrence in Cruzan, Justice O'Connor stated that there is a protected liberty interest in refusing unwanted medical treatment, including artificially delivered food and water. *Cruzan*, 497 U.S. at 287; *see also Vacco v. Quill*, 521 U.S. 793, 807 (1997). A subsequent decision by a federal appeals court read the O'Connor concurrence to "explain that the majority opinion held (implicitly or otherwise) that a liberty interest in refusing medical treatment extends to all types of medical treatment, from **dialysis** or artificial respiration to the provision of food and water by tube or other artificial means." Compassion in Dying v. State of Washington *("Compassion in Dying")*, 79 F.3d 790, 815 (9th Cir. 1996) (emphasis added), *reversed and remanded sub nom., Washington v. Glucksberg*, 521 U.S. 702 (1997).

Several state supreme courts have concluded that the state constitutional right to privacy or autonomy includes the right to refuse life-saving medical treatment. *See, e.g., Rasmussen v. Fleming*, 154 Ariz. 207, 741 P.2d 674, 681-82 (Ariz. 1987); *Bouvia v. Superior Court*, 179 Cal. App.3d 1127, 225 Cal.Rptr. 297 (Cal. 1986); *Satz v. Perlmutter*, 379 So.2d 359, 360 (Fla. 1980); *Hondroulis v. Schuhmacher*, 553 So.2d 398, 415 (La. 1988); *In re Quinlan*, 70 N.J. 10, 355 A.2d 647, 663 (N.J. 1976), *cert. denied sub nom., Garger v. New Jersey*, 429 U.S. 922 (1976); *In re Welfare of Colyer*, 99 Wash. 2d 114, 660 P.2d 738, 742 (Wash. 1983); *In re Guardianship of L.W.*, 167 Wis. 2d 53, 482 N.W.2d 60, 65-66 (Wis. 1992).

In many states, courts have found that the right to refuse medical treatment is encompassed by the common-law right not to receive medical treatment without one's informed consent. *See, e.g., In re Storar*, 52 N.Y.2d 363, 420 N.E.2d 64, 71 (N.Y.), *cert. denied*, 454 U.S. 858 (1981); *Superintendent of Belchertown State School v. Saikewicz*, 373 Mass. 728, 370 N.E. 2d 417 (Mass. 1977); *Bouvia v. Superior Court, supra*, 179 Cal.App.3d at 1137 (Cal. 1986); *In re Gardner*, 534 A.2d 947, 951 (Me. 1987); *Brophy v. New England Sinai Hospital, Inc.*, 398 Mass. 417, 497 N.E.2d 626 (Mass. 1986); *In the Matter of Conroy*, 98 N.J. 321, 486 A.2d 1209, 1222 (N.J. 1985). "The purpose underlying the doctrine of informed consent is defeated somewhat if, after receiving all information necessary to make an informed decision, the patient is forced to choose only from alternative methods of treatment and precluded from foregoing all treatment whatsoever." *Rasmussen v. Fleming*, 154 Ariz. 207; 741 P.2d 674, 683 (Ariz. 1987). "Obviously, if a patient is powerless to decline medical treatment upon being properly informed of its implications, the requirement of consent would be meaningless." *McKay v. Bergstedt*, 106 Nev. 808, 801 P.2d 617, 621 (Nev. 1990). Indeed, the U.S. Supreme Court has noted that the right to refuse medical treatment is "basic and fundamental" to the concept of informed consent. *Cruzan*, 497 U.S. 261, 277.

Some states have statutes providing that a physician need not accede to a patient's request to withdraw or withhold treatment if it would be against the physician's beliefs to do so. However, the physician must try to transfer the patient to another health care provider willing to comply with the request. *See, e.g.*, IDAHO CODE §39-4508 ("Any physician or other health care provider who for ethical or professional reasons is incapable or unwilling to conform to the desires of the patient [or decisionmaker] may withdraw without incurring any civil or criminal liability provided the physician or other health care provider makes a good faith effort to assist the patient in obtaining the services of another physician or other health care provider before withdrawal."); ILL. ANN. STAT. ch. 755, para. 40/35 ("A health care provider who because of personal views or beliefs or his or her conscience is unable to comply with the terms of a decision to forgo life-sustaining treatment shall . . . assist . . . in effectuating the timely transfer of the patient to another health care provider willing to comply with the [patient's or decision maker's] wishes . . . ."; N.H. REV. STAT. ANN. § 137-J:8(II) ("When the direction of an agent requires an act or omission contrary to the moral or ethical principles or other standards of a health . . . care provider . . ., the care provider shall allow for the transfer of the patient to another facility . . . .").

Caselaw provides further examples of this requirement. See *Gray v. Romeo*, 697 F. Supp. 580, 591 (D.R.I. 1988) (holding that a hospital and physicians must withdraw life-sustaining treatment over ethical objections unless the patient can be transferred to another facility that will comply with the patient's request); *In re Jobes*, 108 N.J. 394, 529 A.2d 434, 450 (N.J. 1987) (requiring a nursing home to participate in the withdrawal of life-sustaining treatment due to inability to transfer the patient elsewhere); *Elbaum v. Grace Plaza of Great Neck*, Inc., 148 A.D.2d 244, 544 N.Y.S.2d 840, 847-48 (N.Y. App. Div. 2d Dep't 1989) (per curiam) (holding that physicians must, absent a transfer to a willing health care provider, withdraw life support over ethical objections); *Brophy v. New England Sinai Hospital, Inc.*, 398 Mass. 417, 497 N.E.2d 626, 639-640 (Mass. 1986) (holding that although informed consent doctrine could not justify compelling physicians to withdraw life-sustaining medical treatment as requested, physicians must transfer patient to a place where request would be honored); *Conservatorship of Morrison v. Abramovice*, 206 Cal. App. 3d 304, 312 253 Cal. Rptr. 530 (Cal. App. 1st Dist. 1988) (physicians could not be compelled to remove patient's nasogastric tube provided they were willing to transfer the patient to another provider who would).

The particular issue of whether a competent patient's decision to discontinue dialysis treatments must be honored was addressed by a New York state court in *In re Lydia Hall Hospital*, 116 Misc. 2d 477, 455 N.Y.S.2d 706 (N.Y. Sup. Ct. 1982). There, when he was competent, a dialysis patient expressed a desire (both verbally and in a signed statement) to discontinue dialysis treatments. He subsequently lapsed into a coma. The court found by clear and convincing evidence that the patient had made an informed, rational, knowing decision to forego the treatments. Therefore, the court concluded that the decision was legally permissible. It denied the hospital's petition to continue dialysis treatments on the comatose patient.

Here, the argument for honoring the patient's wishes is even stronger, since she is making the decision presently rather than prior to when the withdrawal would take place, and she is conscious and (presumptively) competent.

Based on the authorities discussed above, if the patient in Case 1 is competent, she has a federal constitutional liberty interest and a right under the laws of certain states to withhold consent to further dialysis treatments.

Countervailing State Interests:

However, a patient's liberty interest in refusing medical treatment may be outweighed by countervailing state interests. The Supreme Court noted in *Cruzan* that the interest of competent patients in refusing medical treatment is not absolute, but must be balanced against relevant state interests. *See* 497 U.S. at 279, 280. Such state interests include the interests in preservation of life, prevention of suicide and the protection of innocent third parties such as minor children or other dependents of the patient. *See Polk County Sheriff v. Iowa Dist. Court ("Polk County")*, 594 N.W.2d 421 (Iowa 1999) (and cases cited therein).

In some cases, the state interests have been found to be paramount under this balancing test. *See Donaldson v. Van de Kamp*, 2 Cal. App. 4th 1614, 4 Cal. Rptr. 2d 59, 62-64 (Cal. App. 2d Dist. 1992) (due to state interest against suicide, competent individual suffering from brain tumor which will be lethal within a few years has no legal right to be placed in premortem cryogenic suspension, which will cause death, nor to enlist assistance of another in ending his life); *In re Hughes*, 259 N.J. Super. 193, 611 A.2d 1148, 1151 (N.J. Super. Ct. 1992) (blood transfusion properly authorized despite prior refusal of competent patient because "transfusion can preserve a healthy young woman's life, not prolong a painful and imminent death"); *University of Cincinnati Hosp. v. Edmond*, 30 Ohio Misc. 2d 1, 506 N.E.2d 299, 302 (Ohio C.P. 1986) (although an incompetent patient's family believed the patient would refuse treatment for religious reasons, the court authorized the hospital to perform blood and plasma transfusions because of "a compelling state interest in [preserving] life").

In contrast, other state court decisions suggest that a competent patient's right to refuse medical treatment outweighs any countervailing state interests - that is, the right is virtually absolute. *See Thor v. Superior Court*, 5 Cal. 4th 725, 855 P.2d 375 (Cal. 1993); *Bouvia v. Superior Court*, 179 Cal. App. 3d 1127, 225 Cal. Rptr. 297 (Cal. App. 2d Dist. 1986); *In re Dubreuil*, 629 So. 2d 819 (Fla. 1993); *Wons v. Public Health Trust*, 500 So. 2d 679 (Fla. Dist. Ct. App. 1987), *aff'd*, 541 So. 2d 96 (Fla. 1989); *In re E.G.*, 133 Ill. 2d 98, 549 N.E.2d 322, 328 (Ill. 1989) (holding that a competent minor aged 17 who is likely to die within a month without blood transfusions, but who is 80 percent likely to achieve remission of the disease with blood transfusions and chemotherapy, may decline treatment); *Norwood Hosp. v. Munoz*, 409 Mass. 116, 564 N.E.2d 1017 (Mass. 1991); *In re Peter*, 108 N.J. 365, 529 A.2d 419, 423 (N.J. 1987) ("The patient's medical condition is generally relevant only to determine whether the patient is or is not competent, and if incompetent, how the patient, in view of that condition, would choose to treat it were she or he competent."); *In re Conroy*, 98 N.J. 321, 486 A.2d 1209, 1225 (N.J. 1985) ("The right to self-determination ordinarily outweighs any countervailing state interests, and competent persons generally are permitted to refuse medical treatment, even at the risk of death ....."); *Fosmire v. Nicoleau*, 75 N.Y.2d 218, 551 N.E.2d 77, 85 (N.Y. 1990) (Simons, J., concurring) (stating that majority defines right of self-determination so broadly that for all practical purposes the right is absolute). *See also* Cal. Probate Code sections 4600 to 4753 (providing that no medical treatment can be given over the patient's objection).

In balancing the state and individual liberty interests in the dialysis context, *Polk County Sheriff v. Iowa Dist. Court*, 594 N.W.2d 421 (Iowa 1999), considered the fact that a dialysis patient was not terminally ill (among other factors) as implicating the state's interest in preserving life. *Id.* at 427. In *Polk County*, the court found that the strength of the state's interest in preserving life corresponds directly to the degree to which the patient's quality of life has diminished due to physical deterioration. *Id.* at 426-237 (citation omitted). Because continued dialysis would permit the patient to have "an otherwise normal and healthy life for perhaps twenty years," the court concluded that the state's interest in preserving life "weighs heavily in the balance." *Id.* at 427. It contrasted the patient's situation with a terminal situation in which "heavy physical and emotional burdens would be imposed to effect a brief and uncertain delay in the natural process of death." *Id.* at 427 (quotations and citation omitted).[Footnote 8]

Additionally, because the patient had minor children, the court found that the state's interest in protecting innocent third parties from the impact of the patient's death was implicated. *Id.* at 428. The court also found that the state's interest in maintaining the ethical integrity of the medical profession weighed in favor of continuing treatment, since practitioners would recommend continuing dialysis assuming the patient would voluntarily submit to it. *Id.* at 428. (Because the patient was a prisoner, the court also considered the state interest in maintaining prison security, order and discipline. *Id.* at 428-29. It found that compelling him to submit to dialysis was reasonably related to legitimate penological interests.) Based on all of these factors, the *Polk County* court concluded that state interests outweighed the patient's interest in discontinuing dialysis treatments.

Under this balancing test, in Case 1 the hospital director would have a legal obligation to honor the patient's decision to discontinue dialysis treatments (or transfer the patient to another health care provider or facility that would do so) unless the state's interests outweighed that decision. It is unclear whether the patient is terminally ill; if not, the state arguably has an interest in preserving life. However, the hypothetical does not mention any "innocent third parties" such as dependent children whom the state has an interest in protecting by forcing the patient to continue dialysis treatments. Nor does it appear that a state interest in upholding a recommendation of the medical profession is at stake. The patient is elderly, blind, deaf, incontinent and unable to walk or care for herself. Under the circumstances, dialysis probably would only prolong her life in its present compromised quality until her inevitable and imminent death.

[8] The court also considered the state's interest in preventing suicide, but found that the interest was not implicated in refusing dialysis treatments, because death would result from natural causes if dialysis were discontinued. *Id.* at 427-28 (citation omitted).

Thus it is doubtful that the medical community would recommend continuing dialysis treatments assuming the patient would submit to them voluntarily. In sum, the patient's competent decision to discontinue dialysis treatments would likely override any state interest in continuing the treatments.

Incompetent Patient:

The one situation in which the daughter's objection might override the patient's decision to terminate dialysis treatments would be if the patient were legally incompetent to make that decision when she made it.[Footnote 9] If so, the patient's daughter might be authorized to make the decision for the patient.

Determining whether a patient would be found legally competent by the court can be a difficult task for a physician. Generally, patients who are unconscious, senile, mentally retarded, disoriented, excessively emotional, or very young are incompetent. The general test for competency is the factual question of whether, "at the time and under the circumstances when his consent is required, [the patient has] the mental ability to make a rational, deliberate decision regarding the proposed treatment." *See* David W. Meyers, Medico-Legal Implications of Death and Dying section 6:8, at 109-110, 11:3 at 267 (1981). However, courts use different criteria to determine whether a patient has that ability. Some courts use expert testimony in determining competency, but often the experts themselves disagree over whether the patient is competent. *See, e.g., In re Quackenbush,* 156 N.J. Super. 282, 383 A.2d 785, 788 (N.J. 1978) (where one expert concluded the patient "has the mental capacity to make decisions, to understand the nature and extent of his physical condition, to understand the nature and extent of the operations, to understand the risks involved if he consents to the operation, and to understand the risks involved if he refuses the operation," but the other expert determined that the patient's mental condition "was not sufficient to make an informed decision concerning the operation").

If the hospital director has any uncertainty about the patient's competence, he may be absolved of liability if he continues the dialysis treatments until a court can address the issue. *See, e.g., Ross v. Hilltop Rehabilitation Hospital ("Ross"),* 676 F. Supp. 1528 (D. Colo. 1987). In *Ross,* the patient, a 34 year old who suffered a stroke after intravenous drug use, stated that he wanted to discontinue nutrition and hydration. His mind was left "intact and functioning," but the medical staff had "serious doubts" as to his mental capacity to make that determination. Given that the patient had tried to commit suicide twice prior to his paralysis, his wife had filed to dissolve their marriage, the INS sought to deport the patient, the patient had been diagnosed with an adjustment disorder with depressed mood, and his sister had threatened a lawsuit against the caregivers if treatment were discontinued, the court found that there was at least a genuine issue of fact as to whether the patient was mentally competent. *Id.* at 1534. Accordingly, it absolved the hospital and treating physician from liability

[9] However, if there is clear and convincing evidence that the patient made the decision sometime in the past, when she was competent, to discontinue dialysis treatments, that decision must be honored even if the patient is now incompetent. *See, e.g., Cruzan,* 497 U.S. 261; *In re Lydia Hall Hospital,* 116 Misc. 2d 477, 455 N.Y.S. 2d 706 (1982).

for refusing to honor the patient's wish to discontinue nutrition and hydration. *Id.* at 1542.

Even if the patient is presently incompetent, she may have a valid advance directive or living will stating her wishes[Footnote 10], or appointing a proxy who will make health care decisions for her when she is incompetent. Most states have statutes affirming the right of a patient or proxy to refuse treatment through advance directives. Those statutes provide that a physician who will not honor the refusal must try to or successfully transfer the patient to another health care provider who will.[Footnote 11]

If the patient is incompetent and did not make an advance directive, she still retains the right to make decisions about her care, but that right is generally exercised on her behalf by a surrogate decisionmaker. The surrogate acquires his or her authority to act on behalf of the patient either by state statute or judicial appointment. In many states, a family member is the preferred surrogate. *See, e.g., Causey v. St. Francis Medical Center,* 719 So. 2d 1072, 1074 (La. Ct. App. 2d Cir. 1998) ("If a patient is incompetent, then the responsibility or authority to make decisions falls to the next of kin. La. R.S. 40:1299.58.5."); *In re Doe,* 262 Ga. 389, 418 S.E.2d 3, 6 (Ga. 1992) ("Medical decision-making for incompetent patients is most often best left to the patient's family (or other designated proxy) and the medical community."); *In re Jobes,* 108 N.J. 394, 529 A.2d 434, 445 (N.J. 1987) ("Family members are best qualified to make substituted judgments for incompetent patients.").

Thus, depending on the applicable rules of the state where Case 1 takes place, the patient's daughter may be her surrogate decisionmaker. However, even if so, that does not necessarily mean that the hospital director is legally required (or permitted) to follow the daughter's instruction to continue dialysis treatments. Generally, the surrogate's decision must comply with one of two standards: it must either be in the patient's "best interests," or be the "substituted judgment" of the patient - i.e., what the patient would have decided if she were competent.[Footnote 12] *See Rasmussen v. Fleming,* 154 Ariz. 207, 741 P.2d 674, 688 (Ariz. 1987) ("Courts have developed two standards to guide surrogate decisionmaking: 'substituted judgment' and 'best interests'."); *In re Jobes,* 108 N.J. 394, 529 A.2d 434, 456 (N.J. 1987) (Handler, J., concurring) (discussing the "two major approaches to the making of medical treatment decisions for incompe-

---

[10] An advance directive is an oral or written statement in which the patient, when competent, expresses her wishes regarding whether she will receive medical treatment under certain circumstances, so that those wishes will be honored if the patient subsequently becomes incompetent to make health care decisions.

[11] Although advance directives are generally accorded great weight in determining whether a patient should receive life-saving treatment, courts have recognized that they do not provide absolute certainty about what the patient would want in the present situation. *See, e.g., In re Westchester County Medical Ctr. ex rel. O'Connor,* 72 N.Y.2d 517, 531 N.E.2d 607, 613 (N.Y. 1988) ("There always exists the possibility that, despite his or her clear expressions in the past, the patient has since changed his or her mind.").

[12] *See, e.g., In re A.C.,* 573 A.2d 1235, 1249 (D.C. Cir. 1990) (en banc) ("The substituted judgment inquiry is primarily a subjective one: as nearly as possible, the court must ascertain what the patient would do if competent.").

tent patients. . . . one focusing upon the patient's right of self-determination, the other emphasizing the patient's best interests"); *In re Guardianship of Myers*, 62 Ohio Misc. 2d 763, 610 N.E.2d 663, 669 (Ohio C.P. 1993) ("Guardianship law has traditionally recognized two methods, the best interest test . . . and 'substitute judgment.' ").

In some states, the right to refuse medical treatment can be exercised by a surrogate decisionmaker only if there is sufficient evidence that the patient herself would have exercised that right if she were competent. *See, e.g., In re Jobes*, 108 N.J. 394, 529 A.2d 434 (N.J. 1987). And in some states the court, as the protector of incompetents, can override a surrogate's choice if that choice goes against the interests of the state, or goes against what the court determines to be in the best interests of the incompetent patient. *See, e.g., In re P.V.W.*, 424 So. 2d 1015 (La. 1982). In other states the court, not a family member, is responsible for applying a "substituted judgment" standard on behalf of the patient in the first place. *See, e.g., In the Matter of R.H.*, 35 Mass. App. Ct. 478, 484-485, 622 N.E. 2d 1071 (Mass. 1993) ("the court dons the mental mantle of the incompetent and substitutes itself as nearly as possible for the individual in the decision-making process").

The hypothetical in Case 1 contains no evidence that the patient would have decided to continue dialysis treatments if she were competent. Thus it is not at all clear that the daughter's instruction would constitute the "substituted judgment" of the patient if she were competent. Nor is evidence presented that it would be in the interests of the state or in the patient's best interests to continue dialysis treatments. Rather, given the compromised quality of her life - unable to walk, see, hear, care for herself or control her bodily functions - it seems more likely that discontinuing treatments is in her best interests. Thus, a court might decide that the daughter's decision, even as the patient's legal surrogate, should not be honored.[Footnote 13]

Conclusion:

If the patient was competent when she made the decision to discontinue dialysis treatments, the hospital director probably has a legal obligation to honor that decision (or transfer the patient to a facility that will honor the decision) despite the daughter's objection and threat of a lawsuit. From the facts presented, the patient appears to be competent, and thus this is the most likely legal outcome.

However, if the patient was not competent to make the decision, the director may be obligated to follow the daughter's instruction to continue dialysis treatments. Whether or not he must follow the daughter's instruction will turn on the answers to several factual questions: whether the daughter is the patient's legal representative or surrogate, whether there is sufficient evidence that the

[13] Indeed, it has been noted that continuing unwanted treatment can as harmful to a patient as discontinuing desired treatment. See In re Jobes, 108 N.J. 394, 529 A.2d 434, 453 (N.J. 1987) (Handler, J., concurring) (holding that " 'abuse' includes not only discontinuing treatment for a patient who would have wanted treatment continued, but also the continuation of treatment for a patient who would have wanted treatment stopped").

patient, if competent, would have chosen to continue dialysis treatments, and/or whether continuing treatments would be in the patient's best interests.

Of course, discontinuing the treatments will lead to the patient's death - a final and irreversible result. If the director has any uncertainty about the patient's competence or his legal obligation to honor her wish, he should order continued treatment of the patient until he can obtain guidance from the court.

Ethical Analysis:

The hospital director has an ethical obligation to honor the patient's decision to stop dialysis treatments and thereby end her life. However, he also has an ethical obligation to make sure that discontinuation is the patient's own, sincere, fully informed, conclusive decision, and that the daughter fully understands that decision.

Thus, before authorizing discontinuation of the patient's dialysis treatments, the director should talk to the patient. He should find out if there are any additional reasons why she has decided to discontinue treatments. He should make sure she understands the ramifications of her decision and has all the information necessary to make it. He should also make sure that she has reached her decision of her own accord, rather than being coerced by anyone else. For instance, the patient says she reached her decision after "months of thought and discussion with her minister." The director should confirm that the patient has adopted any advice she received as her own decision, not out of a sense of obligation to do whatever her minister says. He should also confirm that the patient's decision is sincere and carefully thought out - not something she blurted out in a moment of high emotion, but didn't really mean.

The director also should consider how the patient's decision is affecting the patient's daughter. He should try to identify and clear up any misunderstandings or lack of information that may be causing the daughter to reject her mother's decision to discontinue treatments. He should find out why the daughter wants the patient's treatments continued. Maybe the daughter simply does not want her mother to die. Or, maybe the daughter would feel guilty if she didn't do everything possible to keep her mother alive. Or, maybe the daughter mistrusts the director and nephrologist, and thinks they are trying to get rid of the patient. The director should help the daughter understand why the patient wants to discontinue treatment, and explain the safeguards that are in place to confirm that the decision is the patient's own. To facilitate better understanding between the patient and daughter, he director should encourage them to discuss between themselves the patient's decision and the daughter's objection to it.

The director should make sure all of these communications take place as soon as possible. If the patient's wish is sincere and her own, every day it is not honored is another day she must suffer a potentially humiliating, undignified, low-quality, depressing, undesired life against her will.

Connie Zuckerman, J.D.

Patients with decisional capacity have the legal and moral right to either consent to, or to refuse, any treatment intervention offered to them, even if as a consequence of such refusal their death may result. Such decisionmaking empowerment is based on the philosophic principle of autonomy, and the legal principle of individual self-determination. What is critical in this case is the recognition that despite her increasingly debilitated condition, the patient continues to possess the decisionmaking capacity to exercise such right of refusal, and her decision to discontinue treatment appears to be a well considered, authentic reflection of her wishes. Since the patient still has decisional capacity, the daughter has neither the legal authority to insist on treatment continuance nor any standing on which to sue the hospital and attending physician. Dialysis should be discontinued in accord with the choice of this capable patient.

Amy L. Friedman, M.D.

The desire to end one's life can be either impetuous or developed after careful consideration. In the case of impulse the physician must assume that an acute condition of depression, loss of touch with reality or inability to cope with one or more potentially correctable stressors, exists. Under such circumstances, the suicidal individual is transiently incapable of making rational choices and should be prevented from harming himself (herself). Thus a scorned lover, a person who awakes from an operation to discover a feared colostomy or a rape victim each may acutely react with such desperation that the desire to die becomes transiently overwhelming. Appropriate application of tincture of time together with medical and/or psychosocial intervention often allows sufficient recovery for development of a willful decision to live.

However, when an individual choosing to die has rationally considered the quality of his(her) current and projected life and has no reason to anticipate elimination of the factors that contribute to it's unacceptability, the right to dictate what will and won't be done to his(her) body must be protected. Any coherent, competent adult must maintain control of this right even if that decision differs from what others might have chosen.

Still, healthcare choices are not always so evident. There are times when each of us surrenders control of our destiny to the hands and heart of another. Both the driver and airplane pilot are routinely expected to make such decisions consistent with the wishes of their passengers. Every surgeon has had to judge a patient's competency to accept or decline invasive procedures. When the sensorium is clouded by shock (as in the case of a trauma victim in urgent need of lifesaving surgery), by circulating poisons released during severe infection, or by lingering effects of powerful medications, then the healthcare decision must be made by the family or legally designated representative. Occasionally, when no such individual is available, the surgeon himself (herself) assumes this role. While experienced in making life and death decisions for others, no modern surgeon would intentionally disregard the wishes of a coherent, competent adult. Tools with which this might be done unobtrusively are readily available, and the immediate pain or discomfort of any imaginable procedure obviated. Yet performing an operation or administering a blood transfusion without consent, even if necessary to save her life, would be reprehensible. Similarly, ignoring this woman's refusal to proceed with maintenance hemodialysis would be immoral. Certainly, there is relevance to the daughter's opinion that life must continue under all circumstances. She should be encouraged to advocate this position directly to her mother, even if doing so creates a major confrontation. Without doubt, the hospital director has not personally confronted the patient. To permit entry of an administrator personally removed from the group of people deliberating the most personal of life's decisions would be inhumane unless he/she is prepared to directly inform the patient of his actions. His position represents medico-legal posturing in defense of the institution, not the patient. In my experience, no administrator is prepared to leave the protective cover of his desk to face the patient directly. This is precisely the reason physicians must continue to maintain dominance in the establishment and refinement of ethical policies in medicine.

The ultimate choice to accept or refuse any intervention, even if a pattern of prior acquiescence has been established, rests solely with the individual in question. This woman's determination to decline further dialysis treatments must be respected. Quite simply, her rights take precedent over the desires of her daughter and the interests of the hospital.

Carl M. Kjellstrand, M.D.

The physician's first obligation is to his patient. Once you have ruled out incompetency or trivial external condition in a patient requesting withdrawal, you must obey. To continue treatment is battery. At least two court cases (Cinque and Bartley) have upheld what is self-evident; that patients don't have to accept any treatment (dialysis or respirators) they don't want.

Because of the threat of a lawsuit, you need to be extra clear in your notes in the chart. Your hospital director should get the copies of the precedent setting cases and if needed, you have to take it to the hospital board. In general, hospital directors are cowards and more eager to avoid lawsuits against the hospital than to care about patient autonomy, beneficence or non-maleficence. At the extreme, you should be prepared to go to court on behalf of the patient.

Mildred (Barry) Friedman

When the threat of legal action is more important than granting the wish of a patient, there is something wrong with our priorities. Unfortunately, the desire to allow life to end, is thought to be a result of mental incompetence. A decision to continue life, no matter how painful, embarrassing, or without pleasure that life is, is accepted as coming from a healthy mind. If the decision is to allow natural events to end life, mental ability and stability are questioned. Ceasing dialysis is not pure suicide. It is rather, recognition of the inevitable end to life. Dialysis is not without pain, discomfort, and the expenditure of much energy. Consider only the effort of an outpatient to arrive at a dialysis unit.

This woman is being pushed by her circumstances into what many people dread, an aware mind trapped in an incompetent body. She seems to regard

her "quality of life" as negative. Her life belongs to her and just as we accepted her right to make many decisions (marriage, bearing children), so must we accept her right to make this decision.
Wishes of a daughter or any other relative must be listened to but not allowed to override. If the mother was not competent, then the daughter's decisions would take control. We each are in charge of one life, our own. Recognition of this is inherent in the endorsement of Living Wills.
The hospital director is wrong. Hospitals and physicians have been sued before. Hospitals must be patient friendly places not overly concerned with their perceived own well being.

Judith E. Columbo

I believe the hospital director is wrong in his decision to continue dialysis on an 84 year old blind, widowed housekeeper. Blindness, deafness, urinary and bowel incontinence, and age will not improve with dialysis treatment. The patient is requesting that dialysis treatments be stopped because she realizes that her quality of life is ending and she has the right to die with dignity. The patient is of age and sound mind and can still make decisions. The attending physician should take the daughter's feeling into account but the decision about discontinuing should come from the patient.

Editors Remarks 1

Case 1 illustrates two issues: 1. How far we have come in compromising individual hegemony over one's body, and 2. The intrusion of law over common sense. London's superb analysis of legal precedent ends with hedges over what the hospital director may or may not do. The director "probably will be legally obligated to honor the (patient's) decision," she notes, but because of the daughter's threat of a lawsuit, "if the patient was not competent to make the decision, the director may be legally obligated to follow the daughter's instruction." Kjellstrand, Zuckerman, Amy Friedman, and the two patients see a simpler world, admittedly a place in which cowardice by an administrator mandates defensive note writing, but nevertheless calls for throwing the "off switch" for further dialytic therapy. I concur. A competent individual must not be forced to have a single unwanted venipuncture, radiograph, or procedure including hemodialysis. Here, the patient's physician leads the charge serving as an advocate and champion. Neither Ethics Committees nor hospital directors treat patients. At least for the present, that responsibility and honor are reserved for physicians.
Dr. Amy L. Friedman validly introduces the concept of desperation so severe that the desire to die becomes "transiently overwhelming." I have recognized this condition and have patiently, but not always successfully, awaited return of the will to live.
A derivative question that will arise in subsequent case discussions is whether an 84 year old should have been begun on maintenance hemodialysis. Setting an upper age limit for initiating dialytic therapy is not supportable by out-

come-based trials though as a generalization, few individuals older than 80 will achieve even marginal rehabilitation. Biological aging cannot not be ignored as factor in encroaching on the appropriateness or success of ESRD therapy. Think of the example of James A. Michener, Pulitzer Prize-winning author of "Tales of the South Pacific" and more than 40 other books with combined sales of more than 75 million who developed uremia at the age of 87 and was started on hemodialysis treatments in Austin, Texas. Michener observed that: "A person on dialysis undergoes very heavy and irritating treatment and in time it seems more than you can bear. There's always an easy out, just don't go to the hospital. Then after two weeks, you're dead[Endnote 5]." At the age of 90, after three years of hemodialysis, Michener concluded: "For the first time I could understand how a person could say 'the hell with it.' " Michener died, three days after ordering his doctors to stop dialysis[Endnote 6]. The patient in Case 1 relies on her doctor's recognition that responsibility and honor translate into the immediate cessation of further dialysis. My sensibility is affronted by the thought any physician(s) might do otherwise.

Response to Study Questions

1. The physician proposes and the patient either accepts or declines. Neither the physician nor the family can override a legally competent patient's wishes.
2. Certainly. Whether accepted (standard) or experimental, any treatment can be delivered only with the patient's consent.
3. A legally competent patient has the unquestioned right to stop a treatment at any time.
4. No matter how well meaning a family member, the legally competent individual retains control over every therapeutic maneuver. Lacking consent, therapy may not be applied.
5. The question is too broad. For any reason includes minor side effects that though undesirable do not govern the major decision to use a therapy. For example, cyclosporine imposes risks of infection, induction of diabetes, and cosmetic disfigurement - all disagreeable consequences that may be tolerated in order to hold an organ graft (kidney transplant). If, however, the physician believes that what is about to be done to a patient is wrong, inordinately hurtful, or morally unjustified, the physician must not participate and should communicate the reasoning behind refusal.
6. One hopes that included in the skills of any Part hospital administrator is the ability to moderate disputes and appease family guilt when a patient is dying. Whatever the administrator says or does, however, the legal (and moral) responsibility for protection of the patient remain with the physician.
7. A very tough question. While a threatened law suit is not reason to deliver or deny therapy, a physician who performs a procedure that is "against the law" or prescribes a drug that is not "approved" risks loss of licensure even though the motivation was true concern for the patient.

Case 2

FAILURE TO UNDERSTAND DIALYTIC THERAPY

A 27 year old schizophrenic woman who is permanently hospitalized at a state psychiatric institute developed end-stage kidney disease due to lupus nephritis. It has been over six years since the patient conversed with anyone in a rational manner. Initial hemodialyses were accomplished by sedating the patient who awoke repeatedly, shouting and clashing with her attendants. Both arterial and venous lines were pulled out by the patient during each dialysis, leading to extensive hemorrhage on one occasion. A psychiatric consultant indicates that there is no likelihood of improvement in the patient's psychosis which has not responded to electric shock, large doses of phenothiazines, and other drug regimens. ***The responsible nephrologist states her intent to not perform any further dialytic therapy.***

Study Questions

1. Who has the legal *right/obligation* to make life-determining decisions for a psychotic individual?
2. Was it inappropriate (immoral) to begin hemodialysis in a psychotic non-communicative patient?
3. Once dialytic therapy is started, is it moral/ethical to stop treatment when the patient is unaware of what is happening?
4. Is stopping dialysis, meaning certain death, actually premeditated murder?
5. Can a physician (nephrologist) be ordered by the Court to conduct a specific therapy?
6. How is stopping dialysis any different from turning off a respirator?
7. Must the patient's religion be taken into account when making decisions about continuing life sustaining therapy?

Monique Janelle London, J.D.

The patient appears to be incompetent. However, that fact alone does not give the nephrologist the right to decide to discontinue dialysis treatments. That right is generally exercised by the patient with an advance directive, or on the patient's behalf by her surrogate or other legal representative. The nephrologist faces tort liability for discontinuing life-saving medical treatment without the informed consent of the patient or her legal representative. On the other hand, the nephrologist may be absolved of liability for discontinuing "futile" dialysis treatments. On the facts of this Case, however, dialysis does not seem to be futile. The nephrologist's refusal to continue dialyzing the patient without giving her a chance to seek treatment elsewhere may also constitute abandonment of the patient. In the absence of informed consent from the patient or her legal representative to discontinue treatments, the nephrologist should keep trying to dialyze her, or arrange for her transfer to another facility that will.

Incompetent Patient's Decisionmaking Rights:

The patient in this Case is schizophrenic and unable to converse with anyone in a rational manner. Thus, she is incompetent to make a rational, informed decision about whether to continue dialysis treatments. But the patient's incompetence does not give the nephrologist the unilateral right to terminate the treatments. Incompetent patients do not lose their right to self-determination merely because of an inability to exercise it. *See, e.g., In re A.C.*, 573 A.2d 1235, 1247 (D.C. Cir. 1990) (en banc) ("This right of bodily integrity belongs equally to persons who are competent and persons who are not. Further, it matters not what the quality of a patient's life may be; the right of bodily integrity is not extinguished simply because someone is ill, or even at death's door."); *In re Guardianship of Roe*, 383 Mass. 415, 421 N.E.2d 40, 51 (Mass. 1981) ("To deny this right to persons who are incapable of exercising it personally is to degrade those whose disabilities make them wholly reliant on other, more fortunate, individuals."); *In re Spring*, 380 Mass. 629, 634; 405 N.E.2d 115 (Mass. 1980) (explaining that incompetents do not lose the right to choose by virtue of their incompetence).

Advance Directive:

The patient may have executed an advance directive when competent. As explained in connection with Case 1, if the patient executed a valid advance directive regarding *withholding or withdrawing* treatment, many states require that the treating physician honor the wishes stated therein (or transfer the patient to another health care provider who will honor them). Thus, if the patient has such an advance directive, the nephrologist can and should withdraw dialysis therapy. However, it seems unlikely that the patient would have anticipated the present circumstances when she was competent (if she ever was).

On the other hand, the patient may have an advance directive requesting to have treatment administered (rather than withdrawn) in the present situation. If so, the nephrologist should try to continue dialyzing the patient, unless she believes it would be futile or medically inappropriate to do so. The nephrologist's right to withhold medical treatment she believes is futile is discussed in more detail below.

Surrogate Decisionmaker:

If the patient did not make an advance directive, her right to make medical decisions can still be exercised on her behalf by a surrogate. Generally, the patient's family is considered to be the best surrogate. *See In re Doe*, 262 Ga. 389, 418 S.E.2d 3, 6 (Ga. 1992) ("Medical decision-making for incompetent patients is most often best left to the patient's family (or other designated proxy) and the medical community."); *In re Jobes*, 108 N.J. 394, 529 A.2d 434, 445 (N.J. 1987) ("Family members are best qualified to make substituted judgments for incompetent patients."). If no family exists, a guardian may be appointed by the court to make the decision whether to discontinue treatment. *See In re Moorhouse*, 250 N.J. Super. 307, 593 A.2d 1256, 1261 (N.J. Super. Ct. 1991) (stating that life support should not be terminated in the absence of family without appointing a guardian).

Case 2 does not state whether the patient has any surrogate or appointed guardian. If not, the state psychiatric institute where the patient is hospitalized may have legal authority to make decisions on the patient's behalf. In any event, someone other than the nephrologist has the right to make medical treatment decisions for the patient. Thus, to avoid legal liability, the nephrologist should determine whether the patient has any family, close friends or a designated surrogate or legal representative, and then consult those people about the proposed withdrawal of dialysis.

If any of them opposes withdrawing dialysis, the nephrologist may need to seek a court order prior to discontinuing treatments. *See John F. Kennedy Memorial Hosp. v. Bludworth,* 452 So. 2d 921, 926-927 (Fla. 1984) ("Disagreement among the physicians or family members . . . may require judicial intervention"); *In re Lawrance,* 579 N.E.2d 32, 44 (Ind. 1991) ("When there is not unanimity amongst those with tangible professional or personal interest in the patient, the courts are available to resolve the dispute if need be.").

And even if all relevant parties *agree* that discontinuing dialysis is what the patient would want if competent, or is in the patient's best interests, the nephrologist may still need to seek court approval before discontinuing treatment. Some courts favor court involvement in making decisions on behalf of an incompetent regarding life-sustaining treatment. *See Rasmussen v. Fleming,* 154 Ariz. 207, 741 P.2d 674, 692 (Ariz. 1987) (Feldman, Vice C.J., concurring) ("Even where there is unanimity of opinion between the guardian, the family, and the doctors . . . 'substituted judgment' and 'best interest' decisions should be validated by court order."); *In re A.C.,* 573 A.2d 1235, 1247 (D.C. Cir. 1990) (en banc) ("To protect that right against intrusion by others - family members, doctors, hospitals, or anyone else, however well-intentioned - we hold that a court must determine the patient's wishes by any means available, and must abide by those wishes unless there are truly extraordinary or compelling reasons to override them.").

Other courts do not believe court involvement is necessary if all parties agree on the treatment decision. *See John F. Kennedy Memorial Hosp. v. Bludworth,* 452 So. 2d 921, 925 (Fla. 1984) ("To require prior court approval for termination of the life support systems in this type of case is too burdensome, is not necessary to protect the state's interests or the interests of the patient, and could render the right of the incompetent a nullity."); *In re Longeway,* 133 Ill. 2d 33, 549 N.E.2d 292, 295 (Ill. 1989) ("For many years, members of a patient's family, together with doctors and clergy, have made decisions to withdraw life-sustaining equipment from incompetent, hopelessly ill patients without seeking judicial approval.").

In sum, the nephrologist should protect herself legally by finding out if the patient has an applicable advance directive, obtaining consent from the patient's family or other legal representatives to discontinue treatment, and/or seeking approval from the court prior to discontinuing dialysis treatments.

Futility:

However, the nephrologist may be able to avoid liability for discontinuing dialysis treatments even in the face of an advance directive to the contrary or lack of consent from the patient's legal representatives. There is an ongoing debate in the medical and legal communities over whether, and on what grounds, a physician has the legal and ethical right to make a unilateral decision to limit or withhold medical treatment the physician deems futile or medically inappropriate, when that decision affects the patient's right of self determination or autonomy regarding medical treatments.

In many states a physician may not be compelled to provide treatments which would be "futile," "medically ineffective," or "medically inappropriate." *See, e.g.*, LA. REV. STAT. ANN. § 40:1299.58.1(A)(4) (a physician cannot be required to provide "medically inappropriate treatment . . . to any patient [and a physician's] medical judgment with respect to the application of medical treatment or life-sustaining procedures" may not be interfered with); COLO. REV. STAT. ANN. § 15-14-506(5)(b) (health care providers cannot be compelled to administer "medically inappropriate" treatment at the request of a health care agent appointed under a medical durable power of attorney); MD. HEALTH-GEN. CODE ANN. § 5-611(a)-(b) (physicians cannot be required to prescribe or render "medical treatment [they] determine[] to be ethically inappropriate" or "medically ineffective . . . under generally accepted medical practices"); VA. CODE ANN. § 54.1-2990 ("[A physician cannot be required to] prescribe or render medical treatment to a patient that the physician determines to be medically or ethically inappropriate. However, . . . if the physician's determination is contrary to the terms of an advance directive of a qualified patient or the treatment decision of a person designated to make the decision . . ., the physician shall make a reasonable effort to transfer the patient to another physician."); OHIO REV. CODE ANN. § 1337.16(B)(2)(b) ("If the instruction of a [health care agent] is to use or continue life-sustaining treatment [for a patient suffering from] a terminal condition or in a permanently unconscious state, . . . the attending physician . . . who . . . is not willing . . . to comply or allow compliance with that instruction, [presumably because the physician deems life-sustaining treatment inappropriate,] shall use or continue the life-sustaining treatment . . . until a transfer . . . is made.").

Unfortunately, whether the futility determination is subjective (based solely on the physician's judgment) or objective (requiring some type of consensus from the relevant medical community) seems to vary from state to state. Moreover, universal criteria have not yet developed among the medical community for determining whether a particular medical situation is "futile." Thus, unless binding precedent has already been set by a court deciding an analogous futility question, it may be very difficult for the physician to predict whether a futility argument will be successful.

The futility question was analyzed in the dialysis context in *Causey v. St. Francis Medical Center ("Causey")*, 719 So. 2d 1072 (La. Ct. App. 2d Cir. 1998). There, the patient was a quadriplegic with ESRD who suffered a heart attack and entered a coma. The treating physician believed that continuing dialysis treatments would be futile, since the patient only had a 1-5% chance of regaining consciousness. *Id.* at 1073. The physician and the hospital's Morals and Ethics Board agreed that discontinuing dialysis and other life support procedures was the appropriate course of action, since the care would have no benefit other than prolonging life. *Id.* at 1074. The physician terminated all life-sustaining treatment over the family's objection. *Id.* at 1073-1074.

The issue presented was whether the physician committed malpractice by failing to obtain the informed consent of the patient's family to withdraw life support. The court noted that standards of medical malpractice "require a physician to act with the degree of skill and care ordinarily possessed by those in that same medical specialty acting under the same or similar circumstances." *Id.* at 1076. Therefore, the real question was not whether the physician himself believed that continuing dialysis would be medically inappropriate, but whether that was the consensus of the relevant medical community. The court allowed for the possibility that the hospital's Morals and Ethics Board was a consensus of physicians, representing the prevailing standard of care, who had determined that continuing treatment would be "medically inappropriate." *Id.* It acknowledged that the physician might be absolved of liability for failure to obtain informed consent on grounds that the medical consensus was to discontinue treatment. *Id.*

Ultimately, the *Causey* court did not decide this issue, since the matter had not yet been presented to a medical review panel and was thus premature. *Id.* However, its analysis suggests that the nephrologist in Case 2 might avoid liability for discontinuing dialysis treatments for the patient by obtaining a medical consensus that continuing the treatments would be futile.

On the other hand, getting such a consensus would be difficult on the present facts. The patient in the *Causey* case was comatose and unlikely to regain consciousness. The patient in Case 2, in contrast, is conscious, but merely unlikely to improve her psychotic condition. This writer has found no support for the conclusion that continuing dialysis would provide a schizophrenic patient "no benefit other than prolonging life." In *Causey*, continuing dialysis was expected only to prolong the patient's life by up to two years. In Case 2, there is no indication of any limit on how long dialysis could sustain the patient's life.

Indeed, the only real basis on which the nephrologist in Case 2 could possibly claim "futility" would be the physical impossibility of dialyzing the patient. Despite sedation, she awakens, struggles, and pulls out her needles. However, such difficulties apparently can be overcome. In In re Spring, 380 Mass. 629, 405 N.E. 2d 115 (Mass. 1980), the senile patient's behavior was similar to that of the patient in Case 2. Occasionally he "kicked nurses, resisted transportation for dialysis, and pulled the dialysis needles out of his arm." 405 N.E. 2d at 118. Nonetheless, his disruptive behavior was controlled through heavy sedation, and it was still possible to complete the dialysis treatments. Similarly, dialysis treatments could be continued in the present Case, either by sedation or physical restraints.

In sum, the nephrologist in Case 2 probably could not rely on the futility doctrine to avoid liability for discontinuing treatment.

Federally Prohibited Discrimination and Reasonable Accommodations:

If the nephrologist discontinues dialysis treatments, she could also be liable for discrimination in violation of the Americans With Disabilities Act ("ADA") and § 504 of the 1973 Rehabilitation Act, 29 U.S.C.A. § 794(a). Section 504 of the Rehabilitation Act provides: "No otherwise qualified individual with a disability. . . shall, solely by reason of his or her disability, be excluded from the participation in, be denied the benefits of, or be subjected to discrimination under any program or activity receiving Federal financial assistance. . . ." Presumably the state psychiatric institute where the patient is hospitalized is such a program. The ADA similarly prohibits discrimination by health care providers and hospitals against people with "disabilities," including schizophrenia. *See* 42 U.S.C. §§ 12102 to 12213; 28 C.F.R. § 36.104; 29 C.F.R. § 1630.2.

Under either of these federal statutes, it could be argued that the nephrologist is unlawfully discriminating. That is, she is withdrawing dialytic therapy from the patient in Case 2 solely because of her schizophrenia; if the patient were not schizophrenic, the nephrologist would continue to dialyze her. The nephrologist could counter that she was not discriminating on the basis of the schizophrenia, but rather on the basis of the patient struggling and pulling out her needles. She could argue that a schizophrenic patient would not necessarily pull out her needles, and a patient who pulled out her needles would not necessarily be schizophrenic. This argument seems compelling.

However, even if the nephrologist were found to be discriminating on the basis of the patient's schizophrenia, she could defend against the discrimination claim on grounds that it would be futile to try to dialyze the patient. It is unclear whether this argument would succeed. In one discrimination case, a federal district court suggested that futility is not a defense to medical discrimination against a patient based on the patient's disability. In *In Re Baby K,* 832 F. Supp. 1022, 1029 (E.D. Va. 1993), the court held that physicians violated the ADA by withholding ventilatory treatment from an anencephalic infant suffering from respiratory distress based on her anencephaly, noting that "the ADA does not permit the denial of ventilator services that would keep alive an anencephalic baby when those life-saving services would otherwise be provided to a baby without disabilities at the parent's request."Footnote 14

On the other hand, in *United States v. University Hospital,* 729 F.2d 144 (2d Cir. 1984), a federal appeals court rejected a similar discrimination claim where corrective surgery on a child with multiple birth defects was forgone, on grounds that "Section 504 prohibits discrimination against a handicapped individual only where the individual's handicap is *unrelated to,* and thus improper to consideration of, the services in question." *Id.* at 156 (emphasis added). Under that decision, the nephrologist could defend against a discrimination claim on grounds that dialyzing the patient is futile precisely because the patient has schizophre-

[14] On appeal, the circuit court upheld the decision on other grounds, and did not comment on the discrimination ruling of the lower court. *See Baby K,* 16 F.3d 590 (4th Cir.), cert. denied, 115 S. Ct. 91 (1994). Therefore, the influence of the lower court's decision on future cases is uncertain.

nia which makes her struggle with attendants and pull out her needles. Given the different views of the courts, it is uncertain whether the applicable law and facts in Case 2 would support the nephrologist's futility defense against a discrimination claim.

The nephrologist could also try to argue that dialyzing the patient would require making unduly burdensome accommodations or would require a fundamental alteration of the dialysis service provided. Under the ADA, an entity providing services to a disabled person need only "make reasonable modifications in [its practices] when such modifications are necessary to afford [its services] to individuals with disabilities, unless . . . . making such modifications would fundamentally alter the nature of [the services]." 42 U.S.C. § 12182(b)(2)(A)(ii). However, in Case 2, given that the dialysis is taking place in a state psychiatric institute, it does not seem "unreasonable" or likely to "fundamentally alter the nature of the services" to accommodate the patient by using sedation and physical restraints if necessary. Thus, this argument would likely fail.

All tolled, the nephrologist could probably defend against a claim that she was discriminating against the patient on the basis of the "disability" of schizophrenia. However, if the nephrologist did not successfully defend against that claim, it seems unlikely that she could defeat a discrimination claim on futility grounds.

Abandonment:

Although the nephrologist may not be able to discriminate against the patient on the basis of her schizophrenia, she is not obligated to continue caring for the patient indefinitely. She has the option to end her role as the patient's nephrologist, provided she satisfies certain requirements. Under the long-settled doctrine of abandonment, a physician who is engaged to attend a patient is liable for any damages caused by abandoning the case, unless she provides due notice to the patient and affords her a reasonable opportunity to procure the attendance of another doctor. *See, e.g., Manno v. McIntosh,* 519 N.W. 2d 815 (Iowa Ct. App. 1994) (physician who leaves patient in critical stage of disease without reason or sufficient notice to enable patient to procure another physician is negligent); *Allison v. Patel,* 211 Ga. App. 376, 438 S.E. 2d 920 (Georgia App. 1993), *reconsideration denied* (1993) and *cert. denied* (Ga) slip op.; *Ricks v. Budge,* 91 Utah 307, 64 P.2d 208 (Utah 1937); *Gray v. Davidson,* 15 Wash. 2d 257, 130 P.2d 341 (Wash. 1942).[Footnote 15] If these conditions are satisfied, the nephrologist may sever the relationship. *See, e.g., Lyons v. Grether,* 218 Va. 630, 239 S.E.2d 103, 106 (Va. 1977) (holding physician has right to withdraw from case, provided patient is given reasonable opportunity to acquire needed services from another physician); *Miller v. Greater Southeast Community Hosp.*, 508 A.2d 927, 929 (D.C. 1986) (holding that supplying noncritical patient with a list of substitute physicians to replace attending physician is reasonable means of severing professional relationship).

[15] The policy permitting the physician to stop treating the patient generally applies when a medically stable patient wants continued care but does not need emergency care. One case has indicated that dialysis treatments are not "emergency" care. *See Payton v. Weaver,* 131 Cal. App. 3d 38, 182 Cal. Rptr. 225, 229-230 (Cal. App. 1st Dist. 1982).

Thus, to avoid liability for abandonment, the nephrologist must notify the patient's family or surrogate of the intent to discontinue treating the patient, and allow sufficient time for the patient to be transferred to another nephrologist. If the nephrologist satisfies these requirements and thereby terminates the relationship with the patient, she will also avoid liability for failure to obtain informed consent and discrimination on the basis of a disability.

Conclusion:

To avoid legal liability, the nephrologist must continue to dialyze the patient unless and until she can obtain consent to discontinue treatment from all family members and legal representatives, and court approval to do so. Alternatively, she can terminate her relationship with the patient, and end her obligation to dialyze the patient that way - but first, the nephrologist must provide notice of her intent to stop treating the patient, and a reasonable opportunity for the patient to secure another nephrologist.

Ethical Analysis:

Ethically, there is no basis for the nephrologist to refuse to provide further dialytic therapy. In all likelihood, sedatives and physical restraints can be used to prevent the patient from interrupting her dialysis treatments. The patient is not comatose or in a persistent vegetative state. She is conscious, although psychotic. Her illness is not terminal. Neither she nor anyone acting on her behalf requested or consented to discontinuation of dialysis treatments (in the facts given). The patient may not appear to enjoy dialysis, but there is not enough evidence to suggest she would want to die instead. In the absence of any such evidence from the patient (when she was competent), her family or legal representative, the nephrologist should continue the treatments.

Connie Zuckerman, J.D.

This patient clearly lacks the capacity to understand the nature and consequences of her disease, and is thus unable to consider whether the continuance of dialysis under the current conditions meets her interests, as either she or others would define such interests. Given her decisional incapacity, a surrogate decisionmaker will need to determine the propriety of dialysis withdrawal under the current circumstances. Such surrogate will need to weigh and consider the benefits and the burdens of continued dialysis versus dialysis withdrawal, with the goal of determining what serves the best interests of this patient.

A best interest analysis would consider such factors as the extent to which the treatment prolongs life, the pain and suffering caused by treatment continuance versus withdrawal, the possibility of return to functional capacity, the dignity of the individual patient and, ultimately, the quality of life for this patient, now and in the future, in comparison to her previous quality of life. Given that the dialysis will not cure the patient's underlaying lupus and schizophrenia, and given the burdens the patient endures as a result of dialysis, it may be ethically justifiable to support the withdrawal of dialysis for this patient. From a legal perspective, however, such a decision can only be made by one granted the legal authority to do so, and thus a legal guardian may need to be appointed to make the ultimate determination.

Amy L. Friedman, M.D.

Few would doubt that this unfortunate young woman should receive full treatment for either an injury sustained from a fall out of bed or for acute appendicitis. To withhold urgent care would seem inhumane. What distinguishes the use of chronic dialysis to prolong her life from these acute therapies? To maintain an acceptable quality of care with ongoing renal replacement therapy the patient will require numerous surgical and radiological access procedures over time. She will be at risk of infection or anesthetic complication and will suffer pain and discomfort from the interventions. Her healthcare team will be exposed to risk of physical harm from her blood and bodily fluids, particularly since she is combative. Other dialysis patients will experience stress as they witness her management. Hospitalization in an acute care facility will be required intermittently. There is no doubt that a significant amount of money and other resources will be expended in her care. It seems obvious that these risks to the patient, the healthcare team and society would all be easily outweighed if the benefit she was to derive were highly significant. In the case of a patient apparently unable to perceive reality, however, it is more difficult to interpret benefit. Is the state of life itself enough to justify these risks? As a society we have not yet systematically confronted these issues. Elderly patients unlikely to survive the failure of multiple organ systems continue to be admitted to costly intensive care unit beds. Remarkably premature infants are routinely resuscitated at birth and subjected to extensive management courses even though the outcome is often death and the hope of normal growth and development limited at best. Patients with advanced heart failure but not candidates for heart transplants are provided with endless supplies of oxygen, medications and hospital readmissions. In all these circumstances risk to the patient is high, the cost to society is great and the benefit short term at best. **Dialysis is no less indispensable to the patient with renal failure. Both because of its reimbursement by the government (through Medicare) and by virtue of its historical growth from highly publicized selection processes granting access to a limited supply of machines, this therapy is a more visible target of controversy than other forms of medical treatment. I cannot be comfortable with a different approach to the application of dialytic therapies than to other medical regimens. It would be reasonable to impose limited access to dialysis on the basis of cost and resources or limited direct benefits only if similar judgements are routinely made with regard to other therapies.**

On the other hand, I strongly believe that a relative or guardian willing and capable to determine that this woman is suffering inappropriately without sufficient gain should be supported in determining that all therapies should be discontinued. In the absence (which I have assumed in this case) of a relative or guardian capable of subjectively representing the interests of the patient, institutions and health care providers innately biased towards minimizing their own struggles should have the default setting of continuing to provide dialysis and all other forms of medical therapy to their patient. After all, it is also conceivable that she will be maintained sufficiently long to enter an era in which improved therapy for schizophrenia will allow her to rejoin society!

Carl M. Kjellstrand, M.D.

We have not established contraindications to chronic dialysis. We very much need to do so. Without them, foolish enterprises of hopeless resuscitation efforts will be undertaken that are cruel to patients and their families and abusive of scarce and expensive resources on one hand. On the other, all kinds of artificial obstacles will be placed in the way of patients who could benefit, letting these obstacles masquerade as medical contraindications when they actually are political or financial constraints.

My contraindications are:

i) An expected life of less than 6 months, varied humanely.
ii) Dementia or intellectual capacity resulting in inability to understand the benefits of dialysis, which makes it a meaningless, repetitive procedure of torture to the uncomprehending patient.

This case fulfils criteria number two.
Once you have ruled out any possible remedy to the patient's situation it should be carefully documented in the charts, dialysis withdrawn, and the avenues of death made more smooth.

Mildred (Barry) Friedman

Treatment is meant to help patients, to improve quality of life. The Hippocratic Oath states that physicians should do no harm. In this case, a balance between improving the existing medical condition and causing distress, possibly pain, and possibly fear - must be struck. The patient is obviously troubled - she struggles. She is being harmed. Even if there is a functioning mind deep within, comprehension cannot be there. A reasonable assumption is that no one has explained what is happening to her.

If the therapy could cure the medical problem, a reason to continue treatment might exist. It cannot and only prolongs and deepens the misery of the patient. Discontinuing dialysis would not be euthanasia but only recognizing that death is the result of kidney failure due to lupus nephritis.
Cost of maintaining this life should also be considered. The nation can no longer provide *all available* medical treatment to everyone. Decisions regarding who to treat and who not to treat, must be made. Money should be spent with common sense.

Let me say here that if sufficient funds to treat all the ill were available, I would still agree with the responsible nephrologist to no longer dialyze. My primary

grounds are compassion and a desire to improve the quality of life. Strange, but at times quality of life is bettered by death.
I agree with the decision of the nephrologist.

Judith E. Columbo

It is my feeling that this patient, a 27 year old schizophrenic woman who developed ESRD, not only has a failure to understand dialysis but is incapable of understanding everyday life. Sedating a patient, battling to maintain an uneventful dialysis session every time, and having a patient struggle and shout is dangerous Not only to the patient, but this behavior is above and beyond the call of duty. The situation is not temporary it is permanent and the outlook is not encouraging. I agree with the nephrologist not to perform any further dialytic treatment.

Editor's Remarks2

Divergence in perspective between the attorneys versus the physicians and patients is at the same time instructive and sad. All but Dr. Amy L. Friedman, with direct knowledge of sickness and its treatment (patients and physicians) are comfortable with a response directing cessation of an arduous complex therapy that proffers no humane benefit other than sustaining an unaware existence. She raises the possibility of a near-term effective treatment for schizophrenia as rationale for continuing dialytic therapy in the absence of proscription by family or the court.
By contrast, lawyers call for caution and delay to prepare the paper trail defending the nephrologist. London's observes that: "The nephrologist may still need to seek court approval before (discontinuing dialysis). The courts are split on this point." Such advice is understandable so long as other attorneys prowl for lapses in conduct likely to generate winning suits irrespective of intrinsic merit or potential ruination of a physician's career. But that is a story for another venue.
Our illustrative case might just as well have been an autistic adolescent or a vegetative individual after a failed surgical attempt to remove a brain malignancy. The stratagem centers on the issue of whether a nonthinking, noncommunicating but otherwise physiologically functional "person" manifesting ESRD should be subjected to life prolongation by maintenance hemodialysis (peritoneal dialysis or kidney transplant)? Alternatively, the argument can be posed as whether any procedure drug, or regimen (dialysis) likely to sustain life can be withheld because of psychiatric or organic brain debility.
Given such an ambiguous legal position, the practitioner can either be timid (declining action while calling for hospital administrators to make a binding decision) or "bold" (deciding to act without delay on the basis of intuition, personal values, and common sense). My own course is to neither start nor continue dialytic therapy for any patient lacking hope of becoming a functional person. As poignantly and starkly put by Mildred Barry Friedman: "Strange,

but at times quality of life is bettered by death." For the "creature" that is Case 2 no further dialyses should be imposed.

Response to Study Questions

1. For an adult patient, the court's assignment of responsibility (right) to accept or refuse treatment is necessary before anyone may direct therapy for a mentally incompetent person. All of us know obviously psychotic people who walk the streets and function at a level that has not been brought to the court's attention. Until an individual's control has been removed, the physician is bound by the patient's consent. This does not extend to requests that as judged by the physician are not in the patient's interest.
2. As extensively discussed above, it is the individual physician's decision as whether or not to start a dialysis regimen. I would not.
3. Same answer as to the preceding question. Again, I would not.
4. When dealing with lawyers who find municipalities liable for the risk of monkey bars in children's playgrounds, any finding is possible. It is absurd to raise the issue of murder when deciding that a therapy is not in the patient's interest.
5. Yes. But the physician does not have to comply. The court may direct that a lethal injection be administered to a condemned prisoner but the jail physician may refuse to administer the poison.
6. A semantic but nevertheless challenging argument. In both cases, a vital life sustaining function is being replaced by a machine. I would reluctantly have to admit that stopping dialysis can be like turning off a respirator: in both circumstances, sufficient native organ system function may actually be present. The patient may breath on his/her own and urine production may resume in sufficient amount to delay death in uremia for weeks to months. For the purpose of discussion, neither event is presumed probable and stopping dialysis is equivalent to removing a respirator.
7. In so far as the patient relied on religious guidance to decide whether or not to continue a dialytic regimen, the answer is yes. Physicians must not impose individual religious beliefs on their patients. The complexity of the issue is well illustrated in the practice of obstetrics by an orthodox Jew or Catholic who need to set views on abortion aside (by referral?) when responding to a patient's request for the procedure.

Case 3

DISRUPTIVE PATIENT

A 38 year old unmarried, independently wealthy woman has been on maintenance hemodialysis for two years because of polycystic kidney disease. She has been noncompliant with her treatment regimen in terms of adherence to dietary, fluid, and medication prescriptions. On numerous occasions, she has disrupted the normal function of the dialysis unit by shouting at nurses and other patients. She repetitively engages in masturbation while verbally assaulting other patients. The patient declined consultation with a psychiatrist, psychologist, or social worker and refused eudaemonic medications. She has initiated a number of malpractice suits against the dialysis clinic and two of its nephrologists. Despite her complaints about the quality of dialysis delivered, the patient rejects the proposal that she be transferred to another facility on the grounds that she is comfortable where she is. ***Her nephrologist sends a certified letter discharging the patient and declining any further care effective 30 days from receipt of the letter.***

Study Questions

1. Is disruptive or noncompliant behavior grounds for a physician's discontinuing care for a patient?
2. Does society have the *right/obligation* to mandate physician acceptance of patients?
3. Appreciating federal subsidy of hospital, ambulatory care, and dialysis facilities, can a physician whose dialysis unit receives such support decline the care of a patient beneficiary of Medicare or Medicaid funded dialysis?
4. How is the limit of patient independence and assertiveness to be delimited from noncompliance?
5. What protects the patient from egregious conduct by a dictatorial physician prescribing inappropriate therapy (inadequate dialysis, for example)?
6. Does it matter whether or not the patient's dialysis treatments are funded by Medicare, an HMO, or self payment?
7. By what means may a patient be discharged by a physician?

Monique Janelle London, J.D.

If the patient and nephrologist have an express or implied contract under which the patient must behave in certain ways to continue to dialyze at the unit, the nephrologist may have the right to discharge the patient under the terms of that contract. Even if no such contract exists, the nephrologist may still terminate the relationship with the patient, but must avoid "abandonment" - that is, discharge without due notice and ample opportunity to secure other medical attendance. Here, the nephrologist appears to have satisfied the legal requirements to discharge the patient.

Breach of Contract:

The patient and nephrologist (or dialysis unit) might have a contract or agreement providing for the termination of the dialysis relationship if the patient behaves in certain ways. For instance, in some dialysis units, the patient signs a Treatment Agreement setting forth the consumer's (patient's) and the unit's rights and obligations. Or, a court might find that the patient had an implied contract with the dialysis unit requiring the patient to control her behavior so as not to impede or disrupt the provision of dialysis services. To the extent such an express or implied contract existed, it would govern whether the nephrologist could refuse to continue treating the patient. If the contract included specific requirements for *how* the nephrologist could terminate the relationship with the patient (such as how much advance notice the nephrologist must give of the termination), the nephrologist would also have to satisfy those requirements to avoid liability for breach of contract.

Abandonment:

Even in the absence of a contractual agreement providing for discharge of the patient, the nephrologist has the right to terminate his relationship with the patient. However, he must comply with certain legal requirements to avoid liability for abandonment. As explained in connection with Case 2, a physician may withdraw from a patient's case only after providing "due notice" and an "ample opportunity" to secure the presence of other medical attendance. Otherwise, he can be held accountable for any damages resulting from his abandonment of the case. *See, e.g., Hongsathavij v. Queen of Angels etc. Medical Center,* 62 Cal. App. 4th 1123, 73 Cal. Rptr. 2d 695 (Cal. App. 2d Dist. 1998); *Capps v. Valk,* 189 Kan. 287, 369 P.2d 238 (Kan.1962).

In one case with facts similar to Case 3, the court determined that the nephrologist and hospital were legally within their rights to terminate dialysis treatments for an uncooperative patient, given that they had provided the patient reasonable notice of their intent to discharge her if she continued her disruptive behavior, and had made reasonable attempts to transfer her to another dialysis facility. In *Payton v. Weaver,* 131 Cal. App. 3d 38, 182 Cal. Rptr. 225 (Cal. App. 1st Dist. 1982), the dialysis patient, a 35 year old woman, had heroin and barbiturate addictions and alcohol, weight and emotional problems. Her nephrologist sent her a letter stating the dialysis unit would no longer treat her because of her "persistent uncooperative and antisocial behavior over . . . more than . . . three years, . . . her persistent refusal to adhere to reasonable constraints of hemodialysis, the dietary schedules and medical prescriptions . . . the use of barbiturates and other illicit drugs and because all this resulted in disruption [the dialysis center's program]." *Id.* at 41. The patient applied to two other dialysis centers, but was refused. *Id.* at 42.

The nephrologist continued to dialyze the patient at the dialysis unit on an emergency basis for four months, then notified her again by letter that he would no longer treat her. Id. The patient brought suit for a court order compelling the nephrologist and dialysis facility to continue treatment. *Id.* The parties stipulated to a settlement by which the patient would continue to be dialyzed, provided she keep her appointments at the scheduled time, refrain from using alcohol and drugs, follow her medical regimen, get counseling, and cooperate with her caregivers. *Id.*

Almost a year later, the nephrologist notified the patient that, because she had failed to comply with the settlement agreement, dialysis treatments would be terminated. He provided her with a list of local dialysis providers and offered to work with her lawyer to find alternative care. *Id.* The patient instituted a second court proceeding, alleging that the nephrologist and dialysis unit wrongfully refused to provide dialysis treatments. *Id.* at 42. She did not contend that the doctor had any obligation to continue treating her on the basis of the stipulation[Footnote 16]; rather, she only accused him of improperly abandoning her. *Id.* at 44-45.

The trial court rejected the abandonment claim, finding that the nephrologist had given sufficient notice to the patient of his intention to discontinue her dialysis treatments, and therefore had "discharged all obligations imposed by the patient-physician relationship" with her. *Id.* at 44. The appellate court affirmed that decision, finding no basis for an abandonment claim. *Id.* at 45.[Footnote 17]

Similarly, there is probably no valid basis for an abandonment claim in Case 3. Rather, the 30-day notice given by the nephrologist seems sufficient to constitute "due notice and an ample opportunity to secure the presence of other medical attendance." The patient has already refused the proposal that she be transferred to another unit; thus giving her additional time to secure "other medical attendance" by seeking such a transfer would be useless. Moreover, the patient is "independently wealthy," and thus presumably could afford to hire a nurse to dialyze her at home who could begin working within the 30-day period. Unlike the patient in *Payton*, the patient in Case 3 was unwilling to make any attempt to modify her behavior - she refused to receive consultations or be medicated. Thus, giving her additional time to prove she could behave properly would likely be useless. In sum, it appears the nephrologist has satisfied the requirements for discharging the patient.

Discrimination Under the ADA:

It is unclear from the facts presented, but the patient may have a psychological disorder. If so, under the Americans With Disabilities Act, 42 U.S.C. §§

[16] Indeed, the trial court found that the patient had violated all conditions she had agreed to under the stipulation: she gained up to 15 kilograms between treatments, was late for or missed appointments, appeared for treatments intoxicated or drugged, discontinued the counseling program, cursed, screamed and demanded she be disconnected before her treatment was finished, pulled the dialysis needles out of her arms, and exposed her genitals in a lewd manner. *Id.* at 43. It found that the patient had endangered the rights and privileges of the other patients at the unit to full and adequate treatment, which rights were superior to the patient's rights to behave as she did. *Id.*

[17] Although the appellate court recognized that it could not impose a legal obligation on the nephrologist or hospital to dialyze the patient, it felt compelled to "confront the more fundamental question" of what alternatives existed for ensuring that the patient did not die from lack of dialysis. *Id.* at 47-48. To that end, it suggested that the patient might be assisted by a voluntary conservatorship, whereby the patient would consent to placement in a psychiatric facility which would provide her dialysis treatments. *Id.* at 49.

12101-12213 (1994) (passed after the *Payton* case was decided), the patient could argue that denial of further dialysis constitutes discrimination against her based on a "disability" -- a psychological disorder that makes her disruptive and noncompliant with her medical regimen. However, the nephrologist could defend against that argument on grounds that he is not singling out the patient because of her disability. Rather, he would discharge any patient who was persistently disruptive and noncompliant, regardless of whether he or she had a mental disorder. Therefore, this writer doubts that such an argument would succeed.

Conclusion:

The nephrologist is probably within his rights to discharge the patient upon 30 days notice. However, to avoid any chance of liability, he should first explain to the patient that she will be discharged if her behavior does not change, encourage her to agree to modify her behavior, and continue to suggest that she transfer to another facility.

Ethical Analysis:

Ethically, the nephrologist has an obligation to ensure that the patient continues to receive dialysis. If he cannot arrange for the patient to be transferred to another unit or to her home, he should continue to dialyze her where she is. None of the patient's disruptive behavior creates a sufficient basis for discharging her from the dialysis unit, especially given that she might die as a consequence. Many patients are bitter, frustrated, depressed or angry about being on dialysis, and express their feelings through noncompliance or disruption. However, unless a patient's behavior endangers others, the nephrologist has an ethical obligation to treat the patient.

The patient's noncompliance with dietary and fluid restrictions and medication prescriptions alone would not be sufficient to warrant discharging her - indeed, the vast majority of patients are noncompliant at some time with their dietary and fluid restrictions (i.e., they "cheat" by eating a high-potassium or high-sodium meal, or drink too much and gain too much fluid weight between treatments). Many patients simply do not care enough about their diet and fluid restrictions to comply with the dietician's instructions, or choose an unrestricted diet as part of their quality of life despite the health consequences. These are part of the patient's life choices, do not injure anyone but the patient, and should not be grounds for discharge.

The patient's shouting at and verbally assaulting nurses and other patients would be offensive and disruptive to the staff and other patients, but it would not physically prevent the staff from doing their jobs. Perhaps the patient could be put in isolation until she agrees to stop her verbal assaults. Similarly, the patient's masturbating, although not something a captive audience of fellow dialysis patients and staff should have to tolerate, is not an ethical basis for discharging the patient. Again, if she could be placed in isolation or at least have a curtain put around her, that might prevent some of the offensive behavior. Finally, the patient's refusal to consult with a psychiatrist, psychologist or social worker, and her initiation of several malpractice suits against the dialysis clinic, are not disruptive or threatening behaviors, and thus should not result in her discharge.

Connie Zuckerman, J.D.

While the behavior and actions of this patient constitute a tremendous source of frustration for clinicians trying to administer treatment, patients do have the right to decide whether and how they wish to comply with a prescribed treatment regimen. However, such individual choice does not also empower the patient to disrupt treatment being provided to others, nor do clinicians have any obligation to tolerate what is clearly abusive behavior toward them.

After all reasonable efforts have been made to address the underlaying source of this patient's noncompliance and antisocial behavior, her treating physician would be justified in setting out a formal "contract" with the patient, which should detail the precise conditions under which treatment will continue to be provided to the patient. Should she continue disruptive behavior in defiance of the contractual terms, her nephrologist might then have sufficient justification to discharge her from his service; such discharge, however, ought to be accompanied by efforts to assist her in locating an alternative program, so as not to constitute legal abandonment of the patient. Existing case law supports such physician withdrawal from treatment in certain extreme cases. The continuous threats of malpractice litigation also negatively affect the ability of this physician to deliver competent, objective care to meet the medical needs of the patient, further justifying the decision to withdraw from the relationship.

Amy L. Friedman, M.D.

Any patient doctor relationship is two sided. The physician must behave professionally. Personal judgements about the patient and his (her) lifestyle and behavior patterns, although entirely natural, must not be permitted to compromise the delivery of healthcare. Thus, dislike of an individual should not be allowed to become apparent to the patient and should not preclude any ongoing professional obligation to him. Similarly, any legal action taken by the patient against the physician also represents insufficient cause to terminate the relationship (although I have never understood a patient's simultaneous choice to allege malpractice as he continues to willingly seek ongoing help from that same physician!).

The patient who chooses to accept care should accept and acknowledge the medical expertise and judgement of the physician. He(she) must fully disclose medical history and behavior patterns to the physician whose responsibility to protect this confidential type of information is also intrinsic to this complex relationship. The patient must demonstrate respect of the physician both as a person and as a medical expert. Unrealistic and unethical demands of the physician (requesting that a prescription be written for a family member undergoing treatment from the physician) must not be requested. Behavior should be consistent with the full range of professional responsibilities borne by the physician. Accordingly, the patient should arrive promptly for all appointments, should promptly notify the physician about necessary cancellations and should comport himself in a respectful and courteous manner. None of these expectations however, require the patient's acquiescence to the counsel provided by the physician. Medical advice should be heard and considered but not necessarily accepted. As an individual with free will, the patient has the right to choose to disregard the physician's opinion. Thus, smokers who refuse to quit, Jehovah's witnesses declining blood transfusions, or even hypertensive patients who eat high salt diets and are non compliant with medications should still expect to receive the highest level of care from their chosen physician.

An important distinction should be drawn, however, between scenarios in which emergent rather than chronic medical attention is required. In the setting of urgent illness, the physician from whom medical assistance is requested does have an obligation to provide this care, particularly when no alternative is available. However, when chronic care is provided, some issues may appropriately provoke the physician's unwillingness to provide care. Thus, a surgeon must be able to decline to provide elective surgery anticipated to cause significant blood loss, to the Jehovah's witness. Without the component of urgency, the physician may inform the patient about the reason for the declination of care, and should assist the patient in attempting to identify other available surgeons. In the setting described, a young woman repeatedly chooses to disregard the behavioral standards expected by most healthcare providers. Provided she believes the patient is competent, both to decline neurologic or psychiatric assessment and to fully comprehend the preferred conduct, the nephrologist has every right to decline to participate in an ongoing professional relationship with her. It should also be noted that continued tolerance of the disruptive behavior would unreasonably intrude on the professional behavior and environment that other patients receiving dialysis at this center expect. The unruly patient should receive sequential notifications of impending cessation of services, and should be offered assistance in the identification of alternate dialysis centers. Every responsible effort to avoid this continuity of dialytic therapy should be made.

An additional component of the patient physician relationship that is often disregarded is the respect of each other's time. Patients should plan to arrive prior to scheduled appointment times, and should not expect accommodation if significantly tardy. On the other hand, the patient should be able to expect that the physician also honors the scheduled appointment time. Several issues complicate this issue. First, all physicians are now under significant pressure to shorten the length of time spent with patients and to crowd schedules with more appointments than most would consider reasonable. Nevertheless, every effort to maintain punctuality and schedule the day's appointments with reasonable expectations must be undertaken. The second consideration is the unpredictability of some medical problems. Many physicians practice in situations that must routinely accommodate unpredictable medical circumstances. Thus, the obstetrician can obviously not predict the timing or length of childbirth and labor. Similarly, transplant surgeons are unable to predict the availability of cadaver organs with the accompanying need to transplant. In such practices, the need to cancel previously scheduled patient appointments often arises. The physician's office staff should fully inform patients of the circumstances that are occurring, as far in advance as is feasible. Back up management plans (exam by a knowledgeable nurse, promptly rescheduled appointments, etc) must be provided. In general, patients do respond positively to this approach.

Carl M. Kjellstrand, M.D.

The nephrologist will be sued and he will lose in court. It is a foolish action. A death sentence may have been O.K. for masturbation during the Inquisition in the thirteenth century, but it will be met with incredulity in 1994. We have no good remedy for situations like this in dialysis, however things may change. The National Kidney Foundation has addressed the question of abusive patients, like the one described, and suggested that their care should be shared within the network of various dialyses. This will give units time to recover from energy-sapping conflicts with such patients.

Mildred (Barry) Friedman

Responsibility lies across the shoulders of health care providers and also across the shoulders of patients. People who distract those taking care of them, interfere with more than comfort of others in a dialysis unit. People who are distracted and stressed do not function as well as they should. Squeaky wheels get the grease and so the disruptive get the attention. Each of us has only so much time and energy to spend on our jobs. Therefore, care for the compliant, cooperative patient is downgraded. "Good" patients are essentially punished to benefit "bad" ones.

Certainly attempts to treat disruptive patients should be made but these people cannot be allowed to constantly discomfort others around them.

I would begin by documenting her behavior. Tapes, films, videos of her actions would constitute legal proof of her conduct. The next step might be an attempt to isolate her in the dialysis clinic. If this did not work, she should certainly be transferred to another facility using the procedure detailed.

Staff could explain to her (probably unsuccessfully), that while she feels comfortable, others do not. The reaction she is faced with is a consequence of her actions. She has not lived up to her responsibilities as a patient. Patient responsibility should be clearly explained.

Other alternatives should be explored. Independent wealth might allow her to design a comfortable, friendly environment in her home. A sympathetic person sharing a good relationship with the patient, might be able to engross her in designing a home unit. Involvement in her own care could potentially change her behavior.

In summary, explanations, isolation, and involvement should be attempted. If success does not come to pass then I would agree to legally discharging her with notice. No one patient is more important than others.

Judith E. Columbo

The disruptive patient in a dialysis unit is like chalk rubbing the wrong way on a blackboard. This patient is mad at the world for her problems and even her wealth cannot buy her peace. It is one thing to intentionally abuse her body by not sticking to dietary or fluid restrictions but when other people are the patients target, then enough is enough. Perhaps a home dialysis regimen could have been suggested. As a former dialysis patient I applaud the nephrologist in discharging the disruptive patient, realizing that the remaining patients have rights also.

Editor's Remarks3

Dr. Amy L. Friedman urges reason and respect between patient and physician, an approach that has clearly not worked. Other respondents reach consensus that the disruptive patient can be discharged. However, Kjellstrand appears depressed over the high probability that no matter what: "The nephrologist will be sued and he will lose in court." He laments the reality that: "We have no good remedy for situations like this in dialysis." Both patients, however, side against the woman in Case 3 with Columbo going so far as to "applaud the nephrologist in discharging the disruptive patient." My opinion as to what course is open to a nephrologist desiring disengagement from a patient is consonant with the positions expounded by attorneys London and Zuckerman.

In an advisory bulletin to physicians, the American Medical Association's counsel states: "The obligation to treat non-compliant patients should not be an absolute one." Reverting to the cautious stance more characteristic of attorneys, the AMA counsel warns: "Patients should not have to pay for their non-compliance with their lives[Endnote 7]." Thus, like King Solomon coping with two disputatious women claiming to have mothered the same baby, the patient must not be cut in half in order to restore peace to a dialysis unit. As a last resort, an abusive noncompliant dialysis patient can be discharged to another facility providing that the patient's welfare is protected.

To guide in resolution of an unwanted patient relationship, the steps outlined below have been useful.

1. Inventory potential third party problem solvers (spouse, family, friend, clergy, others).
2. Carefully document incidents and staff responses in the patient's chart.
3. Involve the unit social worker and obtain psychiatric consultation if indicated.
4. Report the growing problem to the unit or hospital "risk management" service.
5. Advise the patient *in writing by certified mail* that a limit in toleration of the patient's action has been defined. Establish a date for compliance.
6. Should the abusive behavior continue beyond the time limit, notify the patient of termination of services *in writing by certified mail* permitting

sufficient time for the patient to seek and obtain alternative dialysis care (at least 30 days). Include in the notification a list of proximal dialysis units and the directors' phone numbers.

Response to Study Questions

1. Compliance is a relative term as discussed above. Obese individuals do not comply with physician's dietary instruction, smokers smoke, and hypertensives do not take potency inhibiting drugs. The severity of noncompliance and its impact on other patients and a program's ability to function are the factors that must be weighed.
2. Under some circumstances yes. Institutions accepting federal funding must comply with guidelines stating who may or may not be turned away as patients. Specific legislation correctly protects minority, women, and disabled people from refusal of theapy because of these characteristics.
3. No. There must be a defensible reason for refusal of dialysis other than the physician's whim.
4. Here the art of medicine weighs the difference.
5. Patients may appeal to state health departments and to several federal agencies. In practice, the autocratic, dictatorial physician is losing the authority to be a despot.
6. It should make no difference. Of course, an HMO that reimburses below the level of cost can be discontinued as a contractual partner.
7. The steps are outlined in detail.

Case 4

ACTIVE HEROIN ABUSE

A 21 year old heroin addict continues his habit by repeated injections of heroin into his arteriovenous access used for maintenance hemodialysis. Heroin addiction began during a three year prison term for armed robbery, his seventh felony arrest and fourth conviction. His dialysis course of two years has been complicated by bacterial endocarditis and multiple skin abscesses, the result of continue use of "dirty" needles and syringes. Neither his family - from which he is estranged - nor his parole officer have been able to "reason" with the patient. Over the preceding five months, the addiction has intensified and the patient has infected and destroyed three surgically created accesses in his arms. Dialysis is currently performed by repeated femoral vein cannulation. ***The responsible vascular surgeon refuses any further access surgery so long as the patient continues to inject heroin into any available vein.***

Study Questions

1. Is self injury a reason for a physician to deny reparative therapy?
2. Is heroin or cocaine abuse to be regarded differently from alcohol abuse in terms of application or refusal of therapy?
3. Does a surgeon have the *right/obligation* to accept patients on the basis of how moral the patient is?
4. Can a limit ever be set for applying "rescue" therapy? If not three destroyed vascular accesses, would five or ten similar episodes provide justification for discontinuing care?
5. Would a forced transfer to peritoneal dialysis be a moral choice?
6. Is the physician obligated to report the parole violation of use of narcotic drugs?
7. Might it be best to permit the patient do lapse into uremia and die quietly?

Monique Janelle London, J.D.

The surgeon is unlikely to face any legal liability for his refusal to perform further access surgery. He may not have an ongoing relationship with the patient that would create a duty of continued care. Even if the surgeon does have an existing relationship with the patient, his refusal to perform another access surgery would satisfy the requirements for termination of the physician-patient relationship without liability for abandonment. Moreover, the surgeon might be able to justify his refusal to perform further access surgery on grounds that the procedure would be futile as long as the patient continues to use dirty needles to inject heroin into surgically created accesses.

Ongoing Physician-Patient Relationship and Abandonment:

The surgeon may not have a relationship with the patient creating a duty to perform additional surgery to create a new access. Even if there were such an ongoing relationship, the surgeon probably has met the requirements for terminating that relationship without incurring liability for abandonment.

Liability for abandonment of a patient requires that there be an ongoing relationship with the patient which includes a need for continuing medical attention. *See, e.g., Johnson v. Vaughn,* 370 S.W.2d 591, 596 (Ky. 1963) (the law of abandonment provides that once a patient engages a physician to treat a condition, the physician is under an obligation to "give [the] patient all necessary and continued attention as long as the case requires"); *Vann v. Harden,* 187 Va. 555, 47 S.E.2d 314, 319 (Va. 1948) ("After a physician has accepted employment . . . it is his duty to continue his services so long as they are necessary."). Generally, when a surgeon "takes charge of a case and is employed to attend a patient, . . . the relation of physician and patient [] continues until ended by the mutual consent of the parties, or revoked by the dismissal of the . . . surgeon, or until his services are no longer needed." *Nash v Royster,* 189 N.C. 408, 127 S.E. 356 (N.C. 1925). Abandonment occurs when a physician unilaterally severs his professional relationship with a patient at time when there is still necessity of continuing medical attention. *See Lee v. Dewbre,* 362 S.W.2d 900 (Tex. Civ. App. Amarillo 1962). Thus, a surgeon is not justified in ceasing to attend a patient after an operation while further care and treatment are necessary. *Gross v Partlow,* 190 Wash. 489, 68 P.2d 1034 (Wash. 1937).

The surgeon could argue that his relationship with the patient was limited to the latest access surgery and the follow up care related to that surgery only. He could contend that once the latest access was created and necessary follow-up care related to the surgery provided to ensure that the access was working properly, the relationship with the patient ended - no "further care or treatment" was necessary in connection with that surgery.[Footnote 18] Accordingly, he could claim that he has no present relationship with the patient, and owes the patient no duty of care to perform any further surgery. The surgeon could further argue that even the destruction of the latest-created access does not mean that this is a time when there is "still a necessity of continuing medical attention." Although the patient infected and destroyed the access, he is still able to dialyze by femoral vein cannulation. Thus, he does not "need" surgery to create another access in his arm for dialysis - he is still able to dialyze without it.

Or, the surgeon may have contractually limited his duty to the patient to perform only the previous access surgery, but no further access surgeries. A "surgeon may agree to perform an operation without undertaking or rendering himself responsible for the subsequent treatment of the case. He thus contracts against liability beyond the exercise of reasonable care, diligence, and skill in the performance of the operation and for such services as are contemplated by

[18] Indeed, in this writer's personal experience at an HMO, the vascular access surgeon's duty was limited to creating a working access, and did not extend to subsequent failure, clotting or destruction of the access.

both parties to the special or limited contract." *Nash v. Royster,* 189 N.C. 408, 127 S.E. 356 (N.C. 1925).

Even if there is an ongoing relationship between the surgeon and patient requiring continuing medical attention, the surgeon may end the relationship without incurring abandonment liability by giving reasonable notice and affording the patient a reasonable opportunity to procure another competent health care provider to continue care. *See, e.g., Katsetos v. Nolan,* 170 Conn. 637, 368 A.2d 172 (Conn. 1976); *Miller v. Greater Southeast Community Hosp.*, 508 A.2d 927, 929 (D.C. 1986); *Capps v. Valk,* 189 Kan. 287, 369 P.2d 238 (Kan. 1962); *Ricks v. Budge,* 91 Utah 307, 64 P.2d 208, 211-12 (Utah 1937); *Lee v. Dewbre,* 362 S.W.2d 900, 902 (Tex. Civ. App. Amarillo 1962). The surgeon appears to have done this: he has advised the patient that he will not perform further access surgery unless the heroin injections stop. The patient is currently dialyzing by femoral vein cannulation, and could continue to do so indefinitely. Thus, there is no urgency for him to have surgery to create a new access. He has potentially unlimited time to find another surgeon to perform the access surgery.

Finally, the surgeon has not unconditionally refused to perform the access surgery. He has only told the patient that he will not perform another surgery "so long as the patient continues to inject heroin into any available vein." If the patient stops the heroin injections, the surgeon is willing to perform the surgery. Thus the surgeon could take the position that he is not terminating the physician-patient relationship, but only putting a reasonable condition on performing another surgical procedure.

In sum, abandonment does not appear to be an issue in Case 4.

Futility:

Even if the surgeon had a present duty to care for the patient, he might have the right to refuse to perform any further access surgery on grounds that to do so would be "futile." As stated previously, in many states a physician may refuse to provide treatment which in his view would be "futile" or "ineffective." *See, e.g., Barber v. Superior Court,* 147 Cal. App. 3d 1006, 195 Cal. Rptr. 484, 491 (Cal. App. 2d Dist. 1983) ("A physician has no duty to continue treatment, once it has proved to be ineffective . . . . There is no duty to continue [treatment] once it has become futile in the opinion of qualified medical personnel.").[Footnote 19]

No uniform definition of futility has been established. However, one group of commentators has suggested that "futile" treatment should be defined as treatment highly unlikely to produce a desired result based on reasoning, experience, or empirical evidence, or treatment that fails to improve the patient's prognosis, merely preserving the patient in a state of permanent unconsciousness or maintaining the patient's dependence on intensive medical care. *See* Lawrence J. Schneiderman et al., Medical Futility: Its Meaning and Ethical

[19] In that case, however, both the physicians and the patient's family agreed that treatment was inappropriate. *Id.* at 486, 492-93.

Implications, 112 ANNALS INTERNAL MED. 949, 950-53 (1990). If this definition were accepted by the court, the surgeon in Case 4 could argue that creating a new access would be highly unlikely to produce the desired result (of a fistula that could be used for long-term hemodialysis), based on the "experience" of the last three accesses created, showing that the patient will infect and destroy the new access within a month or so by injecting heroin into it with dirty needles.[Footnote 20] If the surgeon's past experience with the patient were a certain predictor of the patient's future behavior, the surgeon's futility argument might succeed.

However, the "experience" is probably an insufficient basis to conclude that creating another access will be useless or without benefit. It is not certain that the patient will inject heroin into a new access just because he injected heroin into the last three accesses. Circumstances or his attitude or understanding may have changed. Also, it is not clear that "injecting heroin into any available vein" in and of itself destroys the access. It seems that the patient destroyed prior accesses by using *dirty* needles that caused bacterial infections, not merely by injecting heroin. Creating another vascular access may not be "futile" if the patient uses only clean needles for his heroin injections. On the other hand, the patient has not promised to use only clean needles, and there is no indication that he would start doing so now, after at least two years of using dirty needles. In sum, it is uncertain whether futility would be a valid defense.

Disability Discrimination:

The patient might try to argue that the surgeon's refusal to create a new access is discrimination in violation of the Americans With Disabilities Act because he is "disabled" as a heroin addict. This argument will not succeed. Patients engaged in the use of illegal drugs are not considered disabled under the ADA. *See* 42 U.S.C. § 12102(2).

Conclusion:

The surgeon has no legal obligation to perform surgery on the patient to create a new access - principally because either he has no current relationship with the patient creating a duty of care, or he has taken the proper steps to sever any such existing relationship without facing liability for abandonment.

Ethical Analysis:

Despite the surgeon's likely impunity under the law, there is no ethical basis for him to refuse to perform the surgery. He should not refuse further access surgery to "punish" the patient for his felony arrests and convictions. The patient is

[20] This writer has not been able to find any cases addressing the question of whether a determination of futility can be based on the patient's predicted behavior or addiction, but interprets the futility doctrine to allow for this possibility. One group of commentators has suggested that it would be futile to perform a liver transplant on an alcoholic patient who is unlikely to stop drinking, and who would thereby thwart the operation's therapeutic goals. See John D. Lantos et al., The Illusion of Futility in Clinical Practice, 87 AM. J. MED. 81, 83 (1989).

already being punished by society for breaking the law.

Nor should the patient be denied further surgery for the sole reason that he is a heroin addict. In general, the surgeon should base his decision whether to perform the surgery on whether the patient needs it, not whether the patient has self-abusive habits or addictions. The patient's addiction should only affect the surgeon's willingness to perform the surgery to the extent that it compromises or negates the utility of that surgery. It appears that it is not the addiction itself that is causing the problem, but the patient's use of dirty needles, and possibly his injection of the heroin directly into the dialysis access. Before refusing to perform further access surgery, the surgeon should try to remedy the problem. He should explain to the patient why and how the accesses are being destroyed, and how they can be preserved. He should try to reach an agreement with the patient that the patient will use only clean needles, and will only inject heroin into his non-fistula veins. He should inform the patient about programs to treat heroin addiction. He should find out if the patient is currently taking heroin expressly to endure the pain of dialysis. If so, he should inform the patient of other methods of pain management. He should also advise the patient that if he conquers his addiction, he might be eligible for a kidney transplant, which could obviate the need for dialysis. He should also present the patient with the option of peritoneal dialysis (which presumably is not subject to heroin abuse).

However, even if the patient will ultimately destroy the new access, that still does not ethically justify the surgeon's refusal to create the access. If the patient wants and needs the access, and sufficient resources are available to provide it, the surgeon should perform the operation. Case 4 states that the patient's addiction has intensified over the last five months, and he has infected and destroyed three surgically created accesses in his arms. Thus the patient may get one or two months' use out of each access before it is destroyed. To the patient, that may be sufficient "use" such that the surgery is not futile. It may be that the only time he feels his quality of life is appreciable is when he is using heroin. He may prefer to live out his life using heroin in the latest functioning access, until he has no more veins available for creating an access. If these are the patient's feelings and beliefs, then the surgeon has an ethical obligation to respect the way the patient chooses to live his life.

Connie Zuckerman, J.D.

This patient's continued pattern of drug abuse might understandably tempt clinicians to give up on him, as his self-destructive and anti-social behavior seems to make a mockery of their efforts on his behalf. The obligation of physicians and other treating clinicians in this case, however, rests on a determination of his current medical condition and what can be done to address it. Therefore, while his previous prison record is irrelevant to a determination of his current medical needs, his continued use of heroin, and the resulting medical complications, must necessarily be factored into a medical evaluation of his condition.

The decision of the surgeon to withhold further intervention while the patient continues his drug abuse may be justifiable, not because of any evaluation of his social worth as a drug addict, but rather because the previous three failures indicate the likehood of another failure to maintain access yet again. Some might even argue that additional resources should not be expended on this patient, as such efforts are wasted in the face of his drug addiction. This patient appears to lack the resources and social support system which would allow for successfull maintainance. Any refusal to provide additional access surgery ought then be coupled with serious attempts to assist this patient in gaining access to drug treatment. In an emergency circumstance, however, this patient's needs would require immediate medical intervention, and treatment could not be withheld because of previous behavioral patterns.

Amy L. Friedman, M.D.

Making judgements about the self-destructive behavior patterns of others is a human weakness. As a physician it is difficult to avoid demonstrating disdain of the cardiac cripple or diabetic with gangrenous toes who continues to abuse tobacco. Yet, these ill smokers, the non-abstinent alcoholics with advanced liver disease and the morbidly obese who continue to eat unhealthily all have uncontrolled addictions leading to self injury. I doubt that any single member of these groups would not choose to end the self destructive pattern if a simple, affordable and predictably successful means of doing so was available. But such easy fixes for any of these problems do not exist. Although more difficult for many to comprehend on a personal level, addictive use of illegal drugs does not seem any different. No human can stand up to a standard of never acting in ways not subsequently regretted. Patients cannot be asked to either. Trivializing the challenge of escaping a well established addiction to drugs would be wrong.

In attempting to remain unbiased, the physician's role is still to offer counsel regarding the best way to achieve and maintain optimal health. Failing to address ongoing self destructive acts with the patient would be wrong. But it would also be foolish for the physician to provide the means of furthering the behavior pattern, in most settings. Yet, without the access to the vascular system that might be used for illegal drug delivery, the hemodialysis dependent patient will die. Access is a requisite for his (her) life maintenance. With time, the preservation of precious anatomic access sites in the hemodialysis patient commonly becomes a factor limiting his(her) survival. Thus, damage to the dialysis access through use for drug administration and leading to loss of the site limits the patient's survival. Unfortunately, all currently available types of hemodialysis access provide an easy path of administration for illegal drugs. The only way to completely eliminate this route is to place and then remove a temporary catheter with each dialysis session. This approach would mandate repeated catheter placement, with the consequences of increased cost and risk to the dialysis team. With each insertion, scarring of the skin, subcutaneous tract and catheterized vessel that will ultimately prevent future use of that precious site is caused. Thus, preservation of life through hemodialysis cannot continue indefinitely when each session depends on a new catheterization. For this reason, the surgeon should not decline to create a new, permanent access site in this patient's arm. Nevertheless, it would obviously disturb the provider to facilitate this patient's drug addiction- almost as if functioning as a co-conspirator. Additional guilt can also be associated with the knowledge that provision of this intravenous access might virtually seduce the patient to self inject! Could not the surgeon even be sued for knowingly establishing the patient's means of self-endangerment? Accordingly, the patient must be educated regarding the risks and benefits of use of the access. Instruction should also focus on ways to minimize contamination of the access. He should be urged to follow sterile technique and should be provided with access to clean supplies. Although this tact is unpalatable, it is the lesser evil compared to the available alternatives.

Carl M. Kjellstrand, M.D.

We don't have to accept all kinds of self-destructive behaviour, but we have an obligation to take care of difficult patients who behave in suicidal fashions, e.g. crashing fast red sports cars. This patient at least poses no danger to others. Your obligation is to explain the danger to which he exposes himself. He should be told that his veins are worthless for access and put on peritoneal dialysis. The surgeon has no obligation to perform futile surgery and can rightly refuse to do the vascular access. We however cannot abandon the patient and thus a PD access needs to be created.

Mildred (Barry) Friedman

Young men such as this, long ago declared themselves to be beyond redemption. While his background is not detailed, surely reasons for his behavior can be found. However, many other people have overcome similar circumstances and become valued members of society. If questioned, he would know that his behavior was wrong. His choice was to continue this kind of activity. His choice now is to commit slow suicide. Many chances to conform to normal rules of living have been afforded him. I cite the attempts to reach him, provide dialysis treatment, and the creation of three access sites.
Surgeons seldom sit around. There is plenty for them to do and asking them to use valuable time, OR space, and material on what will undoubtedly be thwarted efforts is senseless.
Rehabilitation treatment should be offered to the patient. If he displays any attempt to learn positive behavior, he should be encouraged and even given another access. If he does not, there is no hope for him. Proof of his ability to be concerned for himself and take helpful action is inherent in his arriving at a dialysis unit.

We spend much time, money, and energy on people who give nothing to our world. They are not worthless but so many others are worth more. Let us put increased exertions into public education, care for old people, feeding the hungry,...
The responsible vascular surgeon is correct in refusing further vascular surgery and is compassionate in basing *his* decision on the patient's decision.

Judith E. Columbo

An active heroin addict is not worried about his or her next dialysis treatment. The patient in this case is not willing to help himself. The continued use of "dirty" needles and syringes into his access has caused infection. The patient has intentionally destroyed three surgical created accesses due to his irresponsibility. The patient has been estranged from his family and even his parole officer cannot reason with him. My feeling about drug abuse is simple. You got yourself into drugs, now get yourself out (or at least try). Perhaps, if a time limit was set and the patient showed his ability to restrain from drug use, a vascular surgeon would agree to try again. Since the past record of this patient speaks for itself, I agree with the vascular surgeon to refuse further access surgery

---

Editor's Remarks4

I was surprised at the absence of a legal compunction to continue surgical attempts at creating a vascular access for hemodialysis. London curiously holds that it is ethically binding on the surgeon to create repeated vascular accesses even if they each function for only one month because that is the way the patient opts to live his life. Dr. Amy L. Friedman, a surgeon, is at variance with the surgeon's decision and calls for indefinite continuation of dialytic therapy. Kjellstrand relegates the patient to peritoneal dialysis. Unexpectedly and harshly, both patients agree with the vascular surgeon's position that no further access surgery is warranted.

Recognizing that the patient harms no one but himself, though (society pays for his surgery and the surgeon has the unpleasant imposition of destruction of his accesses), I do not see how further surgery can be refused. There would be no justification for an emergency room surgeon's declining to sew a drunk's scalp laceration because of multiple previous lacerations. Nor could the renal team refuse hemodialysis for the fourth barbiturate overdosage in a suicidal patient. Fortunately such stressful patients are rare though well remembered. I see no way to disengage. The vascular surgeon does not have the option of walking away from a vexing and self destructive patient.

Response to Study Questions

1. No. We do bad things to ourselves frequently sometimes prompting medical intervention.
2. Once the term substance abuse was introduced, the similarities of abusers using different agents was recognized. I well recall heroin abusers successfully weaned from narcotic drugs who later died of alcoholic liver disease.
3. Physicians have the right to accept or decline any patient. There are categories of patients who if refused consistently would result in court cases won by the declined patient. By subsidizing medical schools, the federal government gains a voice in how the product of that school behaves in society. Phy-

sicians, in general, have to adhere to the standards of society in accepting and treating patients.

4. Probably not. Why 5 and not 6 accesses destroyed as the criterion of refusal of the next access?
5. Unlike Kjellstrand, I do not believe that we have the right to remove one of the options in uremia therapy from an individual because of bad behavior that is limited to self destructive acts. As much as I find the patient's actions contemptible, he has not given up the right to control his destiny. At any time, he may stop injecting heroin at any time, reform, and become a model citizen. Frustrating as it is, the door should be left open to this exigency.
6. A legal question. Unlike gunshots, childhood molestation or injury, or obvious battery, the use of illegal drugs is not the physician's responsibility to report.
7. Wow! In a weak moment, I posed this alternative. No, we cannot punish a difficult patient by withholding treatment whether it be insulin in diabetes or dialysis in uremia.

Case 5

NO DIALYSIS FOR AIDS NEPHROPATHY

A 37 year old homosexual man, known to be infected with the HIV virus for seven years, over the past year, developed a series of devastating life-threatening complications of AIDS, including fungal infection of the brain and Kaposi's sarcoma. During the past month, urinary protein excretion rose above 10 grams per day as kidney function declined inexorably. A nephrologist noting typical large kidneys and normal blood pressure made the diagnosis of AIDS nephropathy and projected survival as likely to be less than six months. ***He stated that based on the poor prognosis, he would not start what would amount to a futile regimen of dialytic therapy.***

Study Questions

1. Can futility be defined?
2. Is futility an acceptable reason to withhold a treatment?
3. When death from malignancy is immanent, should systemic sepsis or renal failure be treated as in an individual without malignancy?
4. Is the position that *the patient has suffered enough* a defensible medical stance when declining further treatment?
5. Recognizing that survival in AIDS nephropathy is improving, is the possibility of limited life expectancy sufficient reason to subject the patient to dialysis?
6. When a physician fears contracting a disease from a patient, can the physician decline further care?

Monique Janelle London, J.D.

Presumably, the patient in Case 5 would need to begin dialysis immediately or face death from renal failure. The nephrologist predicted that even with dialysis, the patient would live for less than six months. Based on that prognosis, the nephrologist stated that he would not start what would amount to a "futile" regimen of dialysis therapy. Presumably, the patient is hospitalized, and the hospital will follow the advice of the nephrologist. This decision, seemingly made without consent of the patient, subjects the nephrologist and hospital to legal liability for failure to obtain informed consent, and possibly for discrimination under the Americans With Disabilities Act. It is conceivable but unlikely that the nephrologist and hospital could avoid this liability based on the nephrologist's conclusion that dialysis would be "futile" under the circumstances. The nephrologist may also face liability for abandonment of the patient.

Informed Consent:

As previously discussed, under the doctrine of informed consent, a physician has a duty to disclose to a competent patient (or an incompetent patient's surrogate) sufficient information to enable the patient to make an informed judgment whether to consent to a medical treatment such as dialysis. The ultimate decision is then left to the patient. *See, e.g., Shine v. Vega,* 429 Mass. 456, 709 N.E.2d 58 (Mass. 1999). It is "for the individual to decide whether a particular medical treatment is in [her] best interests, whether that decision is wise or unwise." *Id.* at 463-464, quoting *Norwood Hosp. v. Munoz,* 409 Mass. 116, 123 (Mass. 1991).

Case 5 does not state whether the nephrologist sought consent to withhold dialysis from the patient (if he is competent) or from a surrogate or legal representative (if the patient is unconscious or otherwise incompetent due to the fungal infection of the brain or Kaposi's sarcoma). If the patient is competent, he must be allowed to determine for himself whether the benefit of prolonging his life for up to six months in his condition exceeds the burden or pain of continuing life in that condition (with dialysis added to it). If the patient is not competent and has not made an advance directive, his surrogate must be allowed to make that decision on his behalf. If the nephrologist does not seek informed consent from the patient or surrogate to withhold dialysis, he may be liable malpractice.

Futility:

On the other hand, also as previously explained, a physician may be absolved of liability for failing to obtain informed consent to withhold lifesaving treatment, if the treatment would be "futile." Many states have statutes providing that a physician cannot be compelled to administer treatment that would be medically inappropriate or futile (although they may be obligated to transfer or try to transfer the patient to another caregiver).[Footnote 21] However, the statutes vary in their requirements.

In some states, all that seems to be required under the statutory language is the physician's subjective opinion that the treatment would be "futile" - however he or she defines that term. *See, e.g.,* VA. CODE ANN. § 54.1-2990 ("[A physician cannot be required to] prescribe or render medical treatment to a patient that the physician determines to be medically or ethically inappropriate."); LA. REV. STAT. ANN. § 40:1299.58.1(A)(4) (a physician cannot be required to provide "medically inappropriate treatment . . . to any patient [and a physician's] medical judgment with respect to the application of medical treatment or life-sustaining procedures" may not be interfered with).[Footnote 22] *See also See Findlay v. Board of Sup'rs,* 72 Ariz. 58, 230 P.2d 526, 532 (Ariz. 1951) (Phelps, J., specially concurring) ("It would not only not be professional but it would be highly unprofessional for a physician to assist in the performance of an operation which he believed to be unnecessary or unwise to perform at that time."); *Grace Plaza, Inc. v. Elbaum,* 183 A.D.2d 10, 588 N.Y.S.2d 853, 859 (N.Y. App. Div. 2d Dep't 1992) ("While we recognize the right of a patient to control the course of his or

[21] Some statutes require that the physician transfer the patient. Other statutes require only that a reasonable effort to transfer be made.
[22] *But see Causey v. St. Francis Medical Center,* 719 So. 2d 1072, 1076 (La. Ct. App. 2d Cir. 1998) (applying the Louisiana statute, but defining "medically inappropriate" to incorporate the consensus of the relevant medical community).

her treatment, we do not recognize any right to force a health-care provider to render treatment which is contrary to his or her own conscience."), *aff'd*, 82 N.Y.2d 10, 623 N.E.2d 513 (N.Y. 1993).

In other states, the standard seems to be more objective, requiring some accord between the physician's belief and generally accepted medical standards. *See* MD. HEALTH-GEN. CODE ANN. § 5-611(a)-(b) (physicians cannot be required to prescribe or render "medical treatment [they] determine[] to be ethically inappropriate" or "medically ineffective . . . under generally accepted medical practices"); In re Farrell, 108 N.J. 335, 529 A.2d 404, 412 (N.J. 1987) ("Even as patients enjoy control over their medical treatment, health-care professionals remain bound to act in consonance with specific ethical criteria. We realize that these criteria may conflict with some concepts of self-determination. In the case of such a conflict, a patient has no right to compel a health care provider to violate generally accepted professional standards."); *Brophy v. New England Sinai Hosp., Inc.*, 398 Mass. 417, 497 N.E.2d 626, 639 (Mass. 1986) (approving of the view that a "hospital and its medical staff 'should not be compelled . . . to [act] contrary to its [sic] moral and ethical principles, when [these] principles are recognized and accepted within a significant segment of the medical profession and the hospital community'").

No clear definition of futility or guidelines to determine whether a particular treatment would be futile have yet been developed in the courts or the medical community. Thus in Case 5, various positions could be taken. For instance, it could be argued that starting dialysis would be futile in that it would not improve the patient's terminal prognosis. *See, e.g.*, LA. REV. STAT. ANN. § 40:1299.58.8(A)(1) (immunizing from liability medical personnel who withhold or withdraw life support from a qualified patient who has a terminal and irreversible condition). If the patient is permanently unconscious, the nephrologist could argue that dialysis would be qualitatively futile in that it would merely preserve the patient in his unconscious state, without restoring any quality of life. Indeed, in one case where a patient was comatose and unlikely ever to regain consciousness, the consensus of the relevant medical community was that dialysis would be medically inappropriate since it would provide no benefit other than prolonging the patient's life. *See Causey v. St. Francis Medical Center*, 719 So. 2d 1072, 1076 (La. Ct. App. 2d Cir. 1998). In another case, a prognosis of no chance of regaining consciousness was a requirement for stopping lifesaving treatment. *See Conservatorship of Drabick*, 200 Cal. App. 3d 185, 245 Cal. Rptr. 840, 852 (Cal. App. 6th Dist. 1988), *cert. denied*, 488 U.S. 958 (1988) (holding that the medical advice that would support a decision to terminate life support "must include the prognosis that there is no reasonable possibility of returning to cognitive and sapient life"). Another type of qualitative futility argument could be made based on the nephrologist's opinion that dialysis would not improve the patient's comfort or overall state of health.

On the other hand, even if the patient is unconscious, it could be argued that initiating dialysis would not be futile, in that it would give the patient up to six additional months of life. And if the patient is conscious, dialysis could provide the benefit of giving him time to achieve certain life goals. Additionally, initiating dialysis could benefit the patient by making him feel better - either physiologically by removing toxins from his blood, or psychologically by giving him hope or the comfort of knowing that the medical team is working to save his life. Further, the nephrologist's prognosis is that survival is only "likely" to be less than six months. It could be argued that as long as there is *any* chance, no matter how small, that the patient is not terminally ill and could live longer than six months, initiating dialysis is not futile. Certainly from the patient's perspective, if he can tolerate the pain of his medical condition, he has nothing to lose and everything to gain by trying to beat the odds.

Finally, if initiating dialysis is considered to be emergency lifesaving treatment, it may be required as a matter of federal law, despite any applicable state futility statute. *See In the Matter of Baby K*, 832 F. Supp. 1022 (E.D. Va. 1993), *aff'd*, 16 F.3d 590 (4th Cir.), *cert. denied*, 115 S. Ct. 91 (1994). There, a federal district court noted that the federal Emergency Medical Treatment and Active Labor Act (EMTALA) states that when a patient seeks care, the hospital must initially determine whether an emergency medical condition exists (i.e., whether the patient will suffer serious impairment of bodily functions or organs if immediate medical attention is not provided). If an emergency condition does exist, the hospital must stabilize that patient to avert material deterioration in his or her condition prior to any transfer to another facility. *See* 42 U.S.C. § 1395dd. The court rejected the argument that providing ventilatory support would be futile, since the federal statute provides no futility exception. The Fourth Circuit Court of Appeals agreed that the statute "does not provide an exception for stabilizing treatment physicians may deem medically and ethically inappropriate." It found that because EMTALA is a federal statute conflicting, it preempts the conflicting Virginia state statute on medical inappropriateness. *See Matter of Baby K*, 16 F. 3d 590, 597.

In sum, it is uncertain whether the nephrologist could avoid liability with a futility argument. If the patient is conscious or initiating dialysis is considered an emergency lifesaving treatment, it is less likely that a futility argument will succeed.

Discrimination Under the ADA and the Rehabilitation Act:

The nephrologist's reason for refusing to initiate dialysis is the patient's poor prognosis based on life-threatening complications of AIDS. This may expose the nephrologist to liability for discrimination against the patient on the basis of a disability.

As set forth previously, § 504 of the 1973 Rehabilitation Act states: "No otherwise qualified individual with a disability . . . shall, solely by reason of his or her disability, be excluded from the participation in, be denied the benefits of, or be subjected to discrimination under any program or activity receiving Federal financial assistance." 29 U.S.C.A. § 794(a). AIDS and HIV have been recognized as within the purview of § 504. *See Martinez v. School Bd. of Hillsborough County, Fla.*, 861 F .2d 1502 (11th Cir. 1988); *Chalk v. United States Dist. Court Cent. Dist. of Cal.*, 840 F.2d 701 (9th Cir. 1988). In 1990, the Americans With Disabilities Act ("ADA") extended the Rehabilitation Act's protections to private settings, including public accommodations and services operated by private entities such as the "professional office of a health care provider, hospital, or other similar service establishment." 42 U.S.C. § 12181(7)(F); 42 U.S.C. § 12182. Presumably, the patient would be covered by these broad protections.

The ADA defines disability to include any "physiological disorder or condition . . . affecting one or more . . . body systems," including HIV disease. 42 U.S.C. § 12102(2); 28 C.F.R. § 35.104. The patient in Case 5 is HIV positive, and so would qualify as "disabled" under the ADA. Therefore, under one group of commentators' reading of the ADA, the nephrologist faces discrimination liability if he refuses to provide a service which he is capable of performing, which he ordinarily would provide, and which the patient needs and will benefit from (namely, dialysis), solely because of the patient's HIV infection. *See* Amir Halevy & Baruch Brody, Acquired Immunodeficiency Syndrome and the Americans With Disabilities Act: A Legal Duty to Treat, 96 Am. J. Med. 282-88 (1994).

The nephrologist could try to invoke the futility defense to a discrimination claim. He could argue that he should not be liable for discrimination if initiating dialysis is not something that the patient will benefit from -- either because it will not affect the prognosis of death within six months, will not restore the patient to consciousness, or will not improve the quality of the patient's life, comfort or health. However, a federal district court rejected such an argument on grounds that denying treatment would discriminate against the disabled patient. *In re Baby K* 832 F. Supp. 1022 (E.D. Va. 1993), *aff'd on other grounds*, 16 F.3d 590 (4th Cir.), *cert. denied*, 115 S. Ct. 91 (1994), was a case involving lifesaving treatment for an anencephalic baby. There, the court explained:

> The Hospital asks this court for authorization to deny the benefits of ventilator services to Baby K by reason of her anencephaly. The Hospital's claim is that it is "futile" to keep alive an anencephalic baby, even though the mother has requested such treatment. But the plain language of the ADA does not permit the denial of ventilator services that would keep alive an anencephalic baby when those life-saving services would otherwise be provided to a baby without disabilities at the parent's request. The Hospital's reasoning would lead to the denial of medical services to anencephalic babies as a class of disabled individuals. Such discrimination against a vulnerable population class is exactly what the American with Disabilities Act was enacted to prohibit. The Hospital would therefore violate the ADA if it were to withhold ventilator treatment from Baby K.
>
> 832 F. Supp. at 1029.

This language appears to prohibit physicians from taking disability into account when making end-of-life decisions. Under this analysis, withholding dialysis from the patient in Case 5 because he is terminally ill with AIDS would violate the ADA.

At the other end of the spectrum, another court suggests that discrimination cases in which the disputed treatment is *related* to the patient's disability should be immunized from judicial scrutiny. *See United States v. University Hospital*, 729 F.2d 144 (2d Cir. 1984). *University Hospital* involved a child born with spina bifida, microcephaly, and hydrocephaly. Physicians predicted "an extremely high risk that the child would be so severely retarded that she could never interact with her environment or with other people." *Id.* at 146. The child's parents decided to forego corrective surgery that would help secondary conditions but would not cure the underlying conditions. The hospital honored the parents' request, and the Department of Health and Human Services (HHS) sued the hospital for discrimination under § 504 of the Rehabilitation Act. The court rejected the HHS discrimination claim on grounds that

> Section 504 prohibits discrimination against a handicapped individual only where the individual's handicap is unrelated to, and thus improper to consideration of, the services in question. As defendants here point out, however, where medical treatment is at issue, it is typically the handicap itself that gives rise to, or at least contributes to, the need for services. Defendants thus argue, and with some force, that the "otherwise qualified" criterion of section 504[Footnote 23] cannot be meaningfully applied to a medical treatment decision.
>
> *Id.* at 156. [Footnote 24]

Applying this holding to Case 5, the nephrologist and hospital could argue that the patient's AIDS gave rise to AIDS nephropathy (and the need for dialysis); without his disability (AIDS), he would not be "otherwise qualified" to receive dialysis treatments.

To this writer, the *University Hospital* decision would only make sense as applied to Case 5 if the rule is that the handicapping condition must be "related" to the condition to be treated in the sense that the handicapping condition (AIDS) is so debilitating that it makes the patient's life not worth living any longer. In *University Hospital,* this appears to have been the case. The parents apparently thought the child's handicapping condition was so dismal that they chose to allow her to die rather than subject her to surgery that would not cure the underlying condition, but would enable her to live longer. Although there was no specific contraindication to performing the surgery, the underlying condition was so unacceptable that the surgery would be useless - the child's life in that condition was not worth saving.[Footnote 25]

In Case 5, it is unclear that the AIDS has rendered the patient's life not worth living any longer. The patient or his surrogate or a court might believe that gaining up to six months of life, even with AIDS, would be worth initiating dialysis. If so, then Case 5 could arguably be distinguished from the *University Hospital,* and the nephrologist and hospital held liable for discrimination on the basis of

---

[23] Section 504 of the Rehabilitation Act provides that no *"otherwise qualified"* individual with a disability shall be discriminated against solely by reason of the disability. *See* 29 U.S.C.A. § 794(a).

[24] Other cases have espoused the *University Hospital* reasoning. *See Johnson by Johnson v. Thompson,* 971 F.2d 1487, 1493 (10th Cir. 1992), *cert. denied,* 507 U.S. 910 (1993) (pointing out that the "otherwise qualified" language of the Rehabilitation Act makes little sense in the medical context because if the person were not disabled, he or she would not need the medical treatment and thus would not "'otherwise qualify' for the treatment"); *Glanz v. Vernick,* 756 F. Supp. 632, 638 (D. Mass. 1991) (indicating that if a person's HIV-related disease decreases the person's ability to benefit from ear surgery, then the HIV disease may disqualify the person as a candidate for the surgery).

[25] In fact, the child ultimately survived. *See* B.D. Colen, What Ever Happened to Baby Jane Doe?, Hastings Center Rep., May-June 1994, at 2.

the patient's disability. However, if the patient were permanently unconscious, that might weigh against a finding of discrimination. *See American Academy of Pediatrics v. Heckler,* 561 F. Supp. 395, 402 (D.D.C. 1983) (rejecting the position that the Rehabilitation Act "requires doctors and parents to undertake heroic measures to preserve for as long as possible, despite expense and a prognosis of certain death within months, the life of an anacephalic [sic] lacking all or part of the brain and with no hope of ever achieving even the most rudimentary form of consciousness").

In short, the nephrologist and hospital may face discrimination liability in addition to malpractice liability if he withholds dialysis without the patient's or surrogate's consent.

Abandonment:

It is unclear from the facts given whether the nephrologist himself was engaged to attend the patient, or was merely called in to provide a diagnosis. If he was engaged to attend the patient, as previously discussed, he may be liable for any damages caused by abandoning the case, unless he provides due notice to the patient and affords him a reasonable opportunity to procure the attendance of another doctor. *See, e.g., Manno v. McIntosh,* 519 N.W. 2d 815 (Iowa Ct. App. 1994) (physician who leaves patient in critical stage of disease without reason or sufficient notice to enable patient to procure another physician is negligent). If the nephrologist is not the only nephrologist at the treating hospital, he can probably meet the requirements for severing the relationship simply by notifying the patient that another nephrologist at the hospital will be working with him instead. In a large hospital, procuring the attendance of another nephrologist could be virtually instantaneous. However, if the nephrologist is the only nephrologist available (and the only physician who can orchestrate the initiation of dialysis), he may need to start dialyzing the patient until a transfer can be arranged, or risk abandonment liability.

To avoid legal liability, the nephologist should first seek informed consent to withhold dialysis from the patient (if competent) or his advance directive or surrogate (if the patient is incompetent). If the consent is not obtained, the nephrologist should initiate dialysis or seek court approval to withhold dialysis prior to the time it becomes necessary. He should not withhold or discontinue dialysis without court approval. In the alternative, he may be able to sever his relationship with the patient and avoid all liability that way.

Ethical Analysis:

Ethically, the nephrologist should begin dialysis therapy unless the patient himself consents to forego it. A prognosis of "likely" survival of less than six months is not a certainty. AIDS patients often outlive their predicted life expectancy. New treatments for AIDS are being developed all the time. It would not be ethical to deprive the patient of a chance of surviving AIDS.

Moreover, even if the prognosis and predicted life expectancy were a certainty, those remaining six or fewer months in themselves might be an important, worthwhile, valuable time for the patient, during which he appreciates his life and/or accomplishes personal goals. Those six months might be worth living for the patient even if the quality of his life during that time is compromised by his health problems and even dialysis itself. It should be up to the patient to decide.

If the patient is incompetent or unconscious, the nephrologist still should initiate dialysis if needed to save the patient's life, then consult family and friends about what the patient would want to do. Even if the ultimate prognosis is grim, allowing the patient to die from kidney failure within a few days is simply too drastic a step to take without consulting the patient and any other relevant parties.

Connie Zuckerman, J.D.

This case highlights the importance of making treatment plans in advance of the loss of decisional incapacity, particularly with patients for whom decisions about life-sustaining treatment will inevitably need to be made. It is unclear what this patient's current decisional capacityis, though it is likely to be impaired. It is also quite likely that this patient may have had strong preferences concerning end of life treatment, and if such preferences had been discussed in advance, then the dilemma concerning the provision of "futile" treatment would never even arise. While decisionally capable, or through an advance directive, this patient could have declined the initiation of dialysis, and that decision would be deserving of respect.

As it is unclear what this patient's wishes were, the determination that dialytic therapy is futile, and therefore unnecessary to initiate, is open to debate. While there is no legal or moral obligation to provide futile treatment to a patient there is no consensus as to the precise meaning of that term. It is true that dialysis at this time will in no way address the patient's underlaying HIV infection and terminal diagnosis; it is also true, however, that dialysis *can* address the immediate concern of kidney function decline, thereby extending his life, even if but for a few months. Whether those additional months will be of any value or benefit to this patient is not solely a medical judgment, but rather one that should be made in consultation with surrogates or loved ones, whose judgment will substitute for that of the patient, and whose decision ought to be based on the values and preferences previously expressed by the patient, or, in light of their determination of what serves the best interests of this patient at this time.

Amy L. Friedman, M.D.

Providing maintenance dialysis therapy for the individual with HIV nephropathy requires the use of healthcare dollars and exposes renal failure team members to substantial personal risk from the patient's blood and bodily fluids. It is destined to result in a shorter patient survival time than for some uninfected patients. Yet, many other patients currently supported indefinitely by dialysis are known to have terminal conditions such as metastatic cancer, severe coronary disease and old age and are expected to die even more quickly. The cost of caring for these and other dialysis patients may be considered excessive by some. Yet, as a society we currently provide complex and highly expensive therapies to treat a wide variety of futile conditions. Any decision to restrict access to therapy should be part of a cohesive public policy not a unilaterally determined hidden agenda.. AIDS should not be approached differently than other diseases. We have already learned that individual providers may not arbitrarily choose to restrict care only to HIV negative patients. Thus, the surgeon is not allowed the prerogative of declining to operate regardless of his(her) legitimate fear of exposure to the HIV virus. Access to dialysis may not be defined differently. This patient must be offered dialysis therapy.

Carl M. Kjellstrand, M.D.

One contraindication to chronic dialysis is a very short expected lifetime (see Case 2). This applies to patients with full-blown AIDS and ESRD. Of 48 patients with full-blown AIDS who started dialysis in New York or Miami, 47 were dead within 90 days, the remaining patient died after 540 days. Dialysis is by this definition, futile. Until new information is forthcoming there is no obligation to offer chronic dialysis to patients with full-blown AIDS. On the contrary, HIV and ARC patients can survive for many months or years and should be offered chronic dialysis. Dialysis of patients like the one described is futility and should be undertaken only as part of a planned research effort to see if the situation can be bettered.

Mildred (Barry) Friedman

No hope exists that dialysis would save the life of a man with a disease that leads in 99.9% of its victims, to death. His wishes are not delineated in this presentation.

Honoring the desires of a patient does not exist as the single deciding factor when a diagnosis of AIDS exists. Other people, patients and health care providers, would be involved if he was dialyzed. A potential for mistakes exists. If I was a dialysis patient, I would refuse to be dialyzed on a machine previously used for an AIDS patient. My right is to know if that artificial kidney had been so used. Isolating certain equipment for use only with AIDS patients would eliminate the problem. Such isolation, however, would not remove danger to the health care professionals who come in contact with fluids from the patient. Risk of infection is present. Stress on the workers is increased. Concern for patients is important but so is concern for those who take care of them.

Application of medical techniques to those who should not be treated is an ethical issue troubling many. Each must make his own decision and mine is to not treat people who are beyond help. Once begun on therapy it is difficult to discontinue. More humane is the judgment to not begin. The nephrologist is correct.

Judith E. Columbo

This decision was one of the toughest. A 37-year-old, infected with HIV, developing serious life-threatening complications is hard enough to cope. Not being medically educated I feel that this nephrologist seems to be making a decision based on an opinion and not fact. True the HIV virus will take the life of this man, but the nephrologist's diagnosis of AIDS nephropathy seems gun happy when the patient has normal blood pressure and typical large kidneys. A poor prognosis is not a death sentence. Seems "Likely" is not the word one expects to hear from their doctor. My decision would allow the man some comfort with the start of dialysis treatment. No one knows when a cure for AIDS will be found.

Editor's Remarks5

Of the cases selected for discussion, Case 5 is the most interesting in the sense that it illustrates remarkable progress in medical management of HIV infection.[Endnote 8] When the question was first posed, life expectancy in renal failure in overt AIDS was limited to days to months.[Endnote 9] Columbo, a patient, could not have been expected to recognize that large kidneys and a normal blood pressure ore two characteristic features of renal failure in HIV infection. Gradually, the outlook has improved to the extent that a survival of years to a decade or longer is not an unreasonable expectation.[Endnote 10] Dialytic therapy for AIDS nephropathy is no longer futile. Thus, this question has become outdated - all contributors agree on continuing dialytic therapy - during the author's overlong preparation of this book.

Response to Study Questions

1. There are multiple attempts at defining futility in medicine.[Endnote 11, Endnote 12] Generally, an anticipated survival below 1% has been applied as a demarcation of the hopeless (futile) patient from the very sick with a poor prognosis. The problem is that physicians may not agree on the presence of a futile illness. When they do, dialysis should be withheld.
2. Yes. But the difficulty is in being sure that the patient truly has a futile disorder.
3. This question goes beyond nephrology and reaches the border of when to "give up". Not treating systemic sepsis or renal failure is equivalent to sending the patient to a hospice. Only when the severity of illness is ineluctably clear can the leap to "no treatment" be made without the uneasiness of worrying over "What if?" In rethinking my own actions under this condition, it has usually been a series of compromises administering the antibiotics but nor performing dialysis. Doctors have a terrible time calling the end the end.
4. When patients assess their quality of life, it is often at a sharply superior level than that judged by their physicians. There is a difference to a patient call-

ing it quits and the doctor deciding to stop treatment. As a generalization, suffering has not been subjected to a reproducible measurement such that "enough" has meaning. Accordingly, the answer is no.

5. Answered above. No.
6. No. From bubonic plague outbreaks of the 14th century to risk of exposure to Ebola virus, physicians cannot walk away from their sick patients. The risk is there but it goes with the profession.

Case 6

FUTILE DIALYSIS

A 72 year old retired school teacher admitted for coronary bypass surgery suffered a massive stroke and became unresponsive to deep pain. Three weeks after admission to the intensive care unit, aspiration pneumonia necessitated placement of an endotracheal tube with mechanical ventilation. After seven weeks of machine support (ten weeks of intensive care) the patient developed a rigid abdomen which was found to be caused by infarction of most of the small bowel. During post-operative management for bowel resection, toxic doses of antibiotics and large doses of vasopressor drugs caused renal failure and anuria. ***A consulting nephrologist declined to initiate hemodialysis pointing out that there was no chance that the patient could be restored to cognitive existence.***

Study Questions

1. As in the preceding case, the dual questions arise: Can futility be defined and if present is futility a reason for excluding dialytic treatment?
2. Frequently, following an operative catastrophe, surgeon and medical consultant differ in advising therapy - surgeons deeply involved hope for even the most unlikely turnaround. Should dialysis be performed to assuage the surgeon?
3. Does the nephrologist "play God" when opting for or against dialysis when the odds of recovery are slim?
4. Is the nephrologist obligated to provide a service (dialysis) upon request or is the nephrologist a thinking consultant who has the *right/obligation* to determine when and under which circumstances dialysis is to be performed?
5. Is the insistence by family or hospital administration that dialysis be initiated a factor that must be taken into consideration when determining which patients to dialyze? This patient?

Monique Janelle London, J.D.

Overview:

At age 72, the patient entered into an irreversible coma after suffering a massive stroke. The treatment of subsequent medical problems while the patient was in intensive care caused renal failure. A consulting nephrologist declined to initiate dialysis on grounds that the patient would never regain consciousness. The facts do not state whether patient or anyone acting on his behalf was ever asked for or ever gave consent to initiate or withhold dialysis. Like with the previous Case, if the nephrologist did not obtain informed consent to withhold dialysis (and thereby let the patient die of renal failure within a few days), he faces tort liability. However, even if no consent was sought or obtained, the nephrologist may be justified in his decision, on grounds that to initiate dialysis under the circumstances would be "futile." Although the futility doctrine has not been fully developed in the courts, it appears that the futility argument would have a good chance of succeeding in this case.

Informed Consent:

The patient is presently in a coma, and thus incompetent to give informed consent to withhold dialysis. However, as has been explained, an incompetent patient does not lose the right to self-determination. That right can be preserved by the patient, through an advance directive, or exercised on his behalf by a surrogate. Thus, the nephrologist[Footnote 26] should find out if the patient has an advance directive that applies to the present situation. If not, the nephrologist should find out who is authorized to act on the patient's behalf (the patient's appointed proxy, family, surrogate, guardian, other legal representative), and discuss the treatment options with the representative(s).

If there is any question as to whether the patient or his representative would consent to withholding dialysis, the nephrologist should seek court approval before declining to initiate dialysis. *See In re Spring*, 405 N.E. 2d 115 (Mass. 1980). In *Spring*, the patient was permanently senile and on dialysis. The patient's wife and son wanted to discontinue dialysis; the legal guardian objected to discontinuation. While the patient was competent, he had never stated whether he would want to discontinue dialysis under these circumstances. *Id.* at 118.

The *Spring* court listed circumstances that should be considered in deciding whether a caregiver should seek advance court approval for withholding or withdrawing medical treatment of an incompetent patient: the extent of impairment of the patient's mental faculties; whether the patient is in the custody of a State mental institution; the prognosis with and without the proposed treatment; the complexity, risk, novelty and possible side effects of the proposed treatment; the patient's level of understanding and probable reaction; the urgency of decision; the consent of the patient, spouse or guardian; the good faith of those who participate in the decision; the clarity of professional opinion on what is good medical practice; the interests of third persons; and the administrative requirements of any institution involved. 405 N.E. 2d at 121. The court did not decide the issue of when court approval should be *required* for withholding of medical treatment, but it noted that such approval could reduce the risk of liability. *Id.* at 122.[Footnote 27]

Similarly, in Case 6, absent informed consent by all parties involved to withhold dialysis treatments, the nephrologist should seek court approval to reduce his risk of liability. On the other hand, if there is a consensus that dialysis should be withheld, the nephrologist may not need to involve the court. *See In re Hamlin*, 102 Wash. 2d 810, 689 P.2d 1372, 1378 (Wash. 1984) (holding court involvement unnecessary where all parties agree).

Futility:

Even if the nephrologist did not obtain informed consent, or the patient's representative asked that dialysis be initiated, the nephrologist may be able to withhold dialysis on grounds that it would be futile to initiate it.

The caselaw regarding the futility doctrine varies widely. In many states, the fact that there is "no chance" that the patient can be restored to cognitive existence weighs in favor of a determination that initiating dialysis would be medically inappropriate. The courts of these states have approved decisions to forego life-sustaining treatment for permanently comatose patients. *See Rasmussen v. Fleming*, 154 Ariz. 207, 741 P.2d 674 (Ariz. 1987); *Foody v. Manchester Memorial Hosp.*, 40 Conn. Supp. 127, 482 A.2d 713, 721 (Conn. Super. Ct. 1984) ("Where the incapable patient's condition . . . is permanent and irreversible and there is no reasonable medical probability that the patient ever will return to a cognitive state [and two other conditions are met], . . . the family lawfully may act as the patient's substitute decision-maker and may decide to discontinue the use of the respirator."); *Severns v. Wilmington Medical Center, Inc.*, 421 A.2d 1334 (Del. 1980); *John F. Kennedy Hosp. v. Bludworth*, 452 So. 2d 921, 926 (Fla. 1984) ("The focal point of such decisions [to terminate life-support] should be whether there is a reasonable medical expectation of the patient's return to a cognitive life as distinguished from the forced continuance of a vegetative existence."); *In re Guardianship of Barry*, 445 So. 2d 365 (Fla. Dist. Ct. App. 2d Dist. 1984); *In re L.H.R.*, 253 Ga. 439, 321 S.E.2d 716 (Ga. 1984); *In re Gardner*, 534 A.2d 947 (Me. 1987); *Brophy v. New England Sinai Hosp.*, Inc., 398 Mass. 417, 497 N.E.2d 626 (Mass. 1986); *Matter of Conservatorship of Torres*, 357 N.W.2d 332 (Minn. 1984); *In re Jobes*, 108 N.J. 394, 529 A.2d 434 (1987); *In re Peter*, 108 N.J. 365, 529 A.2d 419 (N.J. 1987); *In re Quinlan*, 70 N.J. 10, 355 A.2d 647 (N.J. 1976), *cert. denied sub nom Garger v. New Jersey*, 429 U.S. 922 (1976); *In re Storar*, 52 N.Y.2d 363, 420 N.E.2d 64, 438 N.Y.S.2d 266 (1981), *cert. denied sub nom Storar v. Storar*, 454 U.S. 858 (1981); *Delio v. Westchester County Med. Center*, 129 A.D.2d 1, 516 N.Y.S.2d 677 (N.Y. App. Div. 2d Dep't 1987); *Leach v. Akron General Medical Center*, 68 Ohio Misc. 1, 22 Ohio Op. 3d 49, 426 N.E.2d 809 (Ohio C.P. 1980); *In re Guardianship of Grant*, 109 Wash. 2d 545, 747 P.2d 445, 757 P.2d 534 (Wash. 1987); *In re Welfare of Colyer*, 99 Wash. 2d 114, 660 P.2d 738 (Wash. 1983).

The reasoning behind some such decisions is that the treatment merely prolongs the dying process. *See John F. Kennedy Memorial Hosp. v. Bludworth*, 452 So. 2d 921, 923 (Fla. 1984) (noting that procedures which "sustain . . . vital bodily functions . . . can be accurately described as a means of prolonging the dying process rather than a means of continuing life"); *In re Doe*, 418 S.E.2d 3, 6 (Ga. 1992) (noting that "the life support system was prolonging her death, rather than her life"); *American Acad. of Pediatrics v. Heckler*, 561 F. Supp. 395, 400 (D.D.C. 1983); *In re Guardianship of L.W.*, 482 N.W.2d 60, 72 n.15 (Wis. 1992).

Withholding dialysis might also be favored by a court on grounds that doing so would preserve the patient's dignity. *See In re Jobes*, 108 N.J. 394, 529 A.2d 434 (N.J. 1987):

> At some point, such a course of treatment upon the insensate patient is bound to touch the sensibilities of even the most detached observer. . . . When cherished values of human dignity and personal privacy, which belong to every person living or dying, are sufficiently transgressed by what is being done to the individual, we should be ready to say: enough.

Id. at 459 (N.J. 1987) (Handler, J., concurring) (citation omitted); *see also In re Guardianship of Crum*, 61 Ohio Misc. 2d 596, 580 N.E.2d 876, 883 (Ohio P. Ct. 1991) ("It is the opinion of the court that it is in the best interest of Dawn M. Crum to authorize the withdrawal of nutrition and hydration and allow her to die peacefully, painlessly, and with dignity.").

An opposing belief is that all life has intrinsic value, regardless of its quality; it is not merely instrumental toward further life goals. Under this view, the medical community should not be allowed to impose its definition of "benefit" on patients by denying life support to those whose lives they deem unworthy of living. Accordingly, some courts have recognized a state interest in preserving even unconscious life. *See Cruzan by Cruzan v. Harmon*, 760 S.W.2d 408, 419 (Mo. 1988) (en banc) ("The state's concern with the sanctity of life rests on the principle that life is precious and worthy of preservation without regard to its quality."), *aff'd sub nom. Cruzan by Cruzan v. Director, Mo. Dep't of Health*, 497 U.S. 261 (1990).

Additionally, as discussed in connection with Case 5, if initiating dialysis is considered to be emergency lifesaving treatment, it may be required as a matter of federal law, despite any applicable state futility statute. *See In the Matter of Baby K*, 832 F. Supp. 1022 (E.D. Va. 1993), *aff'd*, 16 F.3d 590 (4th Cir.), *cert. denied*, 115 S. Ct. 91 (1994).

Finally, in the present Case, the patient is being kept alive by mechanical ventilation. On the one hand, this may suggest that his life expectancy is short and initiating dialysis would be "futile" even in terms of prolonging the patient's life. However, it may suggest that the hospital (only - not the nephrologist) has some present obligation or recognizes some benefit to keeping the patient alive - otherwise, presumably the mechanical ventilation would be discontinued, and the patient would die from asphyxiation rather than kidney failure. There does not seem to be a rational basis for keeping the patient alive on a ventilator for seven weeks, but then letting him die by not initiating dialysis. Additionally, the patient's renal failure did not result from his original medical condition, but rather was caused by toxic doses of antibiotics and large doses of vasopressor drugs administered during post-operative management for bowel resection. The hospital may have a legal obligation to initiate dialysis, on grounds that the need for dialysis was created by the intensive care unit's treatment of other problems, rather than by the patient's existing condition. It could be argued that it would be negligent for the hospital to cause a medical problem and then not treat it.

The nephrologist should seek consent from the patient's legal representative to withhold dialysis. Even if he is unable to obtain that consent, he may be able to avoid liability for declining to initiate dialysis, on grounds that to do so would be futile. However, if dialysis is considered to be an emergency lifesaving treatment, federal law may require that it be initiated.

Ethical Analysis:

Absent an advance directive or other clear evidence that the patient would not want to continue living in his present state, the nephrologist should consult his next of kin and/or other legal representative about the proposed withholding of dialysis. If there is any objection to withholding treatment, the nephrologist has an ethical obligation to initiate dialysis and continue treatment - at least until he can transfer the patient to another nephrologist at the hospital or another facility that is willing to continue the dialysis treatments.

It is true that initiating dialysis would be "futile" in terms of restoring the patient to cognitive existence. Also, from the perspective of the patient, there will not likely be any benefit to initiating dialysis, since he will never know or understand what has been done, and will never feel any pleasure or pain. However, initiating dialysis may be beneficial in other ways. For instance, keeping the patient alive might give a loved one time to arrive from out of town to say goodbye to the patient. Or, it might give a friend or relative time to come to terms with the grief of losing the patient.

On the other hand, keeping the patient alive by initiating dialysis could tie up scarce resources such as an intensive care unit bed and nursing time. It would be unfair to deny these resources to an otherwise viable patient who could regain consciousness because they are being used by a patient who is permanently unconscious and will likely die shortly. And, once the hospital initiates dialysis for this patient, it must initiate dialysis for all similarly situated patients - including patients who are on ventilators and will never regain cognitive existence. This could be an expensive precedent, resulting in more viable patients being denied treatment.

However, other physicians at the hospital have already determined that preserving life is a sufficient benefit in and of itself such that certain lifesaving measures (putting the patient on a mechanical respirator and operating on the patient's bowel) are not futile. Initiating dialysis might not use up any more scarce resources than those already being used for these measures. There is no ethical basis for the hospital to provide some types of lifesaving treatment but not dialysis.

All arguments considered, this writer believes the nephrologist has an ethical duty to initiate dialysis absent evidence that the patient would not want dialysis or evidence that the family and any other legal representatives favor not initiating dialysis.

Connie Zuckerman, J.D.

Unlike the patient in the previous case, the patient in this case, comatose with major organic systems shutting down, is clearly in the process of dying. No interventions will change that course, though a temporary suspension is hypothetically possible. It would be difficult to argue that this patient's interests would be served in any way by initiating further aggressive treatment, such as dialysis, unless one took the extreme, vitalist position that the benefit of continued life itself outweighed the tremendous burdens the patient now suffers. A best interests analysis of this patient's condition would reasonably conclude that further intervention does not serve the interests of this patient.

In fact, it is quite likely that dialysis treatment in this setting would constitute "futile" treatment by any definition, i.e, it will be ineffective in its specific application and the patient will die even if such treatment is initiated. In such a case, the consulting nephrologist is justified in declining to initiate treatment. As stated previously, there is no legal or moral obligation to provide futile treatment. No other additional aggressive measures should be initiated, and the patient should be kept comfortable as he continues to die.

Amy L. Friedman, M.D.

Most surgeons have had to make and later justify the consequences of countless intraoperative judgements to either extend full or partial treatment or declare a condition hopeless. Thus, the mortally ill patient whose entire bowel is dead must either have aggressive resection of the necrotic tissues or be deemed unsalvageable during the operation. For the surgeon indecisiveness is incompatible with the ability to function. We are therefore more comfortable with making decisions based on reality than many other physicians.

When practical hope that an individual will recover the ability to think, participate in the world around him (her) or experience pleasure has vanished, I believe the prolongation of life through artificial or invasive means represents an indignity. While it would be inappropriate to make any active steps to end this man's life unless our society collectively approves of euthanasia (an approach I would personally endorse), the withholding of medical therapies, particularly those that may be associated with discomfort or suffering is entirely reasonable. If this patient developed a condition that required surgical intervention, I would decline to offer it. Maintenance dialysis should be discontinued with the full anticipation that the end of life will result.

Patients and families are usually inexperienced and therefore uncomfortable in handling the end of life. They expect to receive guidance from us and derive great comfort from the physician who demonstrates confidence in the face of impending death. When family actively participates in the patient's management they must be given every opportunity to fully express their wishes for their loved one. The potential for disagreement between the healthcare providers (who feel treatment would be futile and therefore inappropriate) and the patient's relatives (who may understandably have difficulty accepting the inevitability of death in this circumstance) is significant. Yet, in practice, a compassionate, direct and comprehensive presentation of the diagnosis, prognosis and therapeutic options does not fail to reassure the family that the withdrawal of care, when appropriate, is humane.

Carl M. Kjellstrand, M.D.

The problem with futility in *acute* dialysis is that we have not described or measured it although at least 50 articles looking at prognostic factors exist. None of

them apply to institutions outside that of their creation. People all have come to different conclusions as to which factors are important and which are not.
In this case there are no less than 4 organ systems that have failed, brain, gut, lungs and kidneys. I would also advise against dialysis in this case as it would be a meaningless, cruel and futile effort. However, if someone pleaded for dialysis I recommend the use of a *strict time limit* of 3 weeks, at which time 90% of the people needing dialysis for acute reversible renal failure have either regained normal renal function or died. Do not go into this without setting a time limit.

Mildred (Barry) Friedman

In a case like this, I argue with the concept of *necessitated placement of an endotracheal tube.* Two systems had failed - coronary arteries and brain circulation. Seventy-two years is not a short life. The body was deteriorating. Death is the natural end of life and should be allowed to occur when it comes, without interference.
Another system failed and again invasive therapy was performed. That was wrong. Iatrogenic kidney failure then occurred and was presented to the nephrologist for treatment. The patient should not have been pushed so far down the road. If her life had not been mechanically prolonged, the nephrologist would not have been faced with the decision to treat or not treat her.
The nephrologist made a wise judgement to no longer lengthen what had become an existence not a life.

Judith E. Columbo

This 72-year-old retired schoolteacher has unfortunately been dealt a death sentence. A massive stroke, unresponsive to deep pain, pneumonia, mechanical ventilation, bowel resection, and now kidney failure, appear to be a poor prognosis. Unlike the previous case, I feel that the nephrologist is correct in this case with his decision to decline initiation of hemodialysis. Due to the patient's age and because of the previous medical condition, there is no chance of the patient being restored to a "normal" existence.

Editor's Remarks6

I view the question as the inverse of that posed by Attorney London who discusses whether or not the nephrologist should "obtain consent to withhold dialysis." Any decision to perform dialysis is a positive action requiring patient consent. Deciding not to utilize a difficult intervention (dialysis) should not demand consent. London, while acknowledging that there is no legal obligation to provide "futile" treatment, also holds that objection to withholding dialysis by a next of kin triggers enforced initiation or continuation of dialysis. Arguing that the doctrine of informed consent requires that a patient be presented with all medical treatment options (other than those which are medically inappropriate, such as cough medicine for tuberculosis or "futile," London posits that withholding dialysis and initiating dialysis are both treatment options that must be presented to the patient as part of the informed consent process. Attorney Zuckerman reduces the debate to the bottom-line position that "there is no legal or moral obligation to provide futile treatment." I agree with Zuckerman and the two patients who would decline dialysis. It was a bit disconcerting to find that Kjellstrand would yield to a plea for dialysis by setting a three week time limit for therapy. Why? What evidence would make three weeks better than two, four, or twelve as a limit? I agree with Dr. Amy L. Friedman that further dialysis in this case would represent an "indignity."

Response to Study Questions

1. The concept of futility as an absolute is as elusive here as in Case 5.
2. No. Dialysis is not a plaything to make anyone but the patient feel better. On one occasion, I was asked to consult on a religious leader who was maintained in an intensive care unit. The question was whether or not to start hemodialysis. My evaluation found the patient dead but clergy would not permit this diagnosis and wanted dialysis tried anyway. I departed.
3. No. In many instances, physicians apply therapy with only a minimal chance of success. Sometimes, a "Hail Mary Pass" is caught and wins the football game.
4. If the nephrologist does not act as a thinking consultant, he should not be consulted. No therapy should be provided when a physician does not believe it indicated.
5. Yes. If for no other reason that it may force rethinking of a clinical circumstance that has been incorrectly analyzed. An aspect of medicine that makes it appealing is that continuing reassessment of problems is the correct thing to do.

Case 7

PHYSICIAN BIAS

A 58 year old physician, one of the pioneers in introducing peritoneal dialysis for chronic renal failure, consistently coerces his patients into maintenance peritoneal dialysis rather that maintenance hemodialysis. By contrast, another nephrologist at the same facility, who is expert in hemodialysis, does not even consider peritoneal dialysis in the choices presented to newly uremic patients. At some facilities, home hemodialysis is not mentioned, while at a few others, home hemodialysis is promoted as the therapy most likely to permit long survival during maximized rehabilitation. ***A renal fellow observing the conflicting "hard sells" remarked to the chief of medicine that patients were being denied their rights under pressure to accept one therapy over another.***

Study Questions

1. Is physician bias a major force in determining uremia therapy?
2. Should physicians who believe in one regimen over another so inform their patients?
3. Even though federal regulations insist on appraising ESRD patients of the options of renal transplantation, hemodialysis, or peritoneal dialysis, should physicians with a recognized bias be permitted to advise their patients?
4. Are there means to ensure a patient's informed opinion when deciding on ESRD therapy?
5. How might a dictatorial nephrologist (directing a specific regimen) be handled?
6. In the long run, does the choice of ESRD therapy make any difference?

Monique Janelle London, J.D.

A physician who fails to present a patient with all medically appropriate treatment options faces liability for failure to obtain informed consent.

To comply with the requirement to obtain informed consent for medical treatment, a physician must disclose and explain all material information about the nature, purpose, expected benefits and foreseeable risks of any treatment. *See Causey v. St. Francis Medical Center,* 719 So. 2d 1072, 1075 (La. Ct. App. 2d Cir. 1998). Ultimately, it is for the patient to decide whether a particular medical treatment is in his best interests, and the physician must disclose sufficient information to enable the patient to make an informed judgment whether to give or withhold consent. *See Shine v. Vega,* 429 Mass. 456, 709 N.E.2d 58, 63 (Mass. 1999) (citations omitted).

If a patient is a suitable candidate for hemodialysis, home hemodialysis and peritoneal dialysis, then the physician is legally obligated to present all three options to the patient. However, as previously discussed in connection with the futility doctrine, caselaw suggests that a physician need not provide the patient with a treatment option that would be medically inappropriate. *See Causey,* 719 So. 2d at 1075. Thus, if a patient is not medically eligible for a particular type of dialysis - *e.g.*, the patient's vessels are too weak to support hemodialysis -- the physician may not be legally obligated to present the hemodialysis option.[Footnote 28]

In Case 7, one physician, a peritoneal dialysis pioneer, consistently "coerces" his patients into maintenance peritoneal dialysis rather than hemodialysis. "Coercing" in the sense of presenting both options to each patient and opining or advising that peritoneal dialysis is better would not violate the informed consent requirement. However, "coercing" in the sense of not respecting the patient's decision when it conflicts with the advice of the physician, would raise an informed consent issue. *See Shine v. Vega,* 429 Mass. 456, 709 N.E.2d 58, 63 (Mass. 1999).

Another physician in the hypothetical "does not even consider peritoneal dialysis in the choices presented to newly uremic patients." If peritoneal dialysis is a medically acceptable treatment option for a patient, the physician must present it as an option. Otherwise, he has failed to provide the information necessary for the patient to give informed consent to renal replacement therapy.
Similarly, if home hemodialysis is a medically acceptable option, it must be presented to each patient. On the other hand, there is no legal problem with "promoting" home dialysis as the preferable therapy in terms of survival and rehabilitation.

Ethical Analysis:

The ethical requirements are similar to the legal ones. The physicians have an ethical obligation to respect each patient's right to self-determination and autonomy. To do so, the physicians should inform the patient of all medically feasible treatment options and the risks and benefits of each, given that patient's particular situation. The physicians should then let the patient make the ultimate determination as to the appropriate treatment.

Connie Zuckerman, J.D.

The concern of the renal fellow in this case is justified. The initiation of any treatment intervention must necessarily be based upon the informed, voluntary consent of either the patient himself, or an appropriately appointed surrogate. Such consent must include a thorough discussion of the patient's diagnosis, prognosis, the available treatment options and their consequent risks and benefits. While it is appropriate for a physician to advocate for a specific treatment

[28] However, it is difficult to imagine a situation in which one type of dialysis would be unquestionably inappropriate. In the example of a patient with weak vessels, hemodialysis still might be possible using a goretex graft instead of the patient's own vessels.

regimen which he believes best meets the needs of the individual patient, such advocacy cannot cross the line to coerce the patient into a specified plan, nor is the physician justified in withholding information about other reasonable treatment options, even if the physician finds them less preferable or cannot himself make them available to the patient. In fact, consent obtained under coerced circumstances or without reasonable disclosure of treatment options may constitute malpractice on the part of the physician, and potentially subject the physician to liability.

In this case, patients should be informed of all reasonable options for the delivery of dialysis, and should be free to choose that option which best suits their own individual assessments of their interests. Physician treatment recommendations are appropriate, but not at the cost of withholding information or forcing the patient's choice.

Amy L. Friedman, M.D.

Although the impacts of both medical malpractice and managed care have altered physician behavior in ways our predecessors could not have imagined, I still believe that we are given the privilege of guiding our patients through the healthcare maze. The patient who seeks my counsel and care is rarely as informed about the therapeutic options available to treat his disease, as am I. The physician's role as the healthcare expert is to maintain a level of knowledge about the conditions he(she) treats that is reasonably current. Through published literature, relevant medical meetings and participation in other types of academic activities it is vital that he (she) remains abreast of the state of his art. Regardless of his personal preferences, the entire range of choices must be discussed in a professional and objective way with the patient. After this has occurred, however, introduction of the physician's opinion is appropriate.

A perfect illustration of the importance of maintaining a contemporary approach comes from the laparoscopic revolution that altered the practice of general surgery during the 1990's. Prior to that period, gallbladders were removed via long incisions in the abdominal wall with prolonged morbidity for the patient. Introduction of "non-invasive" approaches to accomplish the same internal objectives (gallbladder removal, demonstration of the biliary anatomy when appropriate, ligation of the cystic duct and artery) via several significantly smaller abdominal portals was so effective in diminishing hospital length of stay and patient discomfort that the vast majority of cholecystectomies are performed this way today. Older, highly experienced surgeons quickly recognized the need to learn this approach in order to maintain their fluency in contemporary surgery. Instructional programs to teach them the techniques of laparoscopy were heavily enrolled and credentialing programs to acknowledge their readiness to use these skills were highly successful. Had they not, many patients would have been inappropriately denied access to modern therapy and denied the care of a whole generation of mature surgeons..

Denial of the patient's right to be fully informed about his options in uremia therapy would also be unreasonable. Hemodialysis must be presented to him (her) without bias. If the nephrologist strongly advocates peritoneal dialysis as the treatment of choice he should certainly share his opinion with the patient, in a non-prejudicial manner. Failing to maintain a professional level of objectivity demeans the physician and unreasonably restricts his patient's access to care.

Carl M. Kjellstrand, M.D.

The renal fellow is right. Patients should have unbiased information of the pros and cons of each procedure but after giving this, the physician is within his full rights to advise what he thinks is best. People always ask for that advice and even if not, should be given it. Like everybody else physicians are biased and one hopes that naturally people understand this. The situation needs to be discussed at a staff-meeting. A trained, unbiased nurse-educator may solve the problem.

Mildred (Barry) Friedman

Wouldn't it be nice if the world was a fair place. Because it is not we must work to better it when we can.

"Hard sell" for their preferred treatments was practiced by several nephrologists in the same institution. Designing and producing a videotape that fairly discussed the pros and cons of *all* available replacement therapies for failed kidneys, as well as the pros and cons of no treatment, could go a long way to solving the problem of physician biases. If appropriate medical administrators mandated that it be shown to new renal patients, education would help in the patient's decision process. A tape rather than a brochure is recommended because it can reach the illiterate as well as the blind.
While such education would help it does not take into account that treatment is probably most effective in the hands of the person who believes in it. A peritoneal dialysis biased physician may not conduct hemodialysis as well as one who is biased in that direction. Medicine is still an art and more is involved than the technical mastery of a technique.

There is nothing wrong with physician bias when it is out in the open and discussed. Reasons for such bias exist. Few practitioners will insist that their way is the true and only way. Patient knowledge must be sought and encouraged.

Judith E. Columbo

The older physician who coerces patients into maintenance peritoneal dialysis is just as wrong as another nephrologist promoting only hemodialysis. The "my dad is better than your dad" theory, belongs in a schoolyard, not in decision making over a patient's life. I feel the renal fellow was correct in confronting the chief of medicine about this problem.

I also feel that this fellow is destined to become a good nephrologist if he can already see what his elder chiefs are mistakenly teaching him.

Editor's Remarks7

Full concurrence has been absent in these discussions until Case 7. Every essayist takes the side of the junior nephrologist complaining to the Chief of Medicine. As aptly put by Dr. Amy L. Friedman: "Failing to maintain a professional level of objectivity demeans the physician," and *is to my thinking unethical.* I share this standard.

Aren't all physicians advocates for their form of therapy? Does the interventional radiologist refer patients to the vascular surgeon for acute hemodialysis access? Do cardiovascular surgeons refer patients with angina to cardiologists for angioplasty rather than vascular bypass? Are there doubts over whether the nephrologists partisan to either hemodialysis or peritoneal dialysis believe in what they are selling? Since we are not likely to change behavior of earnest committed physicians championing one or another therapy, we should seek means of bypassing such prejudice thereby ensuring a fair presentation to the patient. Mildred Barry Friedman's suggestion of a teaching video tape fairly presenting the pros and cons of each option in uremia therapy makes sense. It should be noted that the Health Care Finance Administration directs that every new patient about to start ESRD treatment be exposed to the kidney transplant team as well as to possible treatment at home by dialysis.

Response to Study Questions

1. How can a physician not fairly inform a patient that there is more than one way to manage a medical problem? My question is deceitful as inappropriate conduct by physicians when preparing patients for therapy is not uncommon. What recommendation as to the best means of treating newly detected myopia would be made by an ophthalmologist who has just invested in a laser operating device? Though difficult to fulfill, each nephrology program should portray the major forms of uremia therapy in a neutral perspective to every freshly enrolled patient.
2. Yes. It is not the bias that is wrong, we all have biases, it is the avoidance of fairness that is a concern.
3. Several approaches are now being evaluated. We have a staff member in renal clinic whose sole responsibility is the education of individuals with progressive renal insufficiency. When ESRD supervenes, the therapy elected was chosen after full exposure to the choices. Having regular showings and loan of a neutral but upbeat video would serve a similar purpose.
4. First, the fanatic lacking reason should be distinguished from the partisan with a cause. The former requires a direct "Do it this way or else" order while the later will respond to a chat with the chief. It is the responsibility of the program leader to protect patient interests. Periodic debriefing of

patients will soon permit understanding of what actually happens during the selection of one or another treatments.

5. There have been no prospective, alternate case trials of peritoneal versus hemodialysis. Comparing outcome in kidney transplant recipients with age and gender matched dialysis patients is flawed because of "cherry picking," the selection for a transplant of the fittest least complicated patients. Employing the data base of the United States Renal Data System, enthusiasts for either peritoneal dialysis or hemodialysis claim advantages denied by equally enthusiastic advocates for the other regimen. My own bias is that for patients well enough to withstand the rigors of surgery, kidney transplantation is a superior treatment. Of the dialytic regimens available, my experience and reading favors home hemodialysis by a wide margin.

Case 8

SELF REFERRAL OF DIALYSIS PATIENTS

A newly appointed junior staff member of a large nephrology physicians group in a community hospital indicates his dissatisfaction with the system of referrals. He notes that after stabilizing newly evaluated kidney failure patients, continuing long-term care is arranged with one of several surrounding free standing dialysis units. The unit selected for transfer of the new patient is a proprietary facility owned by a partnership held by three of the senior renal staff members. The same physicians who referred the patient and own the unit then decide on the length of each dialysis treatment as well as other components of care such as whether or not to do nerve testing for a fee. Profits at this dialysis unit become the personal income of its owners. ***Concerned over abrogating his patient's free choice, the junior nephrologist indicates his intention to resign from the group.***

Study Questions

1. Is self referral of dialysis patients ethical?
2. Is there any evidence that the outcome of care in proprietary dialysis facilities is inferior to that in not-for-profit facilities?
3. Is there evidence that the dialysis prescription is influenced by type of dialysis unit ownership?
4. Are physicians who gain personal richness from personally owned health care facilities immoral?
5. In general, is health care provided under a government subsidized comprehensive system superior to that in a capitalistic for profit system?
6. For any of the issues raised above, are there *evidence-based* answers?

Monique Janelle London, J.D.

The physicians in the nephrology group are referring patients to dialysis units after they are stabilized. The physicians are deciding on the length of the dialysis treatments and other components of care. Neither of these actions in and of itself raises a legal issue. However, three of the senior renal staff members own the dialysis units in partnership, and the profits of each unit become the personal income of the three partners. Thus the three renal staff members have an incentive to prescribe a course of care for the patients that maximizes profits for the dialysis units, even if that course of care is not what is best for the patient. There is no indication that any patients actually *have* been prescribed a course of care that maximizes profits at the expense of their best interests. Thus the only legal issue is whether the referral system itself is improper. Many states prohibit or limit self-referral arrangements; whether the self-referral system presented in Case 8 is permitted will depend upon the laws of the state where the system exists. The system might also be prohibited under federal anti-kickback law.

Prohibitions and Limitations on Self-Referral Arrangements:

The arrangement in Case 8 may be absolutely prohibited in some states. For instance, a Michigan statute states that it is unprofessional conduct for a licensed professional to engage in " . . . directing or requiring an individual to purchase or secure a . . . treatment, procedure or service from another person, place, facility, or business in which the licensee has a financial interest." MICH. STAT. ANN. § 14.15 (1101). The Michigan Attorney General has interpreted this statutory provision to prohibit a physician from referring patients to a clinical laboratory in which he has a financial interest, regardless of whether the services are medically necessary and regardless of any disclosure to the patient. *See* Op. Mich. Att'y Gen. 5498 (1979). Other states have similar prohibitions. *See* *Day v. Inland Empire Optical, Inc.*, 76 Wash. 2d 407, 456 P.2d 1011 (Wash. 1969) (determining that Washington's fraud and abuse statute prohibits a self-referral arrangement involving ophthalmology services); 55 PA. CODE § 101.51(c)(5) (Pennsylvania statute prohibiting physician self-referral arrangements involving a Medicaid recipient).

Other states do not prohibit self-referral arrangements outright, but have statutes that control them by requiring physicians to disclose to patients their ownership interests in facilities when referring patients to those facilities. *See* ARIZ. REV. STAT. ANN. § 32-1401(12)(ff); CAL. BUS. & PROF. CODE §§ 654.1, 654.2; 85 Op. Cal. Att'y Gen. 105 (1985); FLA. STAT. ANN. § 458.331(gg); MASS. GEN. LAWS ANN. ch. 112, § 1; MASS. GEN. LAWS ANN. ch. 440, § 2; NEV. REV. STAT. § 631.305; MINN. STAT. ANN. § 147.091 (p)(3), (4); PA. STAT. ANN. tit. 35, §§ 449.21-449.23; N.J. STAT. ANN. 45:9; VA. CODE § 54-278.3; WASH. REV. CODE ANN. § 19.68.010; W. VA. CODE § 30-3-14(6), (7).

In some states, the form of the disclosure is specified by the statute or regulation. For instance, New Jersey requires the following form:

> Public law of the State of New Jersey mandates that a physician, chiropractor or podiatrist inform his patients of any significant financial interest he may have in a health care service. Accordingly, I wish to inform you that I do have a financial interest in _[a health care service] the following health care service(s) to which I refer my patients: [.] (list applicable health care services) You may, of course, seek treatment at a health care service provider of your own choice. A listing of alternative health care service providers can be found in the classified section of your telephone directory under the appropriate heading.
>
> N.J. STAT. ANN. § 45:9.

California allows its statutory disclosure requirements to be satisfied in certain circumstances "by posting a conspicuous sign in an area which is likely to be seen by all patients". *See* CAL. BUS. & PROF. CODE § 654.2(b).

Some state statutes create exceptions to the disclosure requirement. *See, e.g.*, ARIZ. REV. STAT. ANN. § 32-1401(12)(ff) (exempting referrals in group practice); FLA. STAT. ANN. § 458.331(gg)(1)-(3) (exempting equity interests in large publicly held corporations and the physician's own practice or his group's practice); MINN. STAT. ANN. § 147.091(p)(3), (4) (exempting group practices, capitated health care premiums and certain fee-for-service withhold amounts). It is unclear whether any of these exceptions would apply to the present Case.

In sum, depending on where Case 8 takes place, under state law the referral system may be prohibited, or permitted on the condition that the physicians make a disclosure to the referred patients.

On the federal level, the Medicare and Medicaid Program Protection Act prohibits "knowingly and willfully" soliciting or receiving payment in return for referring a patient for services paid for by Medicare, Medicaid or a state health care program. See 42 U.S.C. § 1320a- 7b, which provides in pertinent part:

> (b)(1) Whoever knowingly and willfully solicits or receives any remuneration (including any kickback, bribe, or rebate) directly or indirectly, overtly or covertly, in cash or in kind -- (A) in return for referring an individual to a person for the furnishing of any item or service for which payment may be made in whole or in part under title XVIII or a State health care program . . . shall be guilty of a felony and upon conviction thereof, shall be fined not more than $ 25,000 or imprisoned for not more than five years, or both.

Dialysis is usually paid for in part by Medicare or Medicaid. It could be argued that the renal staff members "indirectly" receive payment in return for referring patients for services at their dialysis units.
However, the federal prohibition might not apply in this situation, since the owners are not receiving payment "in return for *referring*" patients to their dialysis units; rather, they are receiving profits from the dialysis units' treatment of the patients. That is, the "payments" are in return for services rendered, not in return for the act of referring patients. Compare *Hanlester Network v Shalala*, 51 F. 3d 1390 (9th Cir. 1995) (proceedings charging that physician self-referral joint venture violated 42 USCS § 1320a-7b by offering and paying remuneration to physician investors *to induce them* to refer lab tests to certain labs). On the other hand, Case 8 might be an example of "indirect" kickbacks for referring patients. This writer has not been able to find authority clarifying whether the system in Case 8 would be covered under federal law.

Conclusion:

The self-referral system may be prohibited, depending upon the laws of the state in which it is located, whether it satisfies any applicable disclosure requirements, and applicability of the federal Medicare and Medicaid Program Protection Act.

Ethical Analysis:

If the three senior renal staff members offer high quality care at their own units, and sincerely believe their units are the best, there is no ethical problem with their recommending their units to patients. Nonetheless, the physicians have an ethical obligation to disclose their financial interest in the dialysis units, so the patients can make a free choice whether to go to those units. However, the patients probably will still take the physicians' recommendation out of reliance on and trust in the physicians. Thus, the physicians have an even more important ethical obligation to consider only the patients' best interests - not the physicians' financial interests -- when making decisions about the patients' dialysis treatments and care. If the physicians are unable to do this, they should try to modify the system so that some other entity can monitor it and ensure that only services and procedures necessary for the patients are provided. Perhaps the physicians could disclose their financial interest in the dialysis units to the insurance carriers paying for the services, who could in turn monitor the quality of the care provided. If the physicians are unable to put the patients' best interests above their financial interests, they should discontinue their referral system.

Connie Zuckerman, J.D.

While physicians' investment in, and profit from, facilities to which their patients are referred is not automatically unethical, it does raise the concern that physician motives will be influenced by factors other than what serves the best interests of their patients. In circumstances where their financial interests may conflict with the medical interests of their patients, physicians must be sure to remain faithful to the fiduciary relationship they have with patients, and to not exploit patients for their own individual financial gain.
In fact, the American Medical Association recommends that physicians who have a personal financial interest in referral facilities make all possible attempts to refer their own patients elsewhere, or, at a minimum, to reveal this potential conflict of interest to patients, with information about other facilities the patients may access instead. In this specific case, it appears that the concerns of the junior nephrologist are well founded. The senior/owner physicians are clearly violating their ethical duties to the patients who are being self-referred, and they may even be liable for malpractice if it is clear that the interests of their patients are secondary to their own financial gain, and that the patients suffer harm as a consequence.

Amy L. Friedman, M.D.

When physicians were kept on pedestals and accorded a uniquely privileged status in society, profiting from personal stakes in health care facilities would have been wrong. But for better or worse, healthcare has changed dramatically. Doctors now work harder for lower income, are subject to intense censoring of administrative and medical judgements, uniformly express significant frustration and diminished satisfaction with their career choices and are common targets of money seeking attorneys and patients. Permitting physicians to reap financial reward for expertise in this new environment seems entirely consistent with our capitalist society. If intangible reimbursement for the personal sacrifices necessary to become and practice as a doctor is no longer available (accident victims often don't even thank the physician who offers help as a good samaritan!), then granting the freedom to exercise a spirit of innovation and resourcefulness should be.

Although personal profit for the physician is reasonable, it must not be allowed

to become a priority. The principles of care should be modeled after those of anti-trust legislation.
The identity of financial stakeowners should be fully disclosed to patients and other interested parties. Self referral of the physician's patients should not occur exclusively. Co-existence of a fiscal incentive with the need to maintain professional objectivity should be acknowledged by the potentially compromised physician who should err on the side of overcompensation. Every attempt to maintain the patient's access to the full market of dialysis facilities must be undertaken. This junior nephrologist should have sufficient confidence to raise his concerns with his partners who should fully explain all arrangements to him. Together, reasonable guidelines for patient disclosure should be developed and initiated.

Carl M. Kjellstrand, M.D.

Greedy physicians are bad physicians, worse friends and the worst supervisors. The young fellow is right, he should run for his life.

Mildred (Barry) Friedman

The junior nephrologist is correct in being agitated by the situation. Resignation is, however, not the answer. Discussion and solutions are.
Patients should be presented with a choice of facilities they might attend which are appropriate for them on an individual basis. They should be informed of their physicians' medical and financial involvement with these facilities. They may chose the one their doctors attend because they are in a good relationship with these health care providers and trust them.
There is nothing wrong with doctors earning money. The problem arises when a conflict of interest exists. Under these circumstances, it seems to me, connections between money-making establishments and patient care can be out in the open and allowed to become factors in patient decisions.
The junior nephrologist should not resign

Judith E. Columbo

A proprietary dialysis facility unit should not be run by three of the senior staff members of a community hospital. Dedication and money do not mix. Profits at this unit became the personal income of the senior staff members. I would not want to be treated at a unit that put a profit before my well being. The length of dialysis treatment should be based on lab results. I feel that the junior nephrologist was correct in choosing to resign from the group. I feel everyone is human and appreciates a good income but it is clear that the senior staff members are more concerned about their profits and not the well being of their patient's.

Editor's Remarks8

Zuckerman aptly defines the problems of physician ownership of medical facilities to which they may refer patients. Over the past ten years as radiologists purchased expensive imaging machines, nephrologists bought dialysis units, and self advertising became ethically acceptable, business concerns have intruded into the practice of medicine to an extent not previously imagined. On the other hand, physicians have owned laboratories and pharmacies since throughout the twentieth century. Once Medicare and Medicaid began tracking patient expenditures, the question of self referral become a multibillion dollar issue.[Endnote 13] Congress passed the Stark Regulations[Endnote 14] spelling out what was and what was not legitimate in the business of medicine. Because of the limited number of dialysis units and their relationship to academic facilities, referral of ESRD patients to facilities owned by the referring nephrologist has been exempted. A change in this interpretation may be made shortly. Attorney London points out that at least three states presently prohibit self referral by law, a circumstance that could grow to entrap the self-referring nephrologist providing dialysis therapy.

At one extreme, Dr. Amy L. Friedman laments the relatively low income for the amount of training and work expended in their profession. I have not noted any surgeons applying for welfare. At the other end of judgment, Kjellstrand, appears too quick in his condemnation of investing physicians as greedy and bad. In at least some instances known to the author, the only means open for expansion of dialysis within a region was investment by physicians. There is no doubt that some entrepreneureal nephrologist have gained huge wealth via keen investments in dialysis units. What should be monitored is the quality of renal care delivered as judged by survival and rehabilitation. I am not defending the Michael Douglas character in the movie "Wall Street" who proclaimed that "Greed is good." But, under capitalism, the desire to accumulate wealth is not in itself evil. Physicians who regard their contact with patients solely as opportunity for financial gain pervert the objectives of medicine as a profession. Devising a means to benefit from efficient and economic delivery of services whether in a car wash or hemodialysis unit is a legal and moral endeavor attractive to certain people including some physicians.

Response to Study Questions

1. Yes, for the time being there is no legal or ethical constraint.
2. At least two studies purport two have discerned higher mortality in patients dialyzed at for profit facilities compared with those treated at not-for-profit facilities.[Endnote 15, Endnote 16] The problem with this inference is that the cohorts compared were not demographically equivalent (unequal proportion of older patients and diabetics, for example). Other variables including dialyzer reuse and the policy on use of erythropoietin must also be taken into account when examining survival on dialysis.[Endnote 17]
3. A variation on question 2 with the same limitation to any answer.

4. No. But note Dr. Kjellstrand's sharp dissent. There are other ways of extracting excess funding from dealing with ESRD patients that are under examination. For example, vascular access surgeons may either create a primary arteriovenous fistula (longest lasting, good) or insert a prosthetic graft (higher fee, bad).
5. Strongly contentious debate surrounds this issue. Socialized medicine in Canada, Sweden, and the United Kingdom permits treatment of approximately one-half the number of ESRD patients enrolled in the United States. Mortality in American dialysis units is said to be twice as high as in Europe. But, like flawed comparisons between survival of kidney transplant recipients versus hemodialysis patients, the cohorts are not equivalent. I have argued that when all variables are taken into account, US ESRD therapy is unsurpassed in either socialistic or capitalistic systems.[Endnote 18]
6. No. Not a single study in which assignment to a treatment modality was randomized has been reported.

Case 9

GAME PLAYING FAMILIES

The husband of a 35 year old insulin-dependent (type 1) diabetic nursing supervisor insists that the severity of his wife's kidney failure be hidden. In his view, the patient is too fragile to bear the news that she is at risk of near-term loss of vision, dialysis and/or kidney transplantation, with a substantive probability of dying. Despite presentation of the argument that his wife will be better able to bear the stresses ahead if she is informed rather than distanced from the truth, the husband warns that "under no circumstance are you to tell my wife this terrible news." ***A resident states that he is not bound by unreasonable requests and will, indeed, discuss the patient's illness with the patient and family.***

Study Questions

1. Must a physician be bound by instructions from a patient's family?
2. Are there circumstances where the physician should withhold the *truth* from a patient?
3. If a physician fails to comply with a family's demand that a patient not be told (or told some other explanation than the truth), is the physician liable for a bad patient outcome (suicide)?
4. Does a physician have the *right/obligation* to change the truth in order to protect a patient judged to fragile to cope with the reality?

Monique Janelle London, J.D.

Informed Consent:

There is nothing illegal about the resident informing the patient of her condition over her husband's objection. Indeed, if her condition becomes serious enough to require dialysis or any other type of medical treatment, the resident must discuss it with her to obtain informed consent for the treatment. *See Causey v. St. Francis Medical Center,* 719 So. 2d 1072, 1075 (La. Ct. App. 2d Cir. 1998). The patient is described as a nursing supervisor, and so presumed to be competent. Thus the patient's husband has no legal right to make decisions for the patient (as a surrogate), or otherwise interfere with doctor-patient communication.

The only potentially applicable exception to the disclosure/informed consent rule is that a doctor has a "therapeutic privilege" to withhold disclosure of a material risk when he reasonably foresees that disclosure will cause the patient to become ill or emotionally distraught so as to foreclose a rational decision, complicate or hinder treatment, or pose psychological damage to the patient. *See Canterbury v. Spence,* 150 U.S. App. D.C. 263, 464 F.2d 772, 789 (D.C. Cir. 1972) (and cases cited therein), *cert. denied,* 409 U.S. 1064 (1972). In such situations, "[t]he critical inquiry is whether the physician responded to a sound medical judgment that communication of the risk information would present a threat to the patient's well-being." *Id.* It seems unlikely that this exception would apply in the present Case. The patient is a nursing supervisor, and thus certainly familiar with the notion that kidney failure can result from diabetes. The diagnosis would not be nearly as shocking to her as to a patient unfamiliar with this medical condition. Sound medical judgment would not dictate against disclosing the information.

In short, the resident will not face any legal liability for his insistence on discussing the patient's condition with her and her family.

Ethical Analysis:

The resident has made the correct ethical decision. He is obligated to inform the patient about her illness so that she can make autonomous decisions about her care. Moreover, the hypothetical states that the conditions the patient may experience are only "probabilities," not certainties. There may be actions the patient herself could take to minimize the risk of these probabilities materializing, such as modifying her diet to forestall the necessity for dialysis. If so, the patient will need information about her illness so that she can take those actions if she chooses. Even if the patient cannot affect the risk by her own actions, she will still likely want to have the information so she can get her affairs in order. She may need to prepare for blindness by learning braille, getting a talking computer, or explaining household finances to her husband. If the risk of dying is high, the patient may need that information in time to prepare her will and make arrangements for life in her family to carry on without her.[Footnote 29]

Especially in this hypothetical, where the patient is a nursing supervisor, and thus presumably familiar with medical conditions generally, she should be informed of her condition. It is unlikely, given her background, that she will fail to understand the information or be unduly frightened by it. However, before discussing the patient's illness with her, the resident should speak further with her husband. He should find out why the husband believes the patient is "too fragile" to bear the news of her condition. It may be that the patient has a history of reacting psychotically or suicidally to similar news. The resident should take any such information into account when deciding how and when to inform the patient about her illness.

Connie Zuckerman, J.D.

Patients with decisional capacity have the right to be involved in the treatment decisionmaking process, and must be provided with the information necessary to allow them to make informed, voluntary, individually appropriate treatment

[29] Even if the hypothetical had stated that the patient only had a "slight" or "miniscule" risk of going blind or dying, ethically the physician would still have an obligation to inform the patient if there were any possible preventive measures she could take. However, the physician should emphasize that the risk is minimal, or try to give a percentage chance of the risk occurring.

decisions. There are exceptions to this physician obligation to gain the patient's informed consent: primarily, in cases of emergency circumstances, or in cases where the therapeutic privilege may be invoked. The therapeutic privilege temporarily suspends the obligation to disclose information, based upon the physician's reasonable assessment that such disclosure would bring about immediate and severe harm to the patient.

While it is possible that in this case, the husband's concern about his wife's fragility may be legitimate (and must be further explored) it is just as likely that the problem lies with the husband, and his difficulty in dealing with the diagnosis. In fact, given the professional training and background of the patient, it is highly likely that she is already substantially aware of her circumstances. Ultimately, the resident may disclose such information to the patient, despite the husband's threats. The resident, however, should allow for the further exploration of the husband's concerns, and work with this family to tactfully but truthfuly disclose all relevant information to this patient, so that she may be an integral part of the decision process.

Amy L. Friedman, M.D.

My primary role as a physician is to serve the patient, not her family. This allegiance was established when she initiated our professional relationship by choosing to place her trust and very life in my hands. When the interests and wishes of these parties overlap the physician serves as counsel to the collective group. Indeed, the majority of patients prefer the active participation of close relatives and friends in negotiating a unique path through the complex and often intimidating options available to them. Individual patients, however, may choose not to share the full range of medical data, choices or predicted outcomes with anyone else. Regardless of the reason (preservation of privacy and dignity, denial of the severity of illness or a desire to demonstrate independence and courage are common motives), the physician is occasionally directed not to distribute details to anyone.

The physician may not be privy to important nuances of intrafamilial relationships. Is there any motivation for a family member to prefer a shorter versus a longer illness, earlier versus prolonged death? Is one relative trying to outmaneuver another to achieve emotional or financial gain? These and other concepts are likely to remain unknown to the physician. The safest approach is to rely on the patient for guidance. If this is not possible due to an altered state of consciousness, the physician may be forced to trust the judgements of another designated individual. Youth, incapacitating depression or dementia may leave no alternative but reliance on the next of kin/guardian. In either case appropriate levels of information must be disclosed to that individual(s). In some circumstances the patient may never have been capable of independent participation. However, every patient capable of judgement must be provided the opportunity to do so. To restrict the knowledge made available to this woman about the nature and severity of disease, treatment options and prognosis would be entirely inappropriate and frankly unethical in the current era of informed consent. Thus, in an open manner, she must be given the opportunity to review all relevant information with her. She may choose to make preparations for an altered lifestyle (e.g., allowing an employer to make realistic plans for her inability to return to full or part time work) or death (e.g., unresolved issues in personal relationships that she chooses to address while still alive).

Ironically, however, the patient's physician must also be sensitive to indications that she does not want to know. For some individuals, denial is an indispensable component of the coping mechanism. It would be insensitive and wrong to override such a patient's preference to maintain an illusion of well being. In this instance, the physician's judgement and familiarity with the patient are most severely tested. I will often choose to entertain the advice of close family members regarding this particular issue. However, if, as in this case, the husband simply does not want his spouse to know, I would rely on my own judgement. If I reach the conclusion that she is not choosing to avoid awareness, then my allegiance is to the patient, not her husband.

Carl M. Kjellstrand, M.D.

Informed unbiased information is necessary for sound choice, see case 7, it is the right of any patient to receive it. Unless the nurse is an idiot, she needs to know and your obligations are to her, the patient, not her husband. However, to be able to interact in an effective way, you need a long meeting with the husband probing his motives. This is important to understand what is behind such a stupid and odd request. Dialysis is a family affair so his views are important too.

Mildred (Barry) Friedman

Game playing is a derogatory term for what may well be simply well intentioned decisions. While I disagree vehemently with withholding information, I acknowledge the thoughtful, considerate feelings of the person who came to that conclusion.

Personal experience causes me to be very emphatic on this point. The passage of time does not change bad new into good nor does it make acceptance by the patient easier. Indeed, here the sick one will only get sicker, her mental function will deteriorate, and she will be less able to understand.

Certainly if ESRD treatment is begun, as a nurse, she will guess what is happening. If no treatment is started then she will have been condemned to death without the opportunity to cope with her circumstances. Either way she is denied the right to control her own life - not a good situation.

A knowledgeable person, and probably any person, knows when they are sick. Speaking honestly with them must lessen the stress. The unknown is more fearful than the known. The resident is right in deciding to tell her what is going on but perhaps the husband might be convinced that bad news dispensed by him, with love and caring, would be the gentlest, kindest way.

Awareness opens the way to honest communication. It is reassuring to be able to ask questions and to express fears and hopes. I see no downside to telling the truth.

Judith E. Columbo

An insulin-dependent diabetic nurse supervisor had a life in the closet if the complications of diabetes are not in her everyday vocabulary. The patient happens to be a diabetic nurse supervisor who I guess, in her career, has seen the worse of diabetic complications yes, even death. Maybe if the husband gave his educated wife some credit and allows her to cope with her medical condition she would and could. I agree with the resident that the illness should be discussed with the patient and family.

Editor's Remarks9

By the length of their responses, all analysts found this case to be straightforward. Their answers are similar. The patient has a right to know and the husband is wrong in requesting that vital information not be communicated to his wife. Not all cultures agree. In Japan, the Supreme Court upheld a physician who elected to lie to his patient in not telling that a cancer was present. After asking the patient whether they wish full disclosure of findings, I concur with Mildred Barry Friedman who stated: "I see no downside to telling the truth."

Response to Study Questions

1. No. The physician's sworn duty is to the patient. Certainly, advice from family should be obtained, digested, and incorporated into the stance utilized for the patient. There is no obligation to follow requests from a relative that are interpreted as contrary to what is best for the patient.
2. Probably. The truth may be frightening in that extensive brain metastasises indicate a very short duration to future functional life. Or, the kidney biopsy showed destruction of the transplant forcing nephrectomy. In the few instances when I have tried to delay telling my patient the unfavorable truth, some other team member did. It is better for the patient to learn of all events from the most trusted physician.
3. Frightening question. Only the court will decide though I think not.
4. The art of medicine includes knowing how to couch unfavorable information in a form that will not destabilize a fragile patient.

Case 10

PHYSICIAN REFUSAL OF HIV+ PATIENTS

Shortly after beginning duty on a renal service with about 15% of patients who are HIV positive, a 27 year old married medical resident requested reassignment. Reasoning that patients' bodily fluids - peritoneal dialysate and blood - contaminated bed clothes and were frequently spilled on work surfaces, the resident commented that she ought to have control over where and when her life was at risk. She remarked that she would not have asked for removal from the renal service if the HIV patients under her care were "innocent" and had become infected from contaminated blood products as in the case of American hemophiliacs and factor VIII. By contrast, however, she stated that she was not prepared to die for an intravenous heroin addict who used contaminated needles, or a homosexual man unable to resist bath houses. The Chief of the Medical service was unsympathetic to the resident's position. ***"Any resident unwilling to provide first class empathetic care to our HIV positive patients shall be immediately terminated from this Medical Service," he announced, thereby ending the problem by fiat.***

Study Questions

1. Is there any risk of contracting AIDS by medical staff?
2. Given the constant exposure to blood in dialysis apparatus, is the risk of contracting AIDS greater for dialysis personnel?
3. Does the fear of contracting a disease qualify as a legitimate reason for declining patient care?
4. Should the medical resident be discharged?

Monique Janelle London, J.D.

Legal Rights of Resident:

The first legal issue is whether the resident has a right to transfer out of the renal unit because some of the patients there are HIV positive due to certain behaviors. The resident does not refuse to treat all HIV positive patients, but only contaminated needle users and homosexual men. Her discrimination is not based on whether a patient is HIV positive, but rather on the behavior by which the patient contracted HIV. Nor is the resident's refusal to treat certain HIV positive patients based on concerns about her own health and safety; she is willing to expose herself to HIV from patients who were infected by contaminated blood products.

Unless the resident has an employment contract with the medical center specifying that she can refuse certain assignments for any reason, nothing in this Case suggests she has a legal right to reassignment from the renal service.

Legal Rights and Obligations of Chief of Medical Service/Medical Center:

The Chief of Medical Service certainly has the right to grant the resident's request for transfer (although as a practical matter, that could set a difficult precedent at the medical center). If he does not grant that request, however, he may have an obligation to terminate the resident rather than risk having her discriminate against certain HIV positive patients in the renal service. If the resident is employed with the medical center under an at-will employment contract (or no employment contract), she can be terminated for any reason.[Footnote 30] If her employment contract only permits termination for cause, her intended discrimination (if it becomes actual) against certain patients based on their behavior alone is probably sufficient cause to justify termination.

Indeed, if the resident is not transferred or terminated, and subsequently refuses to provide dialysis services only to patients who contracted HIV by heroin use or homosexual behavior, she may subject the medical center to liability for discrimination. Some cities have ordinances prohibiting discrimination against HIV positive persons. For instance, a 1985 Los Angeles ordinance, which expressly applies to the provision of medical services, prohibits discrimination against persons with AIDS or persons suspected of having AIDS. Los Angeles, Cal., Ordinance 160,289 (Aug. 16, 1985). A similar ordinance in San Francisco prohibits AIDS discrimination in business establishments and public accommodations. San Francisco, Cal., Ordinance 49,985 (Dec. 20, 1985). Many states also have anti-discrimination statutes which may protect individuals with AIDS or HIV infection. The Chief would need to examine the provisions of the state and local laws governing his medical center to see if they would apply to the behavior of the resident.

Federal laws prohibiting discrimination based on a disability may also be relevant. As explained in connection with Case 5, § 504 of the 1973 Rehabilitation Act states: "No otherwise qualified individual with a disability ... shall, solely by reason of his or her disability, be excluded from the participation in, be denied the benefits of, or be subjected to discrimination under any program or activity receiving Federal financial assistance." 29 U.S.C.A. § 794(a). Federal courts of appeals have shown a willingness to assume that AIDS and HIV infection are within the scope of § 504. *See Martinez v. School Bd. of Hillsborough County,* Fla., 861 F .2d 1502 (11th Cir. 1988); *Chalk v. United States Dist. Court Cent. Dist. of Cal.*, 840 F.2d 701 (9th Cir. 1988).

Section 302 of the Americans With Disabilities Act (ADA) similarly prohibits discrimination against disabled individuals by "public accommodations." 42 U.S.C. § 12182. The ADA also extends the Rehabilitation Act protections to private settings. *See* 42 U.S.C. §§ 12101-12213. The ADA explicitly prohibits discrimination

[30] The only possible exception to this rule is the "public policy" exception, whereby the employee "has a cause of action for wrongful discharge when the discharge is contrary to a clear mandate of public policy." *See Warthen v. Toms River Community Memorial Hospital,* 199 N.J. Super. 18, 488 A.2d 229 (1985), *quoting Pierce v. Ortho Pharmaceutical Corp.*, 84 N.J. 58, 72 (1980). This exception would not apply in Case 10, as the resident did not (and could not) identify a specific expression of public policy.

on the basis of a disability, including HIV, whether symptomatic or not. 42 U.S.C. § 12102(2). However, the ADA also makes an exception for people who engage in socially unaccepted sexual or other behaviors such as homosexuality. *See, e.g.*, 42 U.S.C. § 12114.

It is unclear from the facts presented in Case 10 whether all, or only some, of the HIV positive patients in the renal service contracted HIV in a way objectionable to the resident. If all the HIV patients contracted HIV through heroin use or homosexual behavior, then the resident's refusal to treat such patients has the effect of discriminating against all the HIV patients, and is likely to be deemed discrimination based on the "disability" of being HIV positive. *See, e.g., United States v. Morvant*, 843 F. Supp. 1092, 1094-96 (E.D. La. 1994) (holding that a dentist who uniformly denied services to patients with HIV infection could be liable for discrimination under the ADA).

In contrast, if only some of the HIV patients in the renal service contracted HIV through behavior objectionable to the resident, she would only refuse to treat some of the HIV patients. It seems less likely that the anti-discrimination laws would apply to a hospital whose resident discriminated against only certain HIV patients, based not on the fact that they are HIV positive, but on how they contracted HIV. *See, e.g., Johnson v. Thompson*, 971 F.2d 1487, 1493 (10th Cir. 1992), *cert. denied*, 113 S. Ct. 1255 (1993) (reasoning that § 504 of the Rehabilitation Act does not prohibit discrimination among persons with the same disability because such discrimination is not solely on the basis of disability).

In sum, the Chief of Medical Service may be obligated to terminate the resident to protect his hospital from liability for discrimination, if the resident is not transferred and in fact discriminates against HIV positive patients.

Ethical Analysis:

The resident should not discriminate against patients based on what behavior they exhibited to contract HIV. There is no ethical basis for a physician to treat HIV positive patients who contracted their disease by "innocent" means, but not those who contracted HIV through intravenous drug use or homosexual relationships. It is appropriate for the Chief of Medicine to advise the resident that she will be terminated if she engages in that discriminatory practice.

The Chief of Medicine has no ethical obligation to transfer the resident out of the renal service under these circumstances. If the resident asked for the transfer because she feared the risk to her health of contact with blood contaminated with any infectious disease contracted by the patient by any means, that might be a valid basis for requesting the transfer (especially, for instance, if the resident had young children dependent on her). But she stated that she is willing to risk her life from the contaminated blood of "innocent" HIV patients. She only objects to the risk to her life caused by contaminated blood of patients who contracted HIV through heroin injections or homosexual activity. This discriminatory reasoning creates no obligation for the Chief to consider the resident's request.

Connie Zuckerman, J.D.

While it is conceivable that a newly assigned medical resident may be unfamiliar with the actual risk of HIV infection she faces while at work on a renal service, it is unethical and unacceptable to allow such ignorance and attendant bias to dictate which patients she will or will not care for. With the use of universal precautions, the risk of infection she faces is minimal and certainly does not justify reassignment while other colleagues carry out their professional responsibilities in the face of similar risk. The assumption of a certain amount of risk, as part of the privilege to practice medicine, is a professional obligation which, if not accepted, challenges the overall professionalism and ability of this resident to practice medicine. No one would require that she expose herself to inordinate risk, but in the given context, professional obligations clearly require her to professionally carry out her responsibilities in a competent and nonjudgmental manner. In fact, refusal to provide appropriate care to HIV infected patients may be cause for legal action against the facility, under both federal and state legislation which forbid discrimination against the disabled (which includes those infected with HIV).

While the fiat may practically forclose the resident's option to withdraw, the Chief of Medical Service ought to more personally explore the understanding and motivations of this resident, who may covertly attempt to do what she has overtly been forbidden to do. While physicians are permitted to object to their participation in certain procedures as a result of a religiously based or moral conscience objection, the resident in this case appears influenced by a prejudicially based judgment concerning acceptable lifestyles. Such judgments not only have no place in the delivery of care, and violate the physician's obligation to deliver care in a just and fair manner, but they are often based on mistaken analyses of cause, effect and responsibility for individual illness.

Amy L. Friedman, M.D.

To the reader sitting in a clean chair, far from the possible spray of blood droplets or tissue fluids inadvertently spread from open wounds or dialysis needles it must be easy to judge this young woman. How selfish and biased she appears! How dare she deny that in choosing to become a physician she accepted the obligation of caring for all those seeking her expertise, without bias and without concern of risk to herself. After all, through the ages, physicians have had to fear death from a variety of infectious diseases. HIV is hardly the first threatening microorganism encountered by those who dedicate their lives to healing. It would seem clear that she is obligated to march in to that dialysis unit, don appropriate barrier protection and deliver compassionate care to each and every patient in need.

My perspective is quite different. The daily heroism we frontline soldiers accept is rarely acknowledged. As a surgeon whose latex covered hands have worked within the virus riddled bodies of such afflicted patients, who has had protective eyewear spattered with their blood, and whose fingers have been millimeters away from the tips of sharp instruments and bloodstained needles, the dilemma she faces seems terribly complex. I have been deeply stuck with such a needle while caring for a high risk patient. To protect my spouse from risk we deferred sexual activity to await the results of my post exposure HIV test. I was already endangered, but he was not. And what would we have done if I were pregnant? Would congenital AIDS be a fair burden to impose on our unborn child simply because his(her) mother chose to be a physician? As a woman of childbearing age this resident has ample reason to be more troubled by her occupational risk than any of her male colleagues. Should she abstain from all sexual activity entirely in order to be 100% certain of avoiding pregnancy? Should she and her husband carefully plan to initiate reproduction while she is rotating on safer services? If so, why must the spontaneity and wonder of parenting be restricted only for female trainees? Perhaps she should involve the program director of her residency in the family planning? Should she become pregnant would it be appropriate, logistically feasible or even legal to interrupt all forms of risky clinical behavior until after delivery, even though her residency would have to be lengthened to fully satisfy all academic requirements?

During each of three pregnancies I continued to perform highly invasive operations, caring both for those known to be HIV infected as well as those not blatantly known to be. All three were marked by constant guilt and worry. I even imagined being sued for the imposition of unreasonable risk by an independent guardian on behalf of my child! The answers are not straightforward, but the questions are quite real. So, while this young woman should return to work and fulfill all of her training responsibilities, her fears are valid and must not be belittled. Unless you have been in her place, very gray truths seem black and white.

Carl M. Kjellstrand, M.D.

The chief is right in his conclusions, wrong in his approach. There is to date no known transmission of HIV from an HIV positive patient to other dialysis patients or staff. The resident needs to know that. The "moralizing" attitude needs discussion and the resident reminded of the old Chinese medical code: "Physicians should relieve suffering among all classes: aristocrat or commoner, poor or rich, aged or young, beautiful or ugly, educated or uneducated, enemy or friend, all are to be treated equally". While physicians of course should have and hold rock bottom ethical standards this stand taken by the resident is one of an immature person. If she still holds to her views after a period of reflection she should be terminated.

Mildred (Barry) Friedman

Conscientious objectors were allowed to not participate in battle situations but to serve their country in other ways. Physician refusal to treat HIV+ patients may be considered in the same light. The question is whether people who have taken an oath to serve others may pick and choose who they will serve.

Perhaps doctors with strong convictions that they should not be forced to treat HIV+ patients should leave the profession and find new careers.
Perhaps they should change to a specialty where less threat exists. Ophthalmology and psychiatry come to mind.
What is not arguable is her right to morally judge her patients and decide which ones to treat. Fear of HIV is understandable. A woman in the midst of her child bearing years may well be more concerned than a male of the same age. Consideration of an unborn does not seem to have been raised by the resident but it is in my mind. My belief in the right of each of us to control our own lives comes into play here. Along with that right is the necessity to live with the results of our decisions.

The Chief of the Medical Service is correct in his decision. No compromise seems possible. Medical residents can give no less than full care to the people in their charge and at this stage in their training they cannot decide who will and who will not be under their care.

Judith E. Columbo

A medical resident, or any person, does have control over where and when a life is at risk. I also believe that it takes a caring and dedicated person to become a good doctor. This resident states that she is unwilling to die from a contaminated needle used by an addict but an "innocent" HIV patient is different. A statement that you would not hear from a dedicated and caring doctor. The Chief of Medicine was correct in dismissing the resident from his Medical Service because it is quite apparent that she is bias in her thinking and I feel is in the wrong profession. I bet that "innocent" HIV patient would not feel too much comfort from this resident's bedside manner.

Editor's Remarks 10

All respondents except Dr. Amy L. Friedman, a woman surgeon, agree that the resident be terminated. Dr. Friedman observes that:"very gray truths seem black and white," recounting her own anxiety of disease exposure during three pregnancies. Others, while expressing empathy for the frightened resident, correctly term her stance immature. Patient Columbo makes the insightful observation that "innocent" HIV patients "would not feel too much comfort from this resident's bedside manner." I agree. As the threat of a rapid horrific death following exposure to HIV patients has receded, I have wondered about the conduct of housestaff and attending physicians assigned to care for Ebola virus infected patients from whom fatal transmission is a true and terrifying risk. Some would flee though others would stay risking life as did the physicians of the "Plague Years" in medieval Europe.

Response to Study Questions

1. Reported staff transmissions of HIV infection have been rare, limited to needle sticks and scalpel injuries. It has happened[Endnote 19] and remains a real risk.[Endnote 20]
2. As noted by Kjellstrand, though hepatitis B transmission has been documented via dialysis contamination, HIV has not. Several kidney transplant recipients contracted HIV from their donor kidneys[Endnote 21, Endnote 22] and it is possible to transmit HIV when the donor is HIV negative.[Endnote 23]
3. No. Fully discussed above.
4. Unhappily, for the reasons presented by London, the Chief has no choice but to discharge the resident.

Case 11

RELIGIOUS CONTROL OF PATIENT

A 20 year old orthodox Jewish student with congenital renal disease had several seizures which were attributed to advanced uremia but persisted in postponing dialytic therapy on the advice of his rabbi. When confronted with his rapidly declining weight and loss of muscle mass, the patient stated that all decisions pertaining to the management of his kidney failure were to be made by his religious leader. Telephone contact with the clergyman confirmed the reality that customary sect behavior called for dominant participation by the patient's rabbi. Previously, the rabbi, who was reluctant to employ dialysis, preferred to wait as long as possible to"avoid artificial means of healing." The Chief of Nephrology at the university hospital caring for the patient after his seizures rejected the rabbi as intermediary and advised that ***unless the patient and his immediate family were free to meet with the medical staff and plan a course of therapy, he would ask the patient to transfer to another facility.***

Study Questions

1. Must physicians agree to religion-based decisions modulating patient care? For example, if life is at stake, is a doctor obligated to transfuse a dying Jehovah's Witness who has given precise instructions that no blood transfusions are to be administered?
2. When faced with a circumstance of a patient under religious control, should the physician disengage or attempt to reason with the religious leader?
3. At the age of 20, this Jewish student is legally responsible for himself. Should the nephrologist discharge him as a patient rather than watch further deterioration as directed by the rabbi?
4. Should resort to the responsible court be attempted?

Monique Janelle London, J.D.

If the patient is competent, the hospital probably has an obligation to honor his delegation of health care decisions to his rabbi. Even if the patient is incompetent, his legal representative or designee has the right to make health care decisions. If that designee is the rabbi, the hospital must obtain informed consent from the rabbi to initiate dialysis treatments. The hospital may also be able to initiate dialysis without the rabbi's consent, if doing so qualifies as an emergency lifesaving procedure. But if the hospital refuses to care for the patient further without providing reasonable notice and a chance for the patient to secure other medical assistance, the hospital may be liable for abandonment.

Assignment of Decision-Making Rights By Competent Patient:

If the patient is competent, he probably has the right to assign his decision-making rights to his rabbi. As set forth in Case 1, many states have advance directive statutes under which a competent patient has the right to make medical decisions, including refusal of treatment, through a designated person (proxy). *See*, e.g., CAL. PROBATE CODE §§ 4600-4753; CAL. HEALTH & SAFETY CODE § 7190. These statutes generally require the treating physician to honor the patient's designation, or transfer the patient to a healthcare provider who will.

There is no prohibition on using the advance directive to have the proxy make decisions for a patient even while the patient is competent. Nor does anything in the law suggest that it would be improper to designate a religious leader as one's agent for health care decisions; on the contrary, such a designation comports with the patient's First Amendment right to freedom of religion. If the patient in Case 11 has executed an advance directive (including a living will, durable power of attorney or other legally valid document) designating his rabbi as his agent for health care decisions, the hospital probably has an obligation to honor that designation, or transfer the patient to another hospital that will honor the designation.

If the patient is competent and does not have an advance directive, the hospital should have him execute one to protect the hospital from liability for failure to obtain informed consent from the patient himself. To ensure further protection, the hospital might also have the patient sign a declaration stating that he has chosen of his own free will to have his rabbi make medical decisions for him, and will not hold the hospital or its physicians liable for any decisions the rabbi makes.

Incompetence:

It is unclear whether the patient is competent. The advanced stage of his renal disease, including seizures and subsequent hospital care, suggests that his ability to make a rational decision may be compromised. If so, as discussed in connection with previous Cases, his legal representative or surrogate has the right to make health care decisions on the patient's behalf. If the legal representative is in fact the patient's rabbi (by virtue of advance directive or otherwise), then the hospital must seek informed consent from the rabbi, not the patient, to initiate dialysis therapy. If the legal representative is someone else, the hospital should seek consent from that person, not the rabbi, to initiate dialysis treatments. However, as also discussed previously, whether a patient is competent or incompetent in a case such as this is a fact-specific question which may require court involvement. And even if the patient were deemed incompetent, some weight would likely be given to his expressed desire to have his rabbi make medical decisions for him in determining what the patient would want if he were competent.

Lifesaving Treatment:

Even assuming the rabbi does have the right to decline dialysis treatments on the patient's behalf, the hospital may be able to initiate dialysis over the rabbi's objection without incurring legal liability.
A patient's religious preferences are not always held paramount when it comes to lifesaving treatments. For instance, in certain situations, courts have ordered

lifesaving blood transfusions to be performed over a patient's religious objections. In *Application of the President and Directors of Georgetown College, Inc.*, 331 F.2d 1000 (D.C. Cir. 1964), *cert. denied sub nom Jones v. President & Directors of Georgetown College, Inc.*, 377 U.S. 978 (1964), the court ordered a hospital to administer a blood transfusion over the religious objections of a 25 year old woman, on grounds that: 1) she had voluntarily sought medical care, exposing the hospital to civil and criminal liability either for administering the transfusion or allowing the patient to die; 2) her mental state was in question since she was in an emergency situation; 3) she was the mother of an infant, so the state had an interest in preserving her life; 4) she did not want to die -- her religion did not command death, but only the refusal of transfusions; and 5) she would have died within minutes without the transfusion. *Id.* at 1009. Similarly, in *Hamilton v. McAuliffe*, 277 Md. 336, 353 A.2d 634 (Md. 1976), the Maryland Supreme Court upheld an order authorizing a transfusion over the patient's religious objection because the patient, a single parent, had a two year old child. In *Powell v. Columbia Presbyterian Medical Center*, 49 Misc. 2d 215, 267 N.Y.S.2d 450 (N.Y. 1965), a New York court ordered a blood transfusion for a Jehovah's Witness because she was the mother of six children.

These cases suggest that a court also would authorize lifesaving treatment over a religious objection expressed by a patient's rabbi to whom the patient has deferred all medical decisions. Case No. 11 does not state whether the patient has children, nor whether the lack of dialysis has yet become an "emergency" or life-threatening situation. At some point, however, if dialysis is not initiated, the patient will die. The patient's religion does not appear to mandate death, but only "avoiding artificial means of healing." This writer has not found a case in which a court ordered dialysis over a patient or surrogate's religious objection; however, an argument could be made that the caselaw regarding blood transfusions should apply in the dialysis context.

On the other hand, some courts have found that the balance tipped in favor of the patient's right to religious freedom. *See Public Health Trust v. Wons*, 541 So. 2d 96, 97-98 (Fla. 1989) (finding that the state's interest in having children raised by two parents does not override the right to refuse blood transfusions); *Norwood Hosp. v. Munoz*, 409 Mass. 116, 564 N.E.2d 1017, 1023 (Mass. 1991) (finding that the state's interest in preserving life does not override the right to refuse transfusion invoked by a Jehovah's Witness). These decisions suggest that the patient (through his rabbi) should be allowed to refuse dialysis in theabsence of an overriding state interest.

Moreover, as a practical matter, the rabbi may not object to initiating dialysis at this point. The Case states that the rabbi previously stated that he preferred to wait "as long as possible" to "avoid artificial means of healing." It is unclear what the rabbi meant by this statement. However, since the rabbi first expressed this preference, the patient's situation appears to have worsened. If the hospital explains that it is not possible to wait any longer without jeopardizing the life of the patient, the rabbi may consent to the treatment as lifesaving, and no longer simply an "artificial means of healing."

Under federal law, the hospital may in fact be obligated to initiate dialysis over the rabbi's objection. As explained in connection with Case 5, under the Emergency Medical Treatment and Active Labor Act (EMTALA), when a patient seeks care, the hospital must initially determine whether an emergency medical condition exists (i.e., whether the patient will suffer serious impairment of bodily functions or organs if immediate medical attention is not provided). If an emergency condition does exist, the hospital must stabilize that patient to avert material deterioration in his or her condition prior to any transfer to another facility. *See* 42 U.S.C. § 1395dd. This law has been found to preempt state law to the contrary. *See In the Matter of Baby K*, 832 F. Supp. 1022 (E.D. Va. 1993), *aff'd*, 16 F.3d 590 (4th Cir.), *cert. denied*, 115 S. Ct. 91 (1994).

Thus, if the patient's condition has reached "emergency" status when he seeks care for his seizures, the hospital may be required to initiate dialysis.

Abandonment:

The hospital also has the option of discontinuing any treatment of the patient. However, it may face liability for abandonment if it acts on the Chief of Nephrology's statement without satisfying certain requirements. The hospital is currently "caring for the patient after his seizures." Given his worsening condition, he will probably need additional treatment there. The Chief of Nephrology will not face legal liability for "asking" the patient to transfer to another facility. However, if the hospital refuses to continue treating the patient, it may be liable for abandonment. As stated previously, a caregiver may withdraw from a patient's case only after providing "due notice" and an "ample opportunity" to secure the presence of other medical attendance. *See, e.g., Hongsathavij v. Queen of Angels etc. Medical Center*, 62 Cal. App. 4th 1123, 73 Cal. Rptr. 2d 695 (Cal. App. 2d Dist. 1998); *Capps v. Valk*, 189 Kan. 287, 369 P.2d 238 (Kan. 1962).

The hospital should first ensure that the rabbi is the patient's proxy or surrogate for health care decisions. If so, the hospital should honor the patient's wish to defer to his rabbi about whether to initiate dialysis. A hospital representative should explain to the rabbi why the patient needs to begin dialysis immediately and try to get the rabbi's informed consent to initiate treatment. If the rabbi continues to refuse consent, the hospital may be obligated to initiate dialysis anyway if it becomes necessary to save the patient's life. If the patient's situation has not yet become life threatening, the hospital can avoid liability by terminating its relationship with the patient, provided it gives the patient due notice of that intention and ample opportunity to transfer to another hospital.

Ethical Analysis:

As long as the patient has decided of his own free will to assign his health care decision-making to his rabbi, the hospital has an ethical obligation to honor that assignment. On the other hand, the hospital should not honor the rabbi's refusal of treatment if it means the patient's life will be threatened as a result. Before acting against the instructions of the rabbi, the hospital should first make every attempt to talk to both the patient and the rabbi about the need for dialysis and the consequences to the patient if it is not initiated. The physician responsible for the patient should try to understand what the parameters are of the sect's belief in "avoiding artificial means of healing," and under what circumstances initiating dialysis would be consistent with that belief. If possible, the physician should devise a solution that comports with the patient's religion but also minimizes the risk to his health.

Connie Zuckerman, J.D.

At the age of 20, this patient is presumed legally competent to make his own decisions about treatment, and to factor into his decision whatever values and preferences are important to him, including the advice and reflection of his spiritual leader. The patient may even waive his own decisionmaking authority and transfer it to another if he so chooses. As long as he possesses the actual capacity to understand his situation and the implications of his choices, he may follow whatever treatment regimen he believes appropriate, even if it leads to an increasingly debilitated state, or even his death. Such an issue often arises in the context of Jehovah's Witness patients, whose refusal of blood transfusions seems medically insupportable, but whose choices must be legally respected so long as they are made in an informed and voluntary manner.

In this case, the patient's choice of advisor, and the decisions he chooses to make, must be respected, even if the Director of Nephrology finds them unacceptable. In fact, the only bases on which to challenge the decisions of this patient are if legitimate challenges can be made to either his decisional capacity or if legitimate concern exists that his choice in not one freely made, as opposed to one with which providers disagree. However, physicians who feel that their ability to practice in a professional manner is being compromised by the patient's choices, may decide to withdraw from a case, and assist the patient in finding another provider who is willing to abide by the patient's treatment wishes. In this case, the Director cannot force the patient to reject his rabbi, nor can he force the patient to involve his family if the patient chooses not to do so. However, the option to transfer care of the patient to another facility willing and able to take on this patient is acceptable, if no mutually agreeable treatment regimen can be developed.

Amy L. Friedman, M.D.

The competent adult is ultimately responsible for choosing his own healthcare just as he (she) defines each aspect of his life. He cannot and should not be forced to select a specific provider, institution, medication or therapeutic modality. When he seeks professional counsel from a physician, comprehensive discussion of all options must occur in a forthright way and should be fully documented. This information is then processed or put into perspective as the patient reaches a decision. Or, if no decision is made (due to procrastination, denial or the absence of intention), a passive failure to act still causes an outcome.

It is reasonable and routine for the patient to involve others as he assesses his medical condition and choices. While members of the immediate family and close friends are the most common participants, religious advisers or leaders may also be important in the patient's personal support system. There is no medical basis for preference or exclusion of one over the other. It should be the patient's discretion to assign each relative importance in his own life. However, it is fundamental that the patient is directly exposed to the physician and his(her) opinion. Transmission of the doctor's message to the patient by his rabbi (or anyone else) is inadequate and likely to introduce inaccuracy. Similarly, the patient must himself state his choice of treatment. The physician must be exquisitely sensitive to a possible need to separate the patient from any of the individuals who may be applying pressure or coercion. Thus, the communal stress felt by a Jehovah's Witness to refuse blood transfusion may be so great that he is unable to conceive of the community rejection that would result from blood acceptance. Yet, privately, he may change his mind if reassurance that his medical care will be kept confidential and a means of administering the blood out of the presence of those trying to judge him, devised. An ultimate decision of the fully informed patient to follow the guidance of his religious leader, no matter how medically foolish it seems, must be respected and honored. This nephrologist should strive to develop higher tolerance of those who differ from him.

Carl M. Kjellstrand, M.D.

Rock-bottom religious and ethical beliefs are non-negotiable. Both patient and physician will hold onto them, and should. Transferring this patient to another unit will not help in his care. It will only move a difficult ethical problem to somebody else potentially causing harm to the patient. I would have told the rabbi that he is jeopardizing the patient's life, that he will be responsible for the shortened life-span, and as I understand Orthodox Jewish law, this is a terrible thing. I would tell the patient and the family that they are violating Judaical law by not carefully doing the best to preserve and prolong life, and if nothing helps, search help from higher Judaic religious authority. The effort should be carefully documented.

Mildred (Barry) Friedman

Irrational religious beliefs are difficult to combat. With tongue in cheek I suggest a rapid course in ESRD for all rabbis of this sect.
Tradition here states that the rabbi is the leader. The leader, therefore must be educated. It would seem easier to change one person than a whole sect. Raising the question of whether the rabbi ever believes in using dialysis as a therapy leads to pointing out that delayed treatment is as much an "artificial means of healing" as immediate treatment. Indeed, if the rabbi is led to a good decision, many people - future patients - might benefit. Rabbis are eggheads. Eggheads can learn. The answer to ignorant religious control is education. The time to help this patient may pass but the future may hold good.
The Chief of Nephrology is demanding compliance with his plan of therapy and is not asking for participation by the patient and family in formulating a strategy. They are free to discuss, but their thoughts will be guided by their beliefs.

If they decide to postpone dialysis it is incumbent upon their physician to guide the continuing events as well as he can.

Judith E. Columbo

I believe that the patient's rabbi was considered an immediate family member who the patient respected and not holding the patient hostage. Since the rabbi, patient and patient's family belief, was to wait as long as possible before starting artificial means of healing, then the Chief of Nephrology should be willing to accept this course of therapy. A course that a family's soul is searched. One of the options given each dialysis patient is death. When and if we decide this action, it is something that the patient and family together must survive.

Editor's Remarks 11

When adults seek and consent to religious control of their lives, there is little that outsiders can or should do. Certainly, government must protect its citizens from religious cults releasing nerve gas in subways or conducting sexual orgies with minors but the promulgation of objectionable ideas is not a crime in a free society. Extreme cults promulgating mass suicide or self destructive actions present unique problems that are not easy to remedy.

Examples of harmful advice from religious leaders seen in my program during the past year include:

1. Discontinuing immunosuppressive drugs in kidney transplant recipients because "God will preserve the kidney." and
2. Refusing blood transfusions during major surgery because "Blood is flesh of another person."

The patient in Case 11 is representative of some sects of orthodox Jews who willingly transfer authority for major life decisions to their rabbi. When the rabbi's medical knowledge is limited, and the limitation unappreciated, religion and medicine may clash as in Case 11. I have been unsuccessful in breaching the blockade to reason imposed by religious conviction. Therefore, even though this patient may die from delayed initiation of dialytic therapy, the responsible nephrologist may do nothing more than advise referral elsewhere. Very complete documentation of the nephrologist's proposed therapy - in the chart and in a letter sent by certified mail - may afford protection against a law suit but the patient remains vulnerable to uninformed and outdated leadership.

Response to Study Questions

1. Yes. Patients have the absolute right to reject medical advice. Bear in mind that it is not a rare event for physicians to be wrong. The entire subspecialty

of bloodless surgery was generated by patient refusal to accept transfusions on religious grounds.

2. Always reason. And, reason again and again. Only rarely is transfer of the patient required to preserve the doctor's sanity.
3. Doctor's choice. I would retain the patient trying repeatedly to break through the barrier of bad advice.
4. From London's thorough analysis it is evident that the courts are of minimal value in altering opinions fixed by religious conviction.

Case 12

EMOTIONALLY RELATED ORGAN DONATION

A 45 year old medically well marine sergeant, the life-long friend of a 48 year old attorney who has a 42 year old wife on maintenance hemodialysis due to hypertensive kidney disease, offers his kidney for transplantation. The potential donor declines payment - in any form - stating that giving his "spare kidney" will make him feel fulfilled. Tissue typing and pre-transplant screening indicate that donor and recipient share two antigens and have no circulating factors which might injure the transplanted kidney. On the day of transplant surgery, ***the anesthesiologist refuses to participate on the grounds that what is proposed is a possibly lethal assault on an otherwise healthy human being.***

Study Questions

1. Can a sane person opt to undergo the pain and discomfort of organ removal for a stranger?
2. What testing is necessary to confirm the validity of the offer of organ donation?
3. Is it within the rights of the anesthesiologist to decline to participate in the transplant surgery?
4. Are there moral constraints on living donor kidney transplantation?

Monique Janelle London, J.D.

Abandonment:

It is possible, but unlikely, that the anesthesiologist would face liability for abandonment of the donor and recipient by refusing to participate in the transplant procedure. Generally, abandonment means unilateral severance of the professional relationship between doctor and patient without reasonable notice, when continuing medical attention is still needed. *See Lee v Dewbre*, 362 S.W.2d 900 (Tex. Civ. App. Amarillo 1962).

In Case 12, the anesthesiologist refused to participate in transplant surgery on the day it was scheduled to occur. Presumably, he had never provided anesthetics or any other medical services to the patients before. Probably, then, no "professional relationship" yet existed for him to sever. Or, the anesthesiologist may have been notified by the hospital only that day that he was expected to participate in the surgery. Again, if he never agreed to help with the transplant in the first place, there was no "existing relationship" for him to sever, and no abandonment issue. Further, the patients may not have been informed that this particular anesthesiologist was to participate in the surgery. It seems unlikely that the anesthesiologist would be deemed to have entered into a "professional relationship" with the patients if they did not even know he had been selected to administer the anesthetics.

On the other hand, prior to the surgery date, the anesthesiologist may have known about and agreed to the transplant and the role he was to perform. The patients may have known that he was to provide their anesthetics. If so, the anesthesiologist might be found to have already entered into some sort of "professional relationship" with the two patients, which he unilaterally severed on the day of the surgery. To avoid abandonment liability under such circumstances, the anesthesiologist would have to give the patients "reasonable notice" of his refusal to participate, and "ample opportunity" to secure the services of another anesthesiologist. If the transplant center is sizeable, these requirements could be satisfied even on the day of surgery. The patients could be notified that the anesthesiologist originally scheduled to attend would not be participating, and another anesthesiologist would be taking his place.

Moreover, for malpractice liability to be found under the abandonment doctrine, it must be shown that the abandonment of the patient proximately caused injury to the patient. *See, e.g., Carroll v Griffin,* 96 Ga. App. 826, 101 S.E.2d 764 (Ga.1958) (no abandonment claim where there was no evidence that any damage resulted from abandonment). Case 12 involves a living donor rather than a cadaver from whom the kidney would have to be procured within a limited time, and the facts do not suggest any other urgency in performing the transplant. It is unlikely that any "injury" to either patient would result from the anesthesiologist's refusal to participate in the surgery - even if the surgery were delayed for several days to secure the services of another anesthesiologist.

In sum, it is unlikely the anesthesiologist would be subject to legal liability for his refusal to participate in the surgery. At best, he might face retribution from the hospital for being an unreliable employee.

Ethical Analysis:

There does not appear to be an ethical basis for the anesthesiologist to refuse to participate in the transplant. He claims his reason for refusing is that the transplant is a "possibly lethal assault on an otherwise healthy human being." He may believe that participating in the transplant would violate the Hippocratic oath to "do no harm." But this cannot be the sole basis for the refusal. Indeed, the very act of anesthetizing a person for any surgery always carries a risk of death. And every time the anesthesiologist anesthetizes a patient for elective surgery such as cosmetic surgery, a "possibly lethal assault on an otherwise healthy human being" takes place. In choosing his profession, the anesthesiologist must have concluded that this risk of a "lethal assault" was outweighed by the potential benefits to the patient of the surgery.

The only difference between most surgeries (on one patient) and the present surgery (on two patients) is that one of the parties undergoing anesthesia and surgery (the donor) will not himself benefit medically from the procedure. If the anesthesiologist performs a cost-benefit analysis separately for each of the two patients involved in the transplant, he may feel ethically justified in refusing to participate in a living kidney transplant, but still participate in other elective surgeries. Separately considered, the recipient patient risks complications and death, but has a chance of benefiting medically by receiving a functioning kidney and curing her hypertension. The donor patient also risks suffering complications or dying, but has no potential medical benefits. His only benefits are the emotional benefits of "feeling fulfilled" by attempting to help his friend's wife, and perhaps strengthening his friendship with the recipient and her husband. The anesthesiologist may feel that these emotional benefits are insufficient to justify the medical risks to the donor.

This writer disagrees. First, if all physicians took the position that the emotional benefits to the donor of donating a kidney were insufficient to outweigh the medical risks of doing so, there would be no kidney donation by living donors. Many more patients would die waiting for a kidney transplant. Given the low level of the medical risk to the donor, these additional deaths could not be ethically justified. Second, the fact that the donor voluntarily offered his kidney (and declined any payment for doing so) shows that he believes the benefits of donation outweigh the risks of harm. His right to self-determination should be honored. The donor, not the anesthesiologist, will actually experience any benefits and burdens that materialize, so the ultimate decision to donate should be left to the donor.

As long as both donor and recipient are fully informed of the risks and benefits of the transplant procedure and have decided to proceed with it of their own free will, the anesthesiologist should participate.

Connie Zuckerman, J.D.

It is clearly understandable that a physician would feel uncomfortable or even unwilling to perform major invasive surgery on an individual who will derive no physicial benefit from the intervention, and who in fact courts significant risk as a result. In fact, such an intervention may seem to violate one of the cardinal principles of a physician's obligation to patients, i.e., First, Do No Harm. The anesthesiologist should be given the option not to participate, although ideally this issue and the ensuing discomfort on the part of the physician should have been addressed prior to the scheduled day of surgery.

Given the continuing gap between the number of available cadaver donor organs, and the demands for kidney transplant, the use of live donor organs has become more acceptable and commonplace. This is particularly so in cases where a biologic link between donor and recipient portends a likely successful result from the transplant. In cases such as this, where the donor's relationship with the potential recipient is not biologic, but rather so personal and intimate as to be almost analogous to a blood relative, there is always concern about the motives of the donor and the context of the decision to donate an organ and to put oneself at such personal risk. Several professional societies have approved of this sort of transaction in limited cases. There must always, however, be the independent establishment that the motives of the donor are purely altruistic, and that the decision was an autonomous, informed and voluntary one on the part of the potential donor. To some individuals, this selfless offer and opportunity to be so generous is its own reward, particularly with the knowledge of the lifesaving gift being given to one with such meaning.

Amy L. Friedman, M.D.

Emotional ties are often stronger than those based on genetics. The clearest example involves spouses, who have made lifelong commitments to each other emotionally, financially and legally. For transplant committee members evaluating one spouse's incentive to donate to the other, justification for the donor's assumed risk includes improved quality of life for the couple as well as the reward of improved health in the beloved recipient. Yet, widespread acceptance of the practice of exchanging kidneys between married individuals only occurred in the late 1980's. During this era it became clear that improvements in the ability to pharmacologically prevent rejection abolished the immunologic requirement for close matching of donor and recipient. With elimination of the medical barrier (rejection) to emotionally based living organ donation, a wide variety of relationships became eligible bases for transplantation. Today, the majority of American transplant centers do consider this practice acceptable.

Evaluation of the suitability of any living donor candidate begins with his(her) first contact with the transplant center which must be initiated by him(her) to avoid a coercion to participate. Are appropriate concerns and questions raised? When specific testing is scheduled does he(she) require unusual encouragement to achieve satisfactory completion of the requirements? The behavior pattern and nuances are carefully observed in an effort to detect reluctance (is the recipient exerting some form of blackmail?) or inappropriate enthusiasm (is financial compensation serving as an unethical incentive?) to participate. The donor and recipient candidates are interviewed independently to confirm suitable motivation for the donation. Psychosocial assessment by an individual with experience in donor related issues is also required. Following fulfillment of the medical and psychosocial criteria for donation (previously established by the transplant team) the team reviews each aspect of the potential transplant. If consensus to proceed is reached, an elective transplant is scheduled.

In general, anesthesiologists do not choose to participate in the extensive evaluation process elaborated above. Accordingly a last minute refusal to care for the donor would inappropriately prevent completion of a carefully planned and considered transplant. Yet, the anesthesiologist should not be forced to participate in a process he(she) considers ethical. For this reason the transplant is always scheduled electively. Anesthesia staffing is usually assigned on the day prior to surgery. Objection to participation should be vocalized at that time so that alternate arrangements can be made. If the anesthesiologist fails to prepare appropriately, he (she) is obligated to respect the judgement of the transplant team and deliver care of the highest quality for the patient.

Carl M. Kjellstrand, M.D.

Physicians have a much more malignant view of mankind's morality than the rest of mankind has.[Endnote 24] Altruism, kindness, goodness of heart and generosity, exist. Unrelated living donor kidneys appear to be the only realistic, untapped source of kidney transplants presently available. After deep and careful penetration of the marine sergeant's motives and no hidden agenda are detected, the planned transplant is O.K. The anaesthesiologist should be talked to and if necessary, another one asked to help in the operation. The general principle should be discussed with the hospital's bioethics committee and their conclusions referred to the hospital staff. In general, bioethics committees have been useless when confronted with reality, but they may be a bit more helpful with generalities.

Mildred (Barry) Friedman

If the anesthesiologist would also refuse to involve himself in a living *related* organ donor transplant, logic would be on his side. If he would not, his bias is showing.

Living organ donors are at minimal risk. Adverse effects are seldom noted. The possibility of maintaining healthy life with much less renal capacity than that provided by a pair of normally functioning kidneys is beyond dispute. Physiologically no reason exists to deny a friend the chance to rehabilitate a loved one.

Our society allows blood donation, egg donation, and sperm donation from living volunteers. Kidney donation is an extension of such actions. Because no payment is involved, the offered organ is a gift, not a sale, and is altruistically motivated.

If the marine had died and his organs were harvested and used to save his friend's wife for a cadaveric transplant procedure, they would match no less well. The moral issue would not be raised. We do not question the propriety of allowing parts of the dead to continue life. Why question ongoing life for two people?

The anesthesiologist is wrong and should be encouraged to rethink his decision. If he still retains his opinion then, perhaps, he should remove himself from working on any transplant case.

Judith E. Columbo

I feel that a 45-year-old willing to become a donor for the wife of a long-time friend is a special person. The anesthesiologist in this case is obvious not aware that many kidney donors take this emotional chance every day, every minute, every second. The decision to donate an organ is not easy. Death, or the chance of needing the organ for oneself, has to cross a donor's mind. In this case, if the anesthesiologist is so sure of his conviction, then this decision should have been made prior to the elective surgery. By the anesthesiologist choosing to wait until the day of surgery to tell the patient, patient's husband and friend his beliefs is not acceptable and by no means professional.

Editor's Remarks12

When first done, emotionally related kidney transplants were reported in newspapers as rare examples of human goodness. Increasingly, this surgery has become routine accepted by the medical and lay press.[Endnote 25] Increasing waits for cadaver donor kidneys prompted the growth of living donor transplants that have not been possible in all families.[Endnote 26] Worry over descending a "slippery slope" from accepting a friend's kidney to purchasing organs on the open market surrounds acceptance of this donor source. The outcome, measured as survival of recipient and allograft[Endnote 27] or life style of donor and recipient are reported to be uniformly positive. As remarked by Mildred Barry Friedman, the anesthesiologist is wrong though he has the right to request removal from the transplant milleau. Usually a background figure, the anesthesiologist is an underappreciated vital member of any team performing big surgery. I would not try to change his mind as subtle subconscious negative pressures may persist inhibiting his actions

Response to Study Questions

1. Not only an organ but life itself can be given to another voluntarily. In the extreme, consider Sydney Carlton's sacraficial action in Charles Dickens' A Tale of Two Cities employing force to substitute for Charles Darney, who is about to be executed, remarking that "It is a far far better thing that I do now than I have ever done before." Twice, I have dealt with mothers pleading to donate a second kidney to a child thereby forcing dialysis for themselves. In neither case, did I agree.
2. A physician not directly involved in the transplant effort should speak with the donor to validate that his/her action is of free will and intact mind and not a subterfuge with payment hidden.
3. Yes. No physician should be forced to perform an elective procedure that is against his/her moral standards.
4. None beyond medical considerations. I am reluctant to countenance kidney donation from a child to a parent because the child may someday need the kidney for his/her own child.

Case 13

DISCRIMINATION IN ORGAN DONATION

The wife, brothers, and parents of a 22 year old black nuclear engineer who was fatally shot in the head refuse to consent to the use of his organs for transplantation. Despite recounting of statistics that the proportion of black patients receiving uremia therapy in the United States exceeds the number of blacks in the general population, the family is united and resolute against giving consent for organ donation. One of the brothers who is a statistician for an insurance company points out that blacks receive less than their share of donated kidneys as is evident from the percent of blacks versus whites on dialysis being higher than the percent of blacks versus whites receiving a kidney transplant. ***A community leader stated that there was justice in the brother's feeling and action.***

Study Questions

1. **Is it true that blacks are discriminated in allocation of cadaver organs?**
2. **Should an organ donor have the right to limit the race of a recipient (black to black or white to white)?**
3. **Are there other possible explanations for the racial disparity in organ allocation?**

Monique Janelle London, J.D.

The family will face no legal retribution for their refusal to consent to donation.

Ethical Analysis:

It is neither ethical nor just for the family to refuse to consent to donation of the deceased's organs for transplantation. The Case does not state that the family is refusing to donate because of religious beliefs or out of respect for the wishes of the deceased family member. The only reason stated in the Case for the family's refusal to donate is that blacks receive less than their share of donated kidneys. The only evidence cited for this assertion is that the percent of blacks versus whites on dialysis is higher than the percent of blacks versus whites receiving a kidney transplant. In numeric terms, this would mean that, for instance, of all the people on dialysis, 50% are black and 30% are white; of all the people receiving kidney transplants, 80% are white and 20% are black.

Apparently, the family is concerned that any organs donated from the deceased are more likely to be transplanted into whites than blacks, thereby perpetuating unfairness to blacks in the organ allocation system. However, the statistics do not necessarily show that blacks are receiving less than their fair share of organs. Moreover, even if the statistics did show that blacks *on dialysis* are receiving proportionally fewer kidneys, they would not warrant the conclusion that blacks *on the transplant waitlist* are receiving proportionally fewer kidneys. Nor would the statistics warrant the conclusion that the deceased's organs would be more likely to go to non-blacks than blacks.

Finally, even if it were likely or even certain that the donated organs would go to non-blacks, it would be unethical for the family to refuse to donate the organs on that basis. The family is opposed to the perceived discrimination against blacks (or, if not intentional discrimination, at least disparate impact on blacks) in the organ allocation system. However, refusing to donate organs for the sole reason that they would be given to non-blacks is discrimination based on race - the very thing the family is protesting.

One of the family members notes that the percent of blacks versus whites on dialysis is greater than the percent of blacks versus whites receiving a kidney transplant. From this, the family apparently concludes that the organ allocation system discriminates against unfair to blacks. However, that conclusion may be based on faulty assumptions. For instance, there may be more blacks than whites on dialysis because blacks are more susceptible than whites to high blood pressure and diabetes - two of the leading causes of kidney failure.
Additionally, not all people on dialysis are waiting for a transplant - the number waitlisted is less than a third of those on dialysis. A dialysis patient is not transplant candidates if: 1) the patient's physician does not know about or believe in transplantation, and thus does not inform the patient about the option of transplantation; 2) the patient is not informed about the possibility of getting on the national transplant waitlist; 3) the patient chooses not to get on the transplant waitlist; or 4) the transplant center where the patient seeks to be listed determines that the patient is not eligible to get on the transplant waitlist.

There may be many blacks on dialysis who are not on the transplant waitlist for reasons listed above, rather than the mere fact that they are black. For example, fewer blacks than whites may be eligible to be waitlisted because fewer blacks have the insurance required to pay for a transplant and the immunosuppressive drugs. Also, fewer blacks than whites may be eligible to get on the waitlist because more blacks have health and compliance issues that prevent them from being transplant candidates. In low-income areas which are more heavily populated by blacks than whites, dialysis doctors may be less likely to know about or believe in the option of transplantation. Thus, they may be less likely to refer their patients to the waitlist. Or, those dialysis doctors working in low-income areas may be less likely to refer patients because they are more concerned about maintaining the income stream (usually through Medicare or Medicaid payments) from dialysis patients. This, too, could result in fewer blacks being listed for transplant.
Additionally, due to the seriousness of the diseases that cause kidney failure more often in blacks, it may be that more blacks than whites die while waiting for a transplant. Finally, just because the statistical differences were observed regarding dialysis and kidney transplants, it does not necessarily follow that comparable differences exist for other donated organs.

In sum, the fact that the percentage of blacks versus whites on dialysis is higher than the percentage of black versus whites receiving kidney transplants may not be significant or relevant to show discrimination against blacks in the organ allocation system. Thus it is unethical for the family to refuse to donate the deceased's organs based solely on that fact.

On the other hand, apart from the flaws in the family's reasoning (that the ratio of blacks to whites on dialysis and receiving kidney transplants proves the organ allocation system is unfair to blacks), it may be true that the organ allocation system does disparately impact blacks - i.e., all tolled, blacks are less likely to receive an organ than whites (or non-blacks). If so, the family is certainly ethically justified in objecting to the system as unfair. However, refusing to donate the deceased's organs may not address the injustice. As this writer understands it, race can affect a recipient's compatibility with a donor organ (at least kidneys). Therefore, blacks are more likely to receive kidneys from black donors, and whites are more likely to receive kidneys from white donors. If the donor pool is predominantly white, more whites will receive kidneys. In Case 13, apparently the family believes that if the deceased's organs are donated, they will go to white recipients, thereby perpetuating the system's unfairness. In fact, refusing to donate the organs probably will not do anything to remedy the injustice. On the contrary, black organs will probably go to black recipients, thereby helping blacks.

Finally, even if the family knew that the donated organs would go to non-blacks, they should still consent to donation. All human lives should be considered equally valuable, regardless of race. To discriminate against potential recipients on the basis of their race would be the very type of discrimination the family opposes.

Connie Zuckerman, J.D.

The obligation to donate one's own organs, or the organ of a loved one, is akin to the notion of charity: that is, it is a morally praiseworthy action, yet it cannot be made morally obligatory. If a given family chooses not to donate the organs of a loved one, even after being apprised of the tremendous good that will result, and the tremendous need within the community, they are clearly within their legal rights to decide as such, and ought not be further pressured or coerced into donating. In fact, in some states, the family retains final authority regarding organ donation, even if the potential donor wished to do so and executed an organ donation card while living.

The concerns voiced by the family and community leader in this case stem from legitimate concerns regarding the equitable distribution of donor organs, particularly among black and other minority communities. Suspicion within minority communities about the use of their donor organs and the potential for less than aggressive care should they indicate a willingness to donate has meant that the need for organs in minority communities far exceeds the donor organ availability, a particularly difficult shortage to address given the need to genetically link donor organs with potential recipients as closely as possible. Further, there is legitimate question about the access which minorities have to transplant waiting lists, as referral to such lists depends on many non-medical factors including general access to care within the medical system, intact support systems for potential organ recipients and sophisticated providers who know how and when to make appropriate referrals. For many members of minority communities the de facto inequities in the system translate into less access to potential donor organs. If such inequities were addressed, it is possible that more committment to donate organs would thus come from minority communities.

Amy L. Friedman, M.D.

Concern about the equity of organ allocation is prevalent among the general population. In practice, refusal to donate is often encountered in scenarios similar to this. In order to explore this issue, some incontrovertible transplant related statistics should be reviewed. First, renal failure occurs more frequently among blacks in the United States than among the general population. Second, the rate of cadaver organ donation among blacks is lower than the rate among the general population. Third, there is a relatively greater percent of candidates awaiting transplantation who are black than the rate among the general population. Fourth, when large samples are studied, the greater the genetic similarity between cadaver donor and recipient (judged by the higher percent of HLA antigens which match), the higher the long-term survival of the transplanted kidney. Fifth, there is a greater likelihood of high degree matching between donor and recipient with racially similar backgrounds (due to the lower frequency of widespread genetic mixing). In summary, it becomes clear that incorporation of HLA matching in any organ allocation scheme regardless of the primary intention of promoting maximal survival of the transplanted organ, does disadvantage black candidates. Since black candidates have a lower chance of close HLA matching to the predominantly white pool of cadaver organ donors, the weighting of HLA similarity by the allocation computer functions as a relative racial barrier. On the other hand, organs from a black cadaver organ would in fact be more likely to benefit black rather than white candidates through the same mechanism.

Requests for organ donation are often doomed to fail when made only at the moment of greatest grief and emotional injury. Unless the donor candidate or his(her) family had already considered organ donation, the likelihood of acquiescence is fairly low. The need for public education about the profound need for organ donation, particularly among minority communities is now widely recognized and has begun to receive a significant component of the limited resources available to address the organ shortage. Although this particular donor's organs will not be made available for transplantation, contact should be maintained with this family. If they ultimately reconsider the decision to decline donation, efforts to enlist their aid in enhancing community awareness should be undertaken.

Carl M. Kjellstrand, M.D.

One does not have to be really smart or subtle to understand that real discrimination exists. However, dialysis is a shining exemption. Even when considering the higher incidence of renal disease in blacks, they get more dialysis than whites![Endnote 28] In transplantation however, whites are much favored over other races. However, as I understand it, still more white kidneys go to blacks than vice-versa. This should be pointed out to the family and a plea made to our common humanity. We are all in this together. If still refused, so be it. Team efforts should be to explain our interdependence and a community education effort undertaken.

Mildred (Barry) Friedman

Thorny issues without sufficient information are difficult to discuss. If black uremic patients are not offered available kidneys for transplantation because they are poorly matched, they are not denied them due to prejudice but rather due to good medical practice.
Obvious inherited differences exist between human races. Visible similarities exhibited by members of one race declare that invisible similarities also exist. Tissue antigens held in common may account for untested tissue compatibility and account, in part, for more successful organ transplantation when donor and recipient are elements of the same group.

Black organ donation must be increased. A logical approach is good but maybe not the best. Introducing a family like this to successful organ recipients, black and white, may teach them the value of transplantation. Enough grateful patients exist to form a set of people who would make themselves available at any hour (traumatic death often does not occur during normal waking, working hours) to meet with shocked family and friends. We teach best with "hands on" techniques and being mentally or physically hugged by a recipient of the gift of life might reach deeper into the grieving mind than an intellectual argument.

Community leaders who lack compassion and understanding for *all* people are not good leaders.

Judith E. Columbo

There was justice in the brother's feelings and actions, if you take into consideration that a child only believes what he has been raised to believe. It is disturbing to read that a statistician, of an insurance company state that blacks do not receive their share of donated kidneys. It is not a black or white pool; it is a match pool. It is evident that there are more blacks than whites on dialysis because there is a greater risk of high blood pressure in the black community. Whether for religious beliefs or fear that life support will be pulled too soon, organ donation is often refused in the black community. Therefore I cannot agree with the community leader that there was justice in the brother's feelings and actions.

Editor's Remarks 13

After an all too recent history of overt discrimination and suppression, it is no surprise that black Americans regard their government with suspicion. Segregation left wounds beyond imagination for whites. As an example, there is a pervasive myth that Charles Drew who advanced the science of blood banking and died at the age of 45 after an automobile accident was denied a life saving blood transfusion in a North Carolina hospital *because he was black.*[Endnote 29] Despite clear statistical reports to the contrary[Endnote 30], blacks believe the system of organ allocation is unfair.[Endnote 31, Endnote 32] Once the problem of white credibility to blacks was appreciated, efforts were begun to bridge the gap.[Endnote 33] Especially effective are efforts to disseminate the value of organ donation by blacks by community meetings, visits to churches, and health fairs. Dr. Amy L. Friedman sensibly advises that contact with the family be maintained as a step at closing the racial divide in health care, whether real or perceived.

Response to Study Questions

1. No. There are too many built in regulations and controls to permit racial bias in organ allocation. In fact, blacks receive a greater proportion of cadaver organs than the proportion donated by blacks.
2. No. Once race is permitted as a factor in allocation of cadaver organs, beyond the biological constraints imposed by race-specific tissue antigens, the system is open to corruption and a complexity beyond resolution. Nevertheless, from time to time, so called "directed donation" from black to black has been proposed.[Endnote 34]
3. Other than racial prejudice, organs are distributed without bias to available, stable, potential recipients who report as requested to the transplant facility when summoned. The fact is the reverse of the question's thrust: blacks receive proportionally more (not fewer) kidneys than donated by blacks.

Case 14

"GIFT" FOR TRANSPLANT PRIORITY

An oil-rich Arabian prince, informed of his 25 year old wife's advanced renal failure due to chronic glomerulonephritis arranged her transfer for life-saving hemodialysis to an American university hospital. Upon completion of medical tests including a renal biopsy, the responsible nephrologist advised that though a kidney transplant is the preferred therapy, the current wait for a cadaver donor kidney exceeds one year. Furthermore, current policy demands that the large majority of donor kidneys be given to American citizens. ***The prince subsequently proposes that in exchange for placing his wife at the top of the waiting list, he will donate a new wing to the hospital at a cost of 2.5 million dollars.***

Study Questions

1. Should rich individuals be able to purchase organs or priority on a cadaver list?
2. Would not the gift of a huge sum alter the care of many poor individuals?
3. Suppose the proposed gift were 250 million would that change the perspective?
4. In reality, is money divorced from organ allocation?

Monique Janelle London, J.D.

It is illegal to buy and sell organs in the United States. 42 U.S.C. § 274e, entitled "Prohibition of organ purchases," states:

> (a) Prohibition: It shall be unlawful for any person to knowingly acquire, receive, or otherwise transfer any human organ for valuable consideration for use in human transplantation if the transfer affects interstate commerce.

Interstate commerce is defined as "commerce between any State or Territory and any place outside thereof." *See* 21 U.S.C. section 321(b)(1) (1988). This writer has not found any cases applying the statute to facts like those in Case 14. The statute does not technically prohibit accepting a monetary gift in exchange for transplant priority, but it would likely be read broadly to cover the situation in which a hospital "transfers" a kidney to a particular patient (by giving that patient priority on the waitlist) for "valuable consideration." The "transfer" of the kidney to the wife would likely be construed to "affect" interstate commerce, since the kidney will be transplanted into a patient from Saudi Arabia (who will presumably return to Saudi Arabia), the kidney may come from a state other than the state where the transplant center is located, and the transplant may affect other patients on the national waitlist who reside in other states. (Even if the statute does not prohibit the prince's proposal, as a matter of policy hospitals generally will not accept remuneration to influence a patient's ability to get a kidney transplant more quickly.)

In short, the proposal is probably illegal.

Ethical Analysis:

Although the proposal may be desirable to the prince, his wife, and patients who will benefit from a new wing at the hospital, overall it is unworkable and unethical.

First, the proposal is unworkable as a practical matter. Hospitals have no control over whether a patient is at the "top" of the kidney transplant waitlist. At present, that list is a national list maintained by UNOS, the United Network for Organ Sharing. To list a patient on the national list, the transplant center submits the necessary information to UNOS, and UNOS lists the patient. When a kidney becomes available, the UNOS computer system determines who is at the "top" of the waitlist for that particular kidney, based on waiting time accrued on the list and the compatibility of the donor and recipient. Thus, even if the hospital wanted to accept the prince's offer, it would not have the power to place the patient at the "top" of the list.

Moreover, there is no real "top" of the list. Even with the highest priority in terms of waiting time accrued, the patient may end up waiting longer than others on the list for a kidney transplant. How long she waits will depend not only on her waiting time accrued on the list, but also on the size of the waitlist at the transplant center where she is listed (which affects the likelihood of other patients being better or perfectly matched to the kidney than the prince's wife), whether she has a rare or common blood type, whether she has any panel reactive antibodies or sensitization from blood transfusions, prior transplants or illnesses, her weight and size, whether the transplant center where she is listed has many kidney "payback" obligations to other transplant centers, and how progressive the transplant center is in accepting "suboptimal" or nontraditional kidneys (such as infant kidneys, kidneys of older people, and kidneys that have a cold ischemic time of over 24 hours).
Going to the "top" of the waitlist may not even be desirable or advantageous for the patient. The Case does not give any indication that the patient is doing poorly on dialysis or has any co-morbid conditions. If the patient is not placed at the "top" of the waitlist, she probably will have to wait at least a year for a transplant in the U.S. The time waited may mean that better immunosuppressive drugs are available by the time the patient is transplanted.

Even if the proposal were feasible, it would raise ethical questions. One such question is whether the proposal would be fair to the other kidney patients who were on the transplant center's waitlist before the prince's wife was listed. That is, would the other patients experience a net benefit, net cost, or no change in their situation? The answer will depend upon many factors, including: whether the new wing of the hospital includes facilities and/or state of the art equipment for kidney transplant patients; whether the new wing is actually completed before the other patients get transplanted; whether the new wing will be adequately staffed and maintained; and whether the present transplant facilities are outdated, run-down, uncomfortable or cramped.
For some patients, these factors might create a sufficient net benefit for them to

prefer to give the prince's wife priority on the waitlist. For those patients who have a different blood type than the prince's wife, their waiting time for a transplant will not be increased by her priority status, but they will get all the benefits of a new hospital wing. Even for patients who have the wife's blood type, their waiting time will not be increased if, for instance, the wife is sensitized to a particular kidney and the other patient is not, or the wife is too big to take the kidney and the other patient is not, the wife is sick when the kidney is offered and cannot take it, or the other patient is sick when the kidney is offered to the wife, and thus would not have been able to take it anyway.

The only patients whose waiting time will be affected by the proposal are: 1) the patient (Patient A) who would have gotten the kidney that is offered to the prince's wife; 2) the patient (Patient B) who would have gotten the next kidney, which was offered to Patient A instead; 3) the patient who would have gotten the kidney offered to Patient B, and so on. Especially if these patients are not doing well on dialysis, this extra waiting time could be detrimental and even life threatening. On the other hand, those patients who are tolerating dialysis may benefit from the development of new, better anti-rejection drugs or completion of the new hospital wing during the extra waiting time.[Footnote 31]

Thus, if the only people involved in the decision were the other patients on the transplant waitlist at that hospital, and the new wing would benefit the waitlisted patients, it would be fair for the hospital to accept the proposal (assuming it had that power). Indeed, the other waitlisted patients themselves would probably request that the proposal be accepted.

From the hospital's perspective, there may also be justification in accepting the proposal. The new wing would benefit many patients, at a potentially minor cost to a few of the other patients on the kidney transplant waitlist. If the hospital is suffering financially and may have to shut down, accepting the proposal could benefit or even save the lives of many patients who rely on the hospital's services.

However, there may be larger costs to the hospital. The local and global community, learning of the proposal, may perceive the transplant system as favoring those who are wealthy enough to offer big gifts to the hospital - those who can pay their way to the top of the list. The community may perceive the hospital as being money-driven without concern for fairness. People who were inclined to be organ donors may no longer want to contribute to what they see as a corrupt system. They may believe that their organs will only go to those who "pay" for them by bribing the hospital.

People who intended to waitlist at the hospital for a kidney transplant may now list at some other center which they consider to be more fair. The hospital might ultimately have to shut down its kidney transplant unit for lack of candidates, to the detriment of potential kidney recipients who live nearby and trans-

[31] Patients of the same blood type as the prince's wife, who knew of the proposal and were considering whether to waitlist at the hospital, could either choose to list there for the new hospital wing, or list elsewhere to avoid any extra waiting time. On the other hand, if there are no other transplant centers as close to where the patient lives of equal caliber, this might not be a real choice.

plant recipients who have their follow-up care at the hospital.

Also, if the hospital accepted this proposal, it would have to devise some principled basis for accepting and rejecting other such proposals. That basis might include a minimum amount of money, a minimum level of benefit to the hospital and future patients, or the urgency of the proposing patient's situation. Regardless, the hospital would be perceived as unfair for drawing the lines where it did.
The public perception of the hospital might also be negatively affected by the hospital accepting a proposal from a Saudi Arabian. Many United States citizens are waiting for a kidney transplant. People who otherwise would consent to organ donation may refuse if they believe the organs are going to non-U.S. citizens.

On balance, these social costs would outweigh the benefits of accepting the proposal. Ethically, the hospital should decline it.

Connie Zuckerman, J.D.

The system of voluntary organ donation in this country rests heavily on the general public understanding that the organ distribution system is a fair and impartial one, based on medical need rather than influence or finances. If distributional decisions drastically departed from this understanding it is likely that there would be even more disparity between the number of donated organs and the number of potential, needy recipients. While the reality does exist that those with more financial resources may be able to "buy" better access to the list (for example, by getting their names put on numerous regional lists), there is every expectation that once on the list, objective, mostly medical criteria are used to actually distribute available organs, rather than because of clout or financial influence.

In this case, the extravagant offer made to 'jump the queue" may be very appealing, especially if one uses utilitarian principles to decide that the net benefit to the public good, given the benefits for the public to be achieved with the use of the donated money, might justify acceptance of the 'gift." However, such a decision would be patently unfair to others on the list in equally as needy a situation who are without the financial means to elevate their position on the list. Finally, the question concerning the foreign status of this potential recipient is a legitimate one, as arguments can be made that organs donated by American citizens are community property or even "national resources" which, from a perspective of reciprocity, ought to be distributed among those from whom the organs are derived. This is as much a political decision as a philosophic one, and most centers now have strict limits on the number of organs available to non- Americans and non resident aliens.

Amy L. Friedman, M.D.

There are no circumstances that would justify the sale of human cadaver organs for transplantation. Such a practice is explicitly prohibited by all of the major medical, surgical and transplantation societies. Introduction of any type of payment scheme would risk creating an incentive for augmentation of the supply of organs through murder or somewhat lesser crimes. Public awareness of even one such act could jeopardize the already scant level of public support for organ donation and compromise the already precariously balanced American transplantation network.
Furthermore, even if a single physician or transplant center acquiesced to this demand, there is no legitimate means through which it could be accommodated in the American organ allocation scheme. Every candidate for a cadaver organ transplant is registered through a central computer currently located and run by the United Network for Organ Sharing. Registration requires entry of a great deal of related data none of which is in any way subjective. The only way in which this listing mechanism could be altered is through fabrication. Both the transplant center and the specific provider responsible would be completely identifiable and liable to punitive actions. In short, the system or list cannot be altered in an unverifiable or unobtrusive manner. The current environment of disclosure and public awareness would certainly lead to a failure to hide such an act. The censure process that would surely follow would likely be sufficiently severe to irreversibly ruin the provider's career and reputation. Acceptance of this bribe would lead to criminal action and be entirely unethical. This Arab princess must wait in line with ordinary American folk in the hopes of legitimately receiving a kidney.

Carl M. Kjellstrand, M.D.

Two philosophical principles - Kantian deontology and Utilitarianism are brawling with each other here and common sense will be treacherous guide in this case. The Utilitarian would reason that the prince's donation would save many lives on dialysis - 2.5 million dollars is almost 60 patient years of dialysis and could thus save twelve 75 year old dialysis patients their entire expected life on dialysis, 5 years each, at the expense of the trivial re-shuffling of the cadaver waiting list. Deontology à la Kant says "Act so that your act can be elevated to a universal law under which all - including you, will have to live". Would you like to live where the rich can buy a national treasure, such as kidneys for transplantation, donated mostly by middle class and poor - **NO**. Unprincipled common sense would lead you down the Utilitarian garden path. However, my common sense tells me that the fact that cadaver donation has stalled or even decreased the world over, is partially due to public distrust of the "medical system". "Now the scoundrel doctors sell our kidneys for profit," DO NOT DO IT, it is bad morally and ethically, bad business, and bad common sense.

Mildred (Barry) Friedman

I would hope that the hospital involved turned down the suggestion of trading a cadaver kidney for a hospital wing in favor of other proposals.

In some nations kidneys can be bought. Whether or not you agree with the morality of the sale, it exists, and the Arabian prince can take advantage of it. If he further insists on American know-how and skills to perform the operation, he may try to make arrangements for the physicians of his choice to be temporarily licensed in the foreign nation. It would probably not be allowed.

The patient and her husband are then left with the prospect of continued hemodialysis. Good years on dialysis are possible and using his money wisely, the prince should arrange construction of a pleasant, even elegant, dialysis arrangement in their home. Furthermore, financing excellent training for several dialysis technicians would insure excellent medical care. Introducing the couple to patients who have lived on dialysis for many years and who maintain good quality of life, might teach them the possiblilty of such a course.

Money entitles people to the best available care. It does not make them more worthwhile than others. The hospital should not allow itself to be bought.

Judith E. Columbo

I am sure that the Arabian Prince's proposal of 25 million dollars to build a new hospital wing, in turn for his wife being top listed on the transplant list is appetizing to the hospital administration. If a hospital ever chooses to allow money to buy life it may just as well close its doors. It is a sad day when prestige and money outweigh the right choice, as in the case of a liver being transplanted to Mickey Mantle. That right choice, which would have been the next in line for that organ, may have one day contributed more to society.

Editor's Remarks 14

Based on an episode known to the author, such a proposal underscores the worst in socioeconomic aspects of kidney transplantation. As reasoned by Attorney Zuckerman: "The system of voluntary organ donation in this country rests heavily on the general public understanding (of fairness). Subverting equity in distribution of a scarce resource (kidneys) leads to further cheating, thievery, and perhaps even murder to gain organs. All respondents turned the concept down. I do not concur with the absolute prohibition of organ purchase espoused by Dr. Amy L. Friedman though I readily admit that the systems that I have observed (India, former Soviet Union) thus far have been "dirty" and not in the general interest of society.

Yet, we all know of the existence of VIP wards and luxurious accommodations for "important" politicians and celebrities in hospitals that receive public funds. Does being a US senator, athlete, or rock star carry the privilege of exceptional health services not open to a Medicaid patient? Certainly, it does. Where is the difference between faster service by more renowned doctors because of fame and accelerated provision of an organ allograft because of wealth? For the time being, the answer will have to be that that is the way it is in our society.

Response to Study Questions

1. Two questions are intermixed. No, the uniform cadaver pool regulated by the United Network for Organ Sharing (UNOS) is inviolate. For the reasons detailed by all respondents above, money should not permit jumping the wait list. Commercialization of organ sales, by contrast is a collateral but distinctly different issue raised by a subsequent case. There the answer is by no means clear to this author.
2. Yes. But, while many poor would derive benefit, as Attorney London remarks, disillusionment with a corrupt system might trigger a reduction in organ donation that could cripple the transplant program.
3. Raise the ante to 2.5 billion dollars and the answer persists as a negative. Honor in health care must not be for sale. Of course, the adage that "every man has his price," is a reality and when the sums of money become enormous as in the drug trade in Mexico or Columbia, every one including the president may yield virtue.
4. Patient Columbo raises the case of Mickey Mantle who despite known malignancy was given a liver within one day of placement on the wait list. While a liver transplant surgeon dear to my heart assures me that it is not so, I worry that the system was subverted in this instance. In fairness, in must be noted that in the "Mickey Mantle Case" no evidence of impropriety has either been formally charged or in any way "proven." Nevertheless, my baseline skepticism over improbable coincidence would have me react with similar unease were the Pope or President to get an organ in under a day. I would assign such an event to chance about as readily as my acceptance of the tooth fairy.

Case 15

CHILD TO PARENT KINDEY TRANSPLANT

A 62 year old obese business executive who developed end-stage renal failure after twenty-three years of non-insulin-dependent diabetes (type 2) has a "troubled" course on maintenance hemodialysis. Repeated infections of his vascular access site and several episodes of pulmonary edema after dietary indiscretion necessitated seven hospitalizations during the first year of dialytic therapy. Depressed over his failed rehabilitation and an anticipated delay of longer than one year for a cadaver donor kidney transplant, the patient proposes that his 22 year old daughter serve as a kidney donor. Recognizing that because both parents are diabetic, she faces a highly probable risk of becoming diabetic in later life, the daughter insists on donating her kidney to "save her father." ***A consulting endocrinologist states that any child-to-parent organ transplant in a diabetic family is dangerous and unethical.***

Study Questions

1. Is the contemplated child to parent organ donation a question of ethics?
2. As a generalization, should children donate organs to parents?
3. If this were not a genetic disease, would the answer be different?
4. Is the transplant surgeon immoral for planning such an operation?
5. Is it ethical for the consulting endocrinologist to present his view to the proposed recipient?

Monique Janelle London, J.D.

Legal Analysis:

There is nothing illegal about the proposed transplant. The donor is a competent adult who apparently has given her informed consent to the transplant.

Ethical Analysis:

It may be unethical for the father to ask his daughter to donate a kidney to him. The potential risks and costs of a daughter-to-father kidney transplant should be weighed against the potential benefits.

On the one hand, the father may be able to improve his health by himself, without subjecting the daughter to the pain, risk, stress and inconvenience of an immediate transplant. The Case states that the father's hospitalizations were due to infections of his vascular access site and pulmonary edema caused by dietary indiscretion. The father may be able to prevent further infections by taking better care of his access site. He could end the pulmonary edema by following the dialysis diet. He could also improve his health by losing weight.
If he does these things, the father probably has the option of safely waiting for a year or longer for a cadaveric kidney or kidney-pancreas transplant. If he waits,

instead of taking his daughter's kidney, he will eliminate the burdens to her of undergoing surgery. These burdens may be serious. For instance, if the daughter is obese, she may be at high risk for diabetes. If she becomes diabetic and stays obese, her risk of getting kidney failure will also increase. If the daughter donates a kidney, this risk may increase even further.

By waitlisting for a cadaveric kidney or kidney-pancreas transplant instead of seeking one from his daughter, the father may also increase his chances of improved health; a successful kidney-pancreas transplant (as opposed to a transplant of his daughter's kidney only, but no pancreas) will eliminate his diabetes. By waiting for a cadaveric transplant, the father also keeps open the option of receiving his daughter's kidney as an emergency backup plan in case the cadaveric transplant fails and his health situation becomes critical.
Moreover, in the father's situation, there is no guarantee that getting a transplant from his daughter will benefit him (or indirectly his daughter or other family members) through his improved health. The surgery may be dangerous or even unfeasible, given that the father is obese. And if the daughter is obese, she may not be a candidate to donate her kidney, either. Second, with only a kidney transplant (and not a pancreas), the father will still be diabetic. Even if the kidney works, the father may still be ill or need hospitalization because of the diabetes. Also, diabetes generally requires strict adherence to dietary restrictions. If the father continues to have "dietary indiscretion," he could stay ill even with a kidney transplant by virtue of his own behavior.

In short, if the father can safely wait for a cadaveric transplant, he has an ethical obligation to do so before seeking one from his daughter.

On the other hand, it may be ethically acceptable for the father to request that his daughter donate a kidney. The father may find that changing his behavior does not alleviate his poor health on dialysis. He may still require constant hospitalization for other dialysis-related problems. If so, getting an immediate kidney transplant from his daughter may be necessary to improve his situation.
Additionally, although there is a risk of the daughter becoming diabetic, she is not actually diabetic. If the daughter follows the medical path of her father, even if she does get diabetes, she might have it for 23 years before developing ESRD. Even if she is genetically predisposed to diabetes, if she is not obese, and is compliant with diet and insulin requirements, the diabetes might never result in kidney failure. Also, the risk of getting diabetes and kidney failure may not be significantly affected by whether the daughter gives up one of her kidneys. And, even if the risk of getting kidney failure eventually materializes, overall the daughter may benefit more from restoring her father to good health than from keeping her kidney. For instance, the father may have been supporting the daughter, her mother, her grandparents, and other siblings emotionally and/or financially, all to the ultimate benefit of the daughter.

Given the overall risks involved, and the limited potential for benefit over waiting for a cadaveric transplant, this writer believes it is at least unwise, if not unethical, for the father to request that his daughter donate a kidney to him. However, armed with complete information about the potential risks and benefits, the daughter should be able to decide to donate a kidney to her father if she wants.

Connie Zuckerman, J.D.

While from a technical perspective this child's match to her father may mean the donation is medically acceptable, the concern of the endocrinologist is legitimate, given the potential harm to this child as a result of her donation. As previously stated, live donor organs have become acceptable and commonplace, especially given the long wait for an acceptable cadaver organ. What is critical to examine in such cases is that the donation be made in a free and informed manner, particularly as the donation from a live donor does pose risk to that donor for no personal benefit, other than the psychological benefit of knowing one has so fundamentally assisted another.

In this case, there is legitimate concern, given the daughter's own medical condition and potential medical complications, that her offer to donate, while selfless and generous, is so personally harmful as to outweigh the benefit she will derive as a consequence. In fact, providers would be obligated to more thoroughly explore this choice to donate, particularly as it comes at the suggestion of the father (thus raising the question of the voluntariness of its nature) and particularly as it seems to be a choice at odds with the medical best interests of the daughter. While her age makes her technically and legally empowered to make her own decisions, her actual decisional capacity in this circumstance is questionable and requires much further inquiry prior to the decision to accept her as an organ donor.

Amy L. Friedman, M.D.

The individual with kidney failure who understands that another living person can choose to accept the risk of a major operation and donate a piece of his(her) body must experience torment. How to raise the topic with potential donors, how to assess the authenticity of an initial offer, how to handle the disappointment of those who do not offer, and how to become comfortable with accepting an offer are all questions he(she) must resolve. The search for answers to these sensitive queries depends heavily on the history and established psychodynamics within the family unit. To pretend that fairly brief interactions between the family members and the experts at the transplant center can adequately assess these complex psychodynamics would be disingenuous.

Transplant team members must serve as independent medical and scientific advisors to the patient and potential donors who turn to us for guidance and validation. It is our role to screen out inappropriate interactions such as obvious fiscal reimbursement or emotional bribery. But there must be no illusion that we can foresee all current and future ramifications of the act of donation. It is certainly unrealistic to suggest that we can comprehend all of the benefits the donor hopes to gain. Redemption for past wrongs, hopes of perpetuating a treasured relationship and denial of one's own mortality may all serve as appropriate components of the donor's decision. Aside from providing the counsel and screening discussed above, the transplant team does not belong in the decision making process, above all, because any practical attempt to referee it would be perfunctory and consequently subject to serious invalidity.

However, from my personal perspective as both a parent and a daughter, it may well be reasonable for the adult offspring to donate a kidney to a parent. Denial of the importance of parental input in the structure and stability of the extended family may well be a root cause of many of our modern societal problems. The beneficial impact of the elder person's maturity on all of the subsequent generations is often profound. To me, a significant opportunity to prolong such input might easily justify the fairly small risk of nephrectomy for the carefully evaluated donor. When the possibility of hereditary disease transmission is relevant, the donor candidate's individual risk for disease development should be fully assessed. If future development of kidney disease is judged a significant possibility, donation should be precluded. On the other hand, if several members are at risk of subsequently developing ESRD, the family should communally assess it's resources (i.e., how many are healthy potential donors) and reach a consensus on how to use them to the collective best advantage.

Carl M. Kjellstrand, M.D.

Never make ethical decisions without knowing and considering technical facts. The endocrinologist is making that error. The chance of a 22 year old developing diabetes is close to 100% if both parents are diabetic. However, if the patient then develops diabetes there is a 50% chance that it will affect the kidneys. What does happen if the unilaterally nephrectomized patient develops diabetes and then kidney disease? Even if the donor develops a need for dialysis it will move up very little - from about 20 years from onset of diabetes to either 15 years or 19 years depending on what mathematical model one believes reflects the physiology of declining renal function. We don't know what the treatments will be in 35 to 40 years from now (I assume she will not get diabetes until age 42) but they certainly will be much better barring civilization catastrophes. Once the patient and the potential recipient understand this and persist in their wish to proceed to the transplant, you must proceed. See also Case 12 Altruism in Disrepute.

Mildred (Barry) Friedman

People who will eventually become diabetic should not consider donating a kidney and certainly should not be coerced to do so. The father's lack of concern for his daughter, his self-concern, his belief that his life is somehow more important than hers, should be discussed with parent and child. Also noted is his status as a noncompliant patient. Failure to follow rules will jeopardize any new kidney he receives.

While it is depressing to go through the hard times of poor response to treatment and a long wait for an organ, many other patients have survived similar circumstances. Treat the depression. Stress the value of compliance. Gently point out that he is the architect of many of his problems. Teach him the realities of diabetes.

Another factor to consider is that his daughter is in her child bearing years. In a diabetic family, the next generation will probably be diabetic as well. If our prediabetic Type II has children who are Type I (as happens) those children might have diabetic kidney failure earlier in their lives. If mother insists on being a kidney donor, she probably would choose to give to her offspring rather than to the man she sprang from.
The dilemma is partly moral and partly medical. On both counts I vote against the procedure and agree with the endocrinologist.

Judith E. Columbo

The consulting endocrinologist is probably correct in stating that transplanting a child to parent organ transplant in a diabetic family is dangerous and unethical. But family emotions play an important part in a family/medical decision. Here we have a business executive who suddenly is faced with a dialysis course he will not accept. He in turn proposes his daughter donates her kidney, not taking into account that the daughter faces a high risk of becoming a diabetic in later life. Although I agree with the endocrinologist, a daughter-father love is strong enough to override the decision not to transplant.

Editor's Remarks15

Every time that I witness a child to parent kidney transplant, I wince. By contrast, reasoning that diabetes in the donor, should it occur, is years away, Kjellstrand concludes that "you must proceed." Likewise, Dr. Amy L. Friedman recognizes circumstances under which: "it may well be reasonable for the adult offspring to donate a kidney to a parent." Patient Mildred Barry Friedman voting no differs from patient Columbo who notes that "daughter-father love" overrides the negative aspects. The facts are clear: the daughter has a high probability of contracting diabetes and with it vascular complications including kidney failure. Optimists weighing research in progress project an improved outlook for diabetic individuals in under a decade. I concur.[Endnote 35]. Other considerations must be weighed. The daughter's future children may develop kidney disease that could benefit from a kidney donation. As a generalization, I am unsuccessful in presenting the negative side of child to parent kidney donation and may have attributed too little moment to the force called love.

Response to Study Questions

1. Hard to say. There is no medical proscription in terms like risk of transmis-

sion of infectious disease or malignancy. In the new world of spare parts medicine, how the parts are obtaind and inserted touches on economics, medicine, and like all human endeavor, ethics.

2. While I am able to state an unequivocal no, equally vehement yes answers are evoked by raising this issue in student teaching sessions.
3. No. My advice is to save the resource for the daughter's children yet to be born.
4. This is the inverse of question 1. No, the surgeon is not immoral and truly believes that he/she is acting properly to benefit a sick patient using a resource (daughter's kidney) that will solve the problem without injury to the donor.
5. While the consultant is called in to assist the primary physician, the advice generated (paid for by the patient) is for the patient. How can the patient be excluded because of what amounts to medical politics?

Case 16

PURCHASED KIDNEY

Reflecting on the long wait for a cadaver donor kidney in the United States, a 53 year old state assembly representative with irreversible renal failure due to membranous glomerulonephritis agreed to a contract with a "kidney broker" in India. For a set fee of $11,000, the broker guarantees that within one week he will deliver an HLA (human leukocyte antigen) matched kidney from a young, healthy donor. The agreed upon fee will cover the cost of the kidney, all physician's charges as well as the total cost of hospitalization and surgical after care. Eager to pursue this opportunity for a new life, the patient requests that his nephrologist prepare a summary of his past course for submission to the broker. Additionally, the patient announces his intent to resume management under the supervision of his local nephrologist upon his return from India in about three weeks post-transplant. ***Stating her unwillingness to participate in an "illegal" operation, the nephrologist declines to prepare the summary or accept the patient upon his return.***

Study Questions

1. In at least six countries, purchased kidneys are routinely used for organ transplants. Is such a transaction immoral?
2. Although classed as illegal in the United States, there is no proscription against a physician sending information or offering assistance for a purchased kidney transplant. Is such assistance immoral?
3. Do you believe that individuals should be able to sell parts of their bodies as they wish as they do for blood, semen, and ova?
4. Should a referendum on the question be held within the medical community?

Monique Janelle London, J.D.

Patient's Legal Liability:

The patient's purchase of a kidney is probably illegal. Federal law makes it illegal "for any person to knowingly acquire, receive, or otherwise transfer any human organ for valuable consideration for use in human transplantation if the transfer affects interstate commerce." 42 U.S.C. § 274e. Interstate commerce is defined as "commerce between any State or Territory and any place outside thereof." *See* 21 U.S.C. § 321(b)(1).

The patient is "knowingly acquiring" a human organ "for valuable consideration" ($11,000) for use in human transplantation. The only issue is whether that transfer "affects commerce between any State or Territory and any place outside thereof."

The patient is American. He is purchasing a kidney from a broker who is in India. The patient is paying in U.S. dollars. The transplant surgery will take place in India. The patient will return to the U.S. with the Indian kidney. The transfer of U.S. dollars from a U.S. citizen to a broker in India for a transplant in India would probably be deemed to affect commerce between the state where the patient lives and India. Thus, the purchase is almost certainly illegal.

Nephrologist's Legal Liability:

The nephrologist refuses to prepare a summary of the patient's past medical history for the kidney broker, and refuses to accept the patient upon return from his transplant in India. The federal statute prohibiting the purchase of kidneys does not prohibit providing medical care or medical records to a patient who has illegally purchased a kidney. Thus the nephrologist probably could provide the summary and follow-up care without legal retribution.

However, she certainly is not obligated to do so. The only legal issue raised by the nephrologist declining to provide the summary and follow-up care is liability for abandonment. As previously explained, a physician may withdraw from a patient's case only after providing "due notice" and an "ample opportunity" to secure the presence of other medical attendance. Otherwise, she is liable for any damages resulting from his abandonment of the case. *See, e.g., Hongathavij v. Queen of Angels/Hollywood Presbyterian*, 62 Cal. App. 4th 1123 (1998); *Capps v. Valk*, 189 Kan. 287 (1962).

Refusal to provide a summary of the patient's medical history probably would not be considered a "withdrawal" from the patient's case, and thus not a basis for an abandonment claim. Moreover, the patient has the right to his entire medical record, and could find another physician to summarize it, or summarize it himself for the broker if necessary.

The nephrologist's refusal to accept the patient upon his return from India is more likely to be deemed "withdrawal" from the patient's case. Such withdrawal does not constitute abandonment as long as the nephrologist provides due notice of her intent to sever the relationship and ample opportunity for the patient to secure other follow-up care. The nephrologist is giving the patient around four weeks advance notice. Also, she is not unconditionally severing her relationship with the patient, but only advising him that she will not treat him further *if* he purchases a kidney in India. On these facts, abandonment liability will not attach.

Ethical Analysis:

The nephrologist is ethically justified in her refusal to provide the medical summary and follow-up care.

Providing these services would be to participate in, and thus condone, an operation that is probably illegal under United States law. U.S. law prohibits the purchase and sale of organs in part because of the concern that brokers will exploit the poor and coerce them into selling their organs despite the medical risks involved. In India, where the average monthly income is $11, donors sell their kidneys for about $275-$550, but brokers charge recipients $1000 over the cost of procurement. *See* Sanjoy Hazarika, India Debates Ethics of Buying Transplant Kidneys, N.Y. Times, Aug. 17, 1999, at A20. Such exploitation is wrong, regardless of whether it occurs in the U.S. or India. The nephrologist should not facilitate that activity.

The health risks to the organ donor and recipient from a transplant may be more serious in India than in the United States. The transplant may not be performed under the same high standards as it would be performed in the U.S. The follow-up care of the nephrologist's patient will be more difficult due to complications arising after the surgery - especially complications caused by unknown problems during the surgery. The nephrologist may face retribution, rejection or disrespect from her colleagues if she facilitates or condones an illegal and potentially harmful procedure for her patient. It is also unethical to support the overseas transplant of a state assembly representative, when other patients who may need a kidney more urgently cannot afford to take such action. Indeed, public opinion may turn against the nephrologist if it is learned that she facilitated such an operation, and the public may be less willing to donate organs as a result.

On the other side of the equation, there is no ethical justification for supporting the patient in his quest to purchase a kidney in India. The Case gives no indication that he is in urgent need of a transplant, or doing poorly on dialysis. In short, the nephrologist should not condone the patient's plan.

Connie Zuckerman, J.D.

Because of the significant disparity between the number of donated organs and the number of potential organ recipients, the use of a market system to procure donor organs has surfaced, both as theoretical discussion in this country, and as an actual reality in such other countries as India. While decried as immoral and unethical in this country, in other, less developed and less wealthy countries the ability to donate an organ in exchange for money has found willing participants. In this country, the debate was effectively curtailed when the 1984 National Organ Transplantation Act (Public Law 98-507) made it illegal for commercial markets dealing in transplantable organs to develop.

While as a society we have tolerated the sale of such renewable "products" as blood and semen, the sale of kidneys or other materials from live donors, which could potentially cause great harm or even death to the donor, has been considered unacceptable. In particular, the use of financial remuneration provides powerful incentives to those less fortunate and is thought to lead to the inevitable exploitation of the poor and disadvantaged, who will sell body parts at even signficiant personal risk for the available financial benefit. In this case, while the physician's preparation of the summary, or resumption of involvement with the patient post-operatively would probably not be illegal, it is clearly within the realm of her personal choice to decide that any participation or fostering of this activity is morally reprehensible and she thus has no obligation to participate. She should, however, provide the patient with a list of other potential physicians who may be willing to take up his case upon his return to the United States. In addition, the patient does have a legal right to gain access to his medical records so as to make them available to another treating or consulting physician.

Amy L. Friedman, M.D.

Organ purchase has been deemed ethically unacceptable by all the major medical, surgical and transplantation societies. Although there is certainly some truth to the argument that poor people may have no means other than sale of a body part in order to provide sustenance and other life staples for an entire family, there can be no compromise. It is widely recognized that individuals who wanted to sell their blood were at especially high risk of carrying serious infectious diseases such as hepatitis or HIV. For the transplant recipient, the safety of organ donation is even more precarious. Financial incentive might well lead a donor to suppress a prior history of malignancy that could well result in transplantation of a malignant cell. In an immunosuppressed host this cell would likely proliferate wildly to death from malignancy. The transplant team could well have no means of identifying this past history other than by report frfom the donor. Similarly, a donor could "neglect" to reveal a history of past treatment of tuberculosis and the recent recurrence of night sweats and fevers. If this donor's organ was used by an uniformed transplant team, the recipient could be seriously jeopardized by uncontrolled tuberculosis. For these reasons payment for blood donations is now disallowed in the United States and most developed nations. The exchange of finances for a solid organ is also illegal in these same countries.

From the perspective of the ESRD patient understandably desperate to receive a kidney transplant, the temptation to travel to another country to purchase an organ must be intoxicating. But it would be foolhardy for the reasons elaborated above. If a pre-transplant patient asks for assistance in facilitating the process, the transplant team should refuse to participate. More importantly the request should be viewed as an opportunity to provide full education about the profound risks involved. If the plans nevertheless proceed and care subsequently sought from the local transplant team the patient should be accepted. Regardless of the organ source the patient should now be given the highest level of care. The unethical transplant has become a fait accompli and the patient remains a human being in need.

Carl M. Kjellstrand, M.D.

The buying and selling of kidneys is repugnant to refined noses. Realize when we prohibit that "we take away the best choice from him that has nothing", to save us from the smell (see Richard JR, "From Him That Hath Not" p.53 in Ethical Problems in Dialysis and Transplantation, Kluwer Academic Publishers, Dordrecht, 1992). A Turkish father wanted to sell his kidney to a British dialysis patient. An outcry led to a law prohibiting such acts. The father complained: "I wanted the money to save the life of my daughter - she needs a heart operation I cannot afford. If I sell my kidney I can buy the operation and my daughter will live. I who love her will be happy, the recipient of the kidney will also be happy. The sum is one life saved and two very happy people. If my daughter had needed the kidney for a transplant and I had donated it no-one would have objected. I would have been praised. To me the risk is the same if my daughter or another patient gets the kidney. By your prohibition you have achieved my daughter's death, my everlasting sorrow, and smashed a dialysis patient's dream of a transplant. You are bad and immoral people and I curse you". The evil in selling kidneys is not in the act itself but in profiteering middlemen and the injustice in giving the advantage to the rich. That can be avoided by regulation.

The representative is availing himself of something anyone rich can buy. Prepare the summary, tell him about the risk of HIV transmission and transfer his care to someone else if you cannot stomach his action.

Mildred (Barry) Friedman

Kidney purchase is not illegal in India and so the patient is breaking no law in opting for this course. Nothing is kept secret. He has a right to a copy of his medical history and the Indian physicians may read it and summarize.
As to resuming care of a patient after treatment in another facility, if the transplant was performed in a United States hospital, collaboration would be forthcoming.

Patient benefit, patient healing, are the aim of the doctor. Adjusting medications or procedures provided by a second physician is acceptable. Therefore, resuming care of a patient is permissible.
Preserving your own life, seeking any kind of legal treatment, is the patient's right. The nephrologist should be complimented that the man is satisfied with her care and again wishes to place his life in her hands. She is wrong in judging her patient's decision and refusing him treatment.

Judith E. Columbo

The idea of a broker getting a kidney for a fee is unethical. A patient making the physician plans for a transplant and his intent to resume management under the supervision of his local nephrologist after the illegal transplant is assuming quite a bit. It is quite clear that this nephrologist is unwilling to participate in an "illegal operation" right from the beginning. If the nephrologist agreed to write a summary for the broker then she would be half-guilty of participating. She neither will write a summary nor agree to follow the patient after the illegal transplant and I feel this nephrologist has the right to make this decision.

Editor's Remarks16

According to UNOS, trafficking in kidneys is illegal, period. All respondents but patient Mildred Barry Friedman side with the nephrologist on legal and moral grounds. She sidesteps the issue of whether marketing kidneys is wrong instead focusing on a patient's right to medical records. Kjellstrand finds the concept of selling kidneys repugnant.

We live in a society in which blood, semen, and now ova are accepted as for sale for a negotiated price. Surgical removal of an ova carries a small - even remote - risk of complication and death. I do not perceive a moral divide between accepting oocyte sale and restricting purchase of a kidney? Donating a kidney is relatively safe and patient and graft survival is equivalent to the best attained with cadaver kidneys. In one small series of purchased kidneys transplanted in children, one- and two-year patient survival was 94.4%, with a graft survival of 83.3%.[Endnote 36] Nevertheless, the stated judgment of just about all who write on the subject is that selling kidneys must be curtailed and punished.[Endnote 37]

Response to Study Questions

1. Here we come to a distinction between morality and legality. Marketing kidneys is illegal in nearly all countries and therefor immoral. I am in the minority who believe that selling one's kidney is a personal right that should not be abridged.
2. Physicians in the United States may not profit from a commercial kidney transplant. Providing records detailing past history and present findings to another physician is appropriate at all times. A patient's record belongs to the patient.
3. Yes. But as discussed above this is a minority view. Among medical students and housestaff asked this question, approximately 45% state that they believe it should be permissible to sell bodily parts including kidneys. When asked openly in an oral discussion, the number of positive replies falls to about 10%.
4. Medicine is a profession that continuously questions its conduct and by that means holds a rolling referendum.

Case 17

SUSPECTED SUBTERFUGE IN PROPOSING KIDNEY DONOR

A 49 year old Indonesian high ranking military officer on peritoneal dialysis because of renal failure due to a congenital horseshoe kidney arrives in the United States with two blood type-identical young men - aged 23 and 25 years old - who are said to be his cousins from another Island. Neither potential donor speaks English and both carry documents stipulating that they are related to the patient. After preliminary testing, both donors are found medically acceptable with two and three antigen matches respectively (equivalent to a closely related sibling). Uneasy over the actual relationship of patient and donors, the transplant nephrologist discusses the matter with the Indonesian counsel who advises that there is no way to clarify the issue. "In our country," he advises, "any high placed person can get whatever papers he needs." ***Upset over what appears to be fakery, the senior surgical resident declines to scrub on the scheduled transplant operation.***

Study Questions

1. In fact, such a charade has played out on several occasions known to the Editor. Is it unethical for a poor person to gain what will amount to twenty years salary by selling a kidney?
6. Suspecting that papers presented do not sustain the stated relationship between intended donor and recipient, should the transplant surgeon pursue the matter?
7. Should rich foreign nationals be able to come to the United States for "private" surgery by the "best professors" providing that they pay high fees?
8. Is there a difference in the level of medical care given to rich compared with poor persons?

Monique Janelle London, J.D.

Legality of Purchasing/Selling Organs:

The two potential donors provided documentation from Indonesia stipulating that they are related to the patient. Apparently, the senior surgical resident suspects that the documentation is falsified (and in fact the donors are not related to the patient). Even if the documentation is falsified, and the donors are not related to the patient, that alone would not make it illegal for the surgeon to perform the transplant. U.S. law does not prohibit transplanting a kidney from a donor who is not related to the patient. Many kidneys are donated by living unrelated donors.

The surgical resident seems to have a bigger concern that the two potential donors not only are unrelated to the patient, but also are being paid to donate a kidney. As stated previously, federal law makes it illegal "for any person to knowingly acquire, receive, or otherwise transfer any human organ for valuable consideration for use in human transplantation if the transfer affects interstate commerce." 42 U.S.C. section 274e. Interstate commerce is defined as "commerce between any State or Territory and any place outside thereof." *See* 21 U.S.C. section 321(b)(1) (1988). This law may apply to the actions of the donors and potential recipient. If the recipient is paying for the kidney, he is knowingly acquiring an organ for valuable consideration for use in transplantation. Likewise, one of the donors will be knowingly transferring an organ for valuable consideration. The transfer could be construed to affect interstate commerce, given that the parties are from Indonesia and the transplant will be performed in the U.S. (and paid for in the U.S., with U.S. dollars).

Legality of Performing Transplant Surgery for Purchased Kidney:

However, the law does not specifically make it illegal for a surgeon to transplant a kidney that was bought or sold in another country. It could be argued that the term "transfer" includes the transplantation of an organ from one person to another. However, this would result in legal liability every time a surgeon transplanted a kidney from outside the state where the transplant occurred. Moreover, this writer has found no situations in which a surgeon was prosecuted for transplanting an organ that was purchased or sold in violation of U.S. law. Thus even if the potential recipient paid the two "cousins" to donate their kidneys, it would probably still be legal for the surgeon to perform the transplant.

Legality of Declining To Scrub on Scheduled Transplant Operation:

There is no statutory law requiring a surgeon to perform a scheduled operation. However, the surgical resident may have a contractual obligation to the transplant center or hospital to perform operations which have been approved and scheduled by the transplant center. Or, performing operations under certain circumstances may be a condition of the resident's continued employment with the transplant center.

A contract to perform an illegal act is not enforceable, so the resident could not be held liable for refusing to scrub if performing the transplant were illegal. However, as discussed above, it is probably legal. If so, the resident may be subject to discharge or liability for breach of contract by the transplant center.
On the other hand, the surgical resident may also have a contractual obligation with the center not to perform any transplants he suspects may be illegal. If so, he would not be subject to discharge or liability for refusing to scrub for the operation.

The resident may also be liable to the donors and recipient for abandonment. This issue was discussed at length in Case 12 in connection with an anesthesiologist's announcement on the day of surgery that he refused to participate. The same considerations would apply in the present Case. On balance, it is highly unlikely that the resident would be found liable for abandonment.

Ethical Analysis:

The surgeon should not refuse to scrub on the mere suspicion that the documentation (stipulating that the donors are related to the patient) is falsified.

First, the only bases set forth in the hypothetical for this suspicion are that the potential donors are from Indonesia, they do not speak English, they would be donating to a high-ranking military officer, and Indonesian counsel advised that in Indonesia, any high-ranking person can get whatever papers he needs. Even combined, these factors do not provide evidence that a fakery occurred in this situation. On the contrary, there is equally strong evidence that the two men really are related to the potential recipient - they have antigen matches equivalent to a closely related sibling). Merely because papers *could* be forged for the patient (since he is a high-ranking official) does not mean that they in fact were forged. If the surgeon refuses to scrub based solely on the fact that it is possible to forge papers in Indonesia, he is discriminating against the patient and donors for being Indonesian.
The surgeon is going to have to get an Indonesian translator anyway, to inform the cousins of the risks associated with the donation, get informed consent, and have them decide which cousin will donate (based on adequate disclosure about the risks and chances of success with two vs. three antigen match), find out if either cousin has a condition such as high blood pressure or diabetes that would create a risk of developing kidney failure and/or needing both kidneys, etc. At that time, the surgeon should also have the translator ask each cousin, separately, detailed questions about the family and the cousin's relationship to the recipient cousin, the possibility of being paid to donate, etc.

However, even if there were more substantive evidence to indicate that the papers were forged and the "cousins" were not in fact related to the patient, such evidence alone would not ethically justify the surgeon's refusal to scrub for the transplant. As noted above, living unrelated kidney transplants are performed in the United States. The Indonesians may not have been aware of this, and may have forged the papers because they believed that only relatives can donate kidneys in the U.S. But regardless of the Indonesians' reasons for falsifying documents, the surgeon should not refuse to perform the transplant merely because the Indonesians lied about something that does not affect their eligibility for a transplant. As long as the potential donors pass the psychological evaluation given to living unrelated donors, give informed consent to donation, and do whatever else is necessary for the transplant to take place, the surgeon should not refuse to perform the transplant merely because the Indonesians falsified papers stating their relationship to each other.

It is also not ethical for the surgeon to refuse to scrub for the transplant on mere suspicion that the two potential donors were paid to donate their organs. Again, there simply is not enough evidence on which to reasonably base that suspicion. To refuse to perform the surgery merely because organs could have been bought and sold in Indonesia is to discriminate unfairly against the patient and donors for being Indonesian.
Even if there were sufficient evidence to suspect that payment was made in Indonesia to the potential donors, the surgeon still should not refuse to perform the surgery. If buying and selling kidneys is legal in Indonesia, then the surgeon's refusal would be discrimination against the Indonesians for following the practices of their country. Moreover, to perform the transplant would not deprive an American of a potential transplant.

Connie Zuckerman, J.D.

Given the lack of ability to communicate with the potential donors in this case, there is no way to verify with certainty that they are in fact cousins of the potential organ recipient. What is, perhaps, of more importance, however, from both a legal and moral perspective, is the inability to determine whether these individuals have given their informed and voluntary consent to donate their kidneys and thus put themselves at risk for the benefit of the military official. It would be unethical and could potentially constitute medical malpractice to accept an organ from either of these donors without being certain that they knowlingly undertake such risk. Furthermore, there is obvious concern that such individuals may be under duress or coercion to become organ donors. They may either have been influenced financially to participate, or perhaps might even be under some threat of physicial harm or other retribution should they refuse to cooperate.

The lack of ability to effectively communicate with these potential donors, and the uncertainty of their understanding of their potential role, support the concerns of the senior surgical resident. In fact, it would be advisable to proceed no further until these fundamental questions were clarified and until it was clear that such donors are knowledgable and willing participants in this organ transfer.

Amy L. Friedman, M.D.

Financial reimbursement for donation of an organ is unethical and dangerous. Tolerance of this practice could easily lead to failure to obtain crucial medical information about the donor, ultimately jeopardizing the recipient. If remuneration is acknowledged or suspected, the team should decline to perform this transplant. As a member of the surgical team, the senior surgical resident does have the right to decline participation in a procedure he considers unethical. He would be wrong to do so without giving adequate warning to the attending surgeon for an alternate assistant to be identified. Fortunately, in practice, this dilemma rarely arises. Training programs usually exist in highly academic environments where peer pressure and intense scrutiny of all decisions rarely permit such anomalous circumstances.

Under no circumstances should the transplant team agree to proceed unless the center's conventional protocols are followed. Even an adequate discussion of surgical risks to the donor will require participation of a translator. If none are available, it would be unethical to proceed with any elective operation lacking informed consent, let alone donor nephrectomy. Although identification of an objective Indonesian interpreter may be challenging, it cannot be impossible. Any costs should be incorporated in the recipient's bill. If further clarification of either donor's incentive or thorough familiarity with the relationship between the pair cannot be made, transplantation should not proceed.

Carl M. Kjellstrand, M.D.

This appears to be a "rock bottom moral belief clash", caused by the beliefs held by the surgery resident. Two things are against accepting his refusal. He assumes it is fakery that the donor is related. It may not be so, the tissue typing speaks against that. This point can also be clarified by an interview of the potential donors by an Indonesian speaking physician, preferably a psychiatrist. Secondly, we do participate in a system that is not perfectly just - the rich do get better care than the poor under some circumstances and can buy care the poor cannot get at all (C.F. the Oregon Plan). Rich people need care too.

Mildred (Barry) Friedman

If living unrelated kidney donors were more accepted there would be no problem here. However, we are in the here and now.

The senior surgical resident has a suspicion, not *apparent fakery*, to deal with. In America we still need proof to be termed guilty. No proof exists. Translators should be asked to hold interviews with the potential donors. Questioning should be directed by the involved physicians and neither the recipient nor his entourage should be present. The Indonesian counsel might be asked to attend.

If the story of the relationship is maintained, surgery should be preformed. As in Case 10, a moral judgement by a doctor may interfere with the care of a patient. When evidence is brought forth to dispute the kinship, then the use of a living unrelated donor will be discussed. It is a different issue since the resident's actions are based not on this question, but on the dishonesty of the presentation.

I feel the resident has overstepped his place and is wrong.

Judith E. Columbo

I feel that the senior surgical resident by making this decision not to transplant the organ showed the human side and not the assembly line aspect of transplantation. When the Indonesian counsel stated that there is no way to clarify the issue leads one to believe that this is what the counsel wanted. With the phrase "In our country" should be answered, well, "In our country". Neither donors understand what was happening and were just doing what they were told. I agree with the surgical resident not to start this practice.

Editor's Remarks 17

Lacking a medical "State Department," there is little to protect a well meaning renal center from subterfuge and/or overt lying when foreign relatives are introduced. After the fact, I learned that the seemingly endless stream of young "cousins" produced by an Indonesian high ranking politician were actually paid live donors waiting to be tissue typed. It is fascinating that the two patients split on endorsing the surgical resident's withdrawal from the transplant team because of suspicion of duplicity: Columbo concurs, Mildred Barry Friedman does not. Unless we devote extensive time to probing the culture and behavior of referred recipients, we will not feel confident that the players are as represented. Well meaning, the suggestion that an interpreter (and investigator?) pursue the suspicion of misrepresentation with their fees added to the patient's bill is impractical and will not work. If the Indonesian counsel is unable to resolve the true identities, neither will the nephrologist or transplant surgeon. I would go ahead with the surgery as requested.

Response to Study Questions

1. Question previously asked and answered. According to prevailing law and custom, it is unethical to buy a commercial kidney. Certainly, in the US, any surgeon dumb enough to operate knowingly using a purchased kidney risks jail.
2. Without investigators, what more can the transplant surgeon do? Nothing. If the stature of the program is sufficient to attract recipients from other countries, the best course is do perform transplants competently providing that all papers appear in order.
3. That is the way the world works. Whether the Shah of Iran with lymphoma or an anonymous rich industrialist, physicians can be "bought" with generous fees - especially in our present era of HMO restricted income.
4. Yes. As remarked by Kjellstrand, that is how we behave. Surgical procedures, drug and doses, and advice may be the same. But, the entire experience for a rich person is easier and indeed, better, because of all the extras supplied by all members of the team once it is known that the patient is rich. This shouldn't be but it is.

Case 18

ACCEPTING ORGAN FROM MENTALLY DEFICIENT DONOR

A 39 year old insulin-dependent (type 1) diabetic social worker develops end-stage renal failure caused by diabetic nephropathy. Noting virulent diabetic retinopathy and serious peripheral vascular disease, the attending nephrologist advocates an immediate kidney transplant rather than dialytic therapy which may permit progression of diabetic complications. The patient has an institutionalized, mentally defective, 37 year old sister, functioning at approximately kindergarten level, who is usually seen only on holiday visits. ***After review of treatment options and in recognition of the two-year or longer wait for a cadaver kidney, the parents - who are legal guardians for the defective sister - direct that she be scheduled as a transplant donor.***

Study Questions

1. Have the parents unfairly exploited the mentally defective potential donor?
2. Should non-comprehending donors be used under any circumstance?
3. Given a gradation in IQ, should there be a minimal level for consent to be an organ donor?
4. Does the genetic nature of the disease (diabetes) make a difference in your decision?

Monique Janelle London, J.D.

The potential kidney donor is mentally ill and functions at kindergarten level. She is legally incompetent to make decisions about her medical care; instead, her parents are her legal guardians. In that capacity, her parents directed that she donate a kidney to her brother.[Footnote 32] Before the attending nephrologist proceeds to schedule the transplant, he should ensure that court approval has been sought and obtained for the procedure. On the limited facts of Case 18 and the sparse caselaw on this issue, it is unclear whether such court approval will be given.

Legal guardians generally have the power to consent to medical and surgical "treatment" on behalf of incompetents. However, organ donation to a relative by an incompetent person is not intended to benefit the incompetent person directly. Therefore, it has been viewed as a procedure that cannot be classified as "treatment." See *Little v. Little,* 576 S.W.2d 493, 498 (Tex. Civ. App. 1979).

Perhaps for that reason, courts with reported cases on the issue have exercised their authority over requests that an incompetent person donate an organ to a relative, applying either the "best interests" test or "substituted judgment"

[32] This writer assumes that the ESRD patient is male.

test. See *In re Doe,* 104 A.D.2d 200, 481 N.Y.S.2d 932 (N.Y. App. Div. 4th Dep't 1984) ("The court under its parens patriae authority is empowered to protect the person and property of an individual who is not capable of making decisions in his own best interests. We conclude that the source of any power that a court may have to authorize an incompetent's participation in a surgical procedure to save the life of another is confined to its parens patriae power; thus such authorization may only be given if it is in the incompetent's best interests. . . ."); *Strunk v. Strunk,* 445 S.W.2d 145, 149 (Ky. 1969) (opining that courts of equity have the power to permit removal of an organ from an incompetent ward of the state for transplantation into the ward's sibling and holding that organ donation was in "the best interest" of the incompetent ward); *Little v. Little,* 576 S.W.2d 493, 498 (Tex. Civ. App. 1979) (stating that whether courts expressly use the doctrine of substituted judgment or not, they primarily focus on the benefits of organ donation to the child donor); *Curran v. Bosze,* 141 Ill. 2d 473, 566 N.E.2d 1319 (Ill. 1990) (denying permission for toddler twins to submit to bone marrow harvesting for the benefit of their half brother because the procedure was not in the best interests of the twins); *In re Richardson,* 284 So. 2d 185, 187 (La. Ct. App. 4th Cir. 1973) (concluding that a mentally retarded teenage boy donating a kidney to his adult sister would be against the boy's best interests).

It is not clear from the facts given in Case 18 whether the parents' decision to have the defective sister donate a kidney would meet judicial approval. As a preliminary matter, the Case does not state whether the potential donor was ever competent, nor whether she gave any indication while competent that she would want to donate a kidney to her diabetic brother should the need ever arise. If the defective sister had given some such indication, it could be argued that her decision when competent should be given some weight. It should at least factor in to a court's application of the substituted judgment standard (i.e., what the sister would decide to do now if she were competent). As discussed earlier, cases have held that a competent patient's decision about her medical treatment must be honored even if the patient is presently incompetent. *See, e.g., Cruzan v. Director, Missouri Department of Health,* 497 U.S. 261 (1990); *In re Lydia Hall Hospital,* 116 Misc. 2d 477, 455 N.Y.S. 2d 706 (N.Y. Sup. Ct. 1982).
On the other hand, it could also be argued that those cases are distinguishable from Case 18 - they dealt with a patient's decision when competent about whether to receive lifesaving treatment if the patient's own medical condition deteriorated. In Case 18, the competent sister may have expressed a decision to donate a kidney to her brother if he ever needed one. This would be a decision about her brother's treatment, not her own. It would be in anticipation of her brother's health deteriorating - not of she herself becoming mentally ill. On balance, a court would probably find that the sister's mental illness so fundamentally changed her situation as to discount any statements she made when competent. This finding would not impinge upon the sister's right to self-determination, since the statements in question would be focused on medical treatment for her brother, not herself.

The Case also does not state whether anyone has approached the sister recently and explained to her the current situation and possibility of donation. The Case states that the sister, although mentally defective, functions "at approximately kindergarten level." At that level, even if she is legally incompetent, she may still be able to understand the proposal to some extent and form an opinion about whether she wants to donate. Her present thoughts as an incompetent about what she wants to do might be considered in a court's application of the substituted judgment or best interests standard. For instance, in *Little v Little*, 576 S.W.2d 493 (Tex. Civ. App. 1979), the court considered evidence that a retarded 14-year old girl was aware of the nature of her brother's illness and her ability to help him by donating her kidney in finding that the sister would receive psychological benefits by donating. *See also In re Hier*, 18 Mass. App. Ct. 200, 464 N.E.2d 959, 964-965 (Mass. 1984) ("The expressions of opposition by Mrs. Hier, while those of an incompetent person, and thus not to be given legal effect, are nevertheless to be taken into consideration in applying the substituted judgment test because they are indicative of the burden that she feels in being subjected to advanced medical technologies."); *In re Swan*, 569 A.2d 1202, 1203 (Me. 1990) (holding that minor's pre-accident decision that he did not wish to be kept alive in a persistent vegetative state should be respected).

In Case 18, it is also unclear whether the brother and sister have (or had) a close relationship such that the sister would benefit by donating a kidney to her brother. The cases deciding whether to approve organ donation by an incompetent person generally require that there be some type of "close" relationship between the donor and recipient, such that the donor will benefit indirectly from the transplant by saving the life or health of the recipient. Cases approving the donation generally conclude that the relationship between the potential organ donor and donee (usually siblings) is sufficiently beneficial to the donor to justify the surgical invasion of the donor for the benefit of the donee. Thus in *Strunk v. Strunk*, 445 S.W.2d 145 (Ky. 1969), a mother requested permission to have her retarded 27-year-old son's kidney transplanted into her competent 28-year-old son. The court decided that the transplant would be in the incompetent son's best interest because the brothers had a close relationship, and the competent brother's death would be devastating to his sibling. In *Hart v. Brown*, 29 Conn. Supp. 368, 289 A.2d 386 (Conn. Super. Ct. 1972), the court approved a transplant between minor twins, based in part on evidence that a successful kidney transplant "would be of immense benefit to the donor in that the donor would be better off in a family that was happy than in a family that was distressed and in that it would be a very great loss to the donor if the donee were to die from her illness." *Id.* at 389. In *Little v. Little*, 576 S.W.2d 493, 500 (Tex. Civ. App. 1979), the appeals court held that a probate court was within its authority to authorize the mother/guardian of a 14-year-old retarded girl to consent to donate one of the girl's kidneys to her brother. There was sufficient evidence of a close relationship between the siblings, such that the sister would benefit from the donation by having her brother alive and by potentially experiencing heightened self esteem, renewed meaning in life, and other positive feelings. See also *In re Doe*, 104 A.D.2d 200, 481 N.Y.S.2d 932 (N.Y. App. Div. 4th Dep't 1984) (determining that it would be in the incompetent's best interest to donate bone marrow to save the life of a brother who was the only family member involved with the incompetent's treatment and placement decisions).

Similarly, cases disapproving donation determine that the relationship is not sufficiently close to benefit the donor. *See Curran v. Bosze*, 141 Ill. 2d 473, 566 N.E.2d 1319, 1343 (Ill. 1990) (determining that bone marrow testing would not

benefit psychological interests of toddler twins because they did not share a close family with the potential recipient - their half sibling); *In re Pescinski*, 67 Wis. 2d 4, 226 N.W.2d 180 (Wis. 1975) (denying petition to remove mentally incompetent schizophrenic's kidney to donate to his sister in absence of evidence that ward would benefit from the procedure).
It is possible that a 39-year old brother could be sufficiently "close" to a sister with the mentality of a five-year old for the sister to benefit from donating a kidney to him. For instance, in *Strunk v Strunk*, 445 S.W. 2d 145 (Ky. 1969), the court found a sufficiently close relationship to authorize a transplant between 27- and 28-year old brothers, even though the donor brother had the mentality of a six-year old. Case 18 states that the brother usually only sees the institutionalized sister "on holiday visits." This indicates that the two are not close. However, current circumstances may be creating a temporary distance between the siblings. They may have been in closer contact before the brother developed diabetes or before the sister became mentally ill. If the sister donates a kidney to her brother, the brother's improved health and/or gratitude to his sister for donating her kidney may cause the two to become close, thereby creating a benefit for the sister. This writer was unable to find any case in which the *potential* for a close relationship (without a presently existing close relationship) was sufficient to find that an incompetent person would benefit from donating a kidney to a family member. Nonetheless, such an argument seems feasible.

Additionally, the facts of Case 18 do not state whether the defective sister is the only family member who would be an acceptable donor. Caselaw suggests that kidney donation by an incompetent will be approved only if no competent family members are medically acceptable donors. *See, e.g., Little v. Little*, 576 S.W.2d 493, 500 (Tex. Civ. App. 1979) (approving transplant from mentally ill sister in part on grounds that sister was the only living related donor with acceptable matching characteristics); *Strunk v Strunk*, 445 S.W. 2d 145 (Ky 1969) (finding transplant was in best interests of incompetent donor ward where recipient brother was dying of kidney failure, and ward was the only family member medically acceptable to donate a kidney); *In re Richardson*, 284 So. 2d 185, 187 (La. Ct. App. 4th Cir. 1973) (disapproving transplant where incompetent was a perfect antigen match with the donee, but other family members were half-matches with the donee); *but see Hart v. Brown*, 29 Conn. Supp. 368, 289 A.2d 386 (Conn. 1972) (approving transplant from twin sister although both parents had offered a kidney, where the transplant from the identically matched twin had the best chance of success). Thus, the presence of competent family members who are also candidates would probably weigh against court approval of donation by the mentally defective sister.

Even if the sister were the only medically acceptable candidate for donation, in certain situations donation might still be found to be contrary to her best interests. For instance, the sister may be the only family member "medically acceptable" to donate because she is the only non-obese family member. However, she and her brother might be a zero-antigen match. In that case, the chances of the transplant being successful might be statistically less than if the brother were to wait for a cadaver kidney with a better antigen match. It could be argued that it is not in the sister's interests to donate a kidney where the chances of graft survival may be less than with a cadaveric kidney. If the transplant rejects, the sister does not benefit from having her brother in better health or still alive as a result of her donation.

Case 18 also does not inform the reader whether the sister has diabetes, hypertension, or any other warning signs that she might be at risk of developing kidney failure or needing both of her kidneys. Even if the sister is the only family member medically acceptable to donate in terms of matching characteristics, it may be against her best interests to donate if her own health would suffer as a result.

Nor do the facts of Case 18 state whether the transplant is needed to save the brother's life. This may also be a factor in whether a court approves a transplant from an incompetent to a sibling. For instance, in *In re Richardson,* 284 So. 2d 185, 187 (La. Ct. App. 4th Cir. 1973), although the court found "no doubt that . . . a kidney transplant [from a mentally retarded teenage boy] would be more beneficial to [his sister] than any other known remedy," it was not an "absolute immediate necessity" because dialysis could preserve her life.

In recent years, dialysis technology has improved to the point that dialysis has become a workable alternative (or even preferable) to transplantation for many people. The cases cited above date back to times when dialysis took much longer and was tolerable by fewer people than it is today. Thus a court today would be less likely to find that a transplant from an incompetent is necessary to save the life of a relative (and thereby preserve a "close" relationship for the benefit of the incompetent person). However, Case 18 does state that the brother risks "progression of diabetic complications" if he does not get a transplant immediately. This alone might be sufficient for a court to find that the transplant is necessary to the brother's health or perhaps his life. Thus it might be necessary for the sister to donate a kidney in order to obtain the "benefit" of having her brother's health or live preserved.

In sum, not enough information is presented in Case 18 to allow for a reliable prediction of whether a court would approve the proposed transplant. The attending nephrologist should learn more information about the situation first. He should explore the nature of the relationship between the brother and the sister, how the sister feels about the transplant as she understands it, whether undergoing the transplant would be safe for the sister, whether the transplant has a strong likelihood of succeeding, and whether there are any acceptable alternatives to having the sister be the donor. If the nephrologist finds sufficient information to indicate that on balance the sister would benefit from donating a kidney to her brother, he should seek court approval to proceed with the transplant.

Ethical Analysis:

Case 18 does not present enough information to reach an ethical conclusion. Generally, an incompetent should only be considered as a donor if there are no other medically acceptable donors available (related or unrelated), and the donee faces a serious threat of medical deterioration or death if he does not receive a kidney transplant immediately. Assuming this is the situation in Case 18, someone who knows how to communicate with the mentally defective sister should explain very carefully and slowly to her the situation and what it would mean for her to donate a kidney. The discussion should take place over several days or even weeks, to be certain the sister understands, to the extent she is capable, what would happen. If she expresses any reluctance, that should weigh heavily against using her as a kidney donor.

This writer does not find the closeness of the relationship between donor and donee (even if it were shown in Case 18, which it is not) to be a particularly compelling factor in favor of a kidney transplant. Even if the donor and donee are close prior to the transplant, there is no guarantee they will remain so thereafter. On the one hand, the act of donation, the sacrifice, the gratitude, the health benefits it may bring, the loyalty it shows, all may draw the siblings closer. However, it is also possible that the brother would subsequently reject the kidney, or continue to have deteriorating health from the diabetes despite the kidney transplant. If the sister donates, the brother is only getting a kidney (as opposed to possibly getting a kidney and pancreas from a cadaveric donor). Thus his diabetes will persist. Feelings of resentment, wasted effort, failure, lost opportunity to cure the diabetes, etc. could be detrimental to the relationship between the siblings.

On balance, the best ethical approach would be to avoid having the defective sister donate a kidney unless it is necessary to save the brother's life.

Connie Zuckerman, J.D.

In this case there is no question that the potential donor is unable to give informed, voluntary consent to the donation of a kidney for the benefit of an ailing sibling. Her limited capacity renders her incompetent to make such a decision. The question then becomes whether, as her legal guardians, the parents of this potential donor have the legal authority to subject this incompetent patient to invasive surgery, with no direct benefit to the patient, for the benefit of their other ailing child?

There is reported case law which upheld the authority of parents to consent to an organ donation by a retarded child for the benefit of the child's sibling (*Strunk v. Strunk. Ky. 1969*). In that case, however, the court somewhat disingenuously argued that the surgery did benefit the retarded child, given that child's close attachment to the ailing sibling. Still, that authority seems to violate the prevailing ethical consensus that individuals who cannot consent on their own behalf ought not be put at risk unless the benefit directly accrues to them. In this specific case, there is no evidence that the mentally incompetent donor would derive any benefit from the donation, and would likely court significant risk. While some may argue that she should not be denied the opportunity to act altruistically and for the benefit of her sibling, by no means would the parents automatically have authority to make such a decision on the incompetent patient's behalf. It would thus be necessary to seek judicial approval before the organ donation could actually proceed.

Amy L. Friedman, M.D.

Mental deficiency should not be viewed as an absolute contraindication to living organ donation. In fact, the ability to save the life of a loved one may represent an unparalleled means of raising the sister's self-esteem. The judgement to be made when organ donation may benefit both the donor and the recipient versus sacrificing the interests of a mentally deficient individual solely to benefit a relative is challenging. Thorough psychosocial evaluation of the motivation of the potential recipient independently from the motivations of the parents must be undertaken. To whatever extent possible, the wishes of the disabled relative must be assessed. Even most kindergarten aged children, for example, are able to clarify the extent of their love for an individual to experienced observers. Denial of the disabled sister's right to help her brother might actually be discriminatory. After careful assessment of the family interactions, provided there is no excessive risk to the sister beyond that expected for any other donor, use of her kidney to stabilize her brothers health and the well being of the entire family is reasonable.

Carl M. Kjellstrand, M.D.

This case is best resolved by a court who appoints the patient advocate for the mentally defective sister and resolves it after having heard all pros and cons for the recipient and weighs it against the pros and cons of the donor. Yes! There are pros of being a donor: increased self-esteem and happiness (see RG Simmons, "Gift of Life", p.58. Transactions Inc, New Brunswick 1987). Of course this feeling may not be available with someone of kindergarten levels.

Mildred (Barry) Friedman

A few years ago a child was conceived for the stated purpose of becoming a bone marrow donor for an older sister. When the new daughter was old enough she indeed gave bone marrow and saved her sister's life. Case 18 proposes using a mentally deficient sibling as a kidney donor. Both dilemmas raise the same question.

Parents are legally responsible for decisions affecting both proposed donors. Arguing that their conclusions are those that would be made by the immature sisters if they were mentally responsible, seems illogical. There is no way of knowing what the girls would decide if they were adult. Accountability for the conclusions rests on the parents

Kidney donation and bone marrow donation are minimally physically risky for the donors. Psychological gains may lie in the future for both girls. Gratitude from the recipients may foster closer relationships. More attention may be paid to the givers. In a family where one child is sick and the other well, the sick one receives more attention. When the differences between siblings are made more equal, concern for them will even out.

Under these circumstances the moral question lies before the ill daughters. When they ask for the donation they signal their resolution of the problem. A

feeling of guilt will probably remain for the rest of their lives. Guilt is not always avoidable or bad. Out in the open and discussed, it can be dealt with.
My moral judgement would be different but I do not disagree with the decision.

Judith E. Columbo

This is a case that pulls at the heart. Trying to explain to a normal kindergarten level child the course of transplantation is difficult but a mentally defective patient is heartless. The parents and social worker/sister should not have a problem telling the mentally defective sister of **their** decision for transplantation. The family feelings are quite clear. They visit the potential donor only 12 holidays out of 365 days. This action speaks for itself. Since the parents are the legal guardians they along will decide. A decision that I cannot accept.

Editor's Remarks18

I've never understood the genesis of the phrase "pushing the envelope" though the issues in Case 18 does just that. Is a mentally deficient (institutionalized) adult to be regarded as a child in terms of hegemony over her body? If so, why not volunteer organs (kidney, ova, liver segments) for unrelated recipients? When a couple conceives a child to act as a bone marrow donor for a fatally afflicted sibling, is this avant guard medicine or Hitlerish denial of human dignity? London recounts court decisions on both sides underscoring the confrontation to discern what is right and moral. London pleas for more information before making a decision. Zuckerman, citing the same Stunk v. Strunk decision also wants more information. Dr. Amy L. Friedman projects organ donation by a mentally deficient donor as offering "an unparalleled means of raising the sister's self-esteem.." Kjellstrand defers to the court while patients Mildred Barry Friedman and Columbo reach divergent decisions agreeing and dissenting from the parents willingness to use the subnormal sister as a donor. I do not agree. But, the whole question of which individuals should be kept alive under what conditions is vexing.

To test your own feelings, consider the plight of a newborn lacking major organs including genitalia and kidneys and having microcephaly indicative of profound mental deficiency. Should that infant be started on dialysis with the knowledge that a "normal" life will never be possible? Is it just to retrieve (harvest) organs from persons afflicted with terminal illness? Should the "opting out" regulations now in place in some European countries be adopted here. Under this regulation, unless a family member says no, organs are presumed utilizable for transplantation. Refer to the earlier discussion by Pristave and Watson for a detailed consideration of legal precedents pertinent to Case 18.

Response to Study Questions

1. Torn by the tragic afflictions of both children, the parents should not be judged harshly for trying to salvage the life of one based on the donation of another.
2. I would not. London has reviewed available court cases but no clear answer is possible.
3. A frightening question. Why not an IQ test before voting. Or marriage? Or any other activity? For the present, I will accept the judgment of the renal team giving the presumption that they want what is best for their patient and mean the donor no harm.
4. Yes and no. Survival in diabetic hemodialysis patients is progressively improving. Nevertheless, fewer than 1 in 25 will live a decade. At the same time, kidney transplantation delivers a strikingly more favorable outcome. Giving the 39 year old social worker a functioning kidney transplant provides a return to productive life. Even the best dialysis outcome, by comparison, is a continuing drag with sub-optimal rehabilitation the usual outcome.

Case 19

CONSENT FROM CHILD FOR ORGAN DONATION

An 8 year old student develops chronic glomerulonephritis and is begun on continuous ambulatory peritoneal dialysis (CAPD) with fair rehabilitation. Over two years of dialytic therapy, his growth is maintained by injections of recombinant human growth hormone. The patient's monozygotic (identical) twin brother shows no sign of kidney disease. After a series of dialysis access infections, and a worsening depression in the patient, the parents request that a kidney transplant be performed between their twin sons. The donor twin states that he wishes to do everything for his brother but that he is afraid of being hurt by the surgeon-doctor. ***His parents request that the kidney transplant be performed promptly, advising their donor son that he will feel no pain once the surgery is finished.***

Study Questions

1. Is a child ever a suitable organ donor?
2. A tissue donor (bone marrow)?
3. Can parents consent to organ donation by their child or must the court be involved?
4. Will the child at the age of 18 have a legal basis for a suit against the consenting parents?

Monique Janelle London, J.D.

The legal analysis of this Case is similar to that of Case 18. This Case involves potential kidney donation from one sibling to another. Like in Case 18, the potential donor is legally incompetent to make his own medical decisions (although here, it is because he is a minor rather than because he is mentally ill). To avoid legal liability, the nephrologist should ensure that judicial approval is sought and obtained before proceeding with the transplant. The court will likely apply either the "best interests" test or the "substituted judgment" test to determine whether to approve the transplant between the twins.

As noted in the discussion of Case 18, the factors courts consider in this analysis include the closeness of the donor and donee siblings, whether the transplant is necessary for the ill sibling's survival, whether the potential donor would benefit from saving the life of the donee (or suffer if the donee sibling died), and whether the donor, although incompetent, understands and consents to the procedure. For instance, in *Hart v. Brown,* 29 Conn. Supp. Ct. 368, 375, 289 A.2d 386, 390-391 (Conn. 1972), a Connecticut court held that under its equitable powers, it could permit parents to authorize organ donation by one child to another, if the donor and donee would benefit, there would be minimal risk to the donor, the donor consented, and the donor would suffer if the recipient died. In that case, the court found that a kidney transplant was necessary for the 7-year old twin's survival, the prognosis was excellent, the risks were negligible for both twins, and the donor twin would benefit from saving her sister's life. Courts have also considered whether the incompetent sibling is the only medically suitable donor. *See Little v. Little*, 576 S.W.2d 493, 500 (Tex. Civ. App. 1979) (approving transplant from mentally ill sister in part on grounds that sister was the only living related donor with acceptable matching characteristics).

In Case 19, the brothers are eight-year old twins. Presumably they have grown up together in the same household and continue to live together (although the Case does not specify whether the parents are separated or divorced). The potential donor brother has stated that he "wishes to do everything for his brother." This situation and the brother's statement of desire to help his twin suggest that the brothers are close, and the donor brother would benefit by saving the life of his ill twin brother. The brother's statement also suggests that he would consent to donate a kidney to his brother.

However, it is unclear from the facts presented whether a kidney transplant is actually necessary to save the ill brother's life or even prevent serious deterioration in his health. The Case does not state that a nephrologist or other medical professional recommended that the boy get a transplant from a living donor. It only states that the boy's parents requested that a transplant be performed promptly.

The facts presented allow for the possibility that a transplant is not an immediate necessity. The Case indicates that the boy has had "fair rehabilitation" during most of the two years he has been on CAPD, but has recently experienced "a series of dialysis infections" and "a worsening depression." No explanation is given for the infections and depression. The likely cause of the infections is that the boy has not taken sufficient care to keep his access site clean, and has gotten peritonitis as a result. Peritoneal dialysis requires diligent care of the access site, using extreme precautions and hygiene to prevent infection. Keeping the peritoneal access clean and infection-free would be difficult for many eight-year old boys. The likely cause of the boy's depression is the peritonitis, which is often extremely painful and debilitating and can require hospitalization.

It appears that the boy's problems with dialysis could be remedied for the present without a transplant. He could be given extra training and supervision in keeping his access clean so that he stops getting infections. If that strategy is unsuccessful, the boy could be switched to hemodialysis. It is true that surgical creation of a hemodialysis access is a serious procedure, and hemodialysis requires adherence to a stricter diet. However, the hemodialysis access is less likely to become infected. Either solution would buy some time for the boy to wait for a cadaveric transplant. (Indeed, if he was placed on the transplant wait-list when he first began dialysis, he should have received a cadaveric transplant already.) A court would probably favor a cadaveric transplant unless the evidence showed that an immediate transplant was necessary. Although the cadaveric transplant would have a lower chance of long term success than a transplant from the boy's twin brother, it would let the court avoid authorizing major surgery on a healthy eight-year old boy from which he will only benefit indirectly at best.

However, if the transplant is found to be "necessary" for the ill brother's life (or health), that factor favors authorizing a kidney transplant from the brother's twin. As identical twins, the brothers are a perfect antigen match, and a transplant between them has a statistically better chance of succeeding than a transplant from any other person (unless there is another, non-twin sibling who is also a perfect or six-antigen match with the ill brother). The potential donor brother will receive the greatest benefit from donating a kidney to his twin if the transplant is successful and thus saves the ill brother's life or health. The fact that the brothers are a perfect match thus further weighs in favor of donation from one twin to the other if an immediate transplant is necessary.

If the twin is the only medically acceptable donor in the family, the argument in favor of authorizing the transplant is very strong. However, the Case leaves open the possibility that there are other relatives who are also medically suitable organ donors for the ill boy. If there are (such as the boy's parents or older siblings), that fact would weigh against authorizing donation by the twin brother. An adult relative could legally consent to the surgical procedure herself, thus avoiding the issues raised by the parents consenting to organ donation on behalf of a minor. An older, more mature donor relative might not be as traumatized by the transplant surgery. Finally, using a different relative would enable the family to save the identical twin as a "back-up donor" in case his brother ever needed another transplant in an emergency situation.

Early cases reached different conclusions on this issue. Compare *In re Richardson,* 284 So. 2d 185, 187 (La. Ct. App. 4th Cir. 1973) (disapproving transplant where incompetent was a perfect antigen match with the donee, but other family members were half-matches with the donee), with *Hart v. Brown,* 29 Conn Supp 368, 289 A. 2d 386 (Conn. 1972) (approving transplant from twin sister although both parents had offered a kidney, where the transplant from the identically matched twin had the best chance of success). Courts might view this question differently today, now that advancements in immunosuppressive medication have improved the chances of success of a transplant from a relative other than an identical twin. However, this writer has been unable to find any current judicial guidance on the issue.

Still weighing against the transplant is the fact that the potential donor is only eight years old. The transplant may be particularly traumatic to him because of his young age. He stated that he is afraid of being hurt by the surgeon. He may suffer physically and/or emotionally from the pain he feels after the surgery, the scar the surgery leaves, the exposure to the hospital and other patients, the effects of the anesthesia and painkiller medication, the invasion of his privacy and impersonal nature of the physicians, time away from school, and questions from his friends and strangers about his absence and the scar.
Moreover, the fact that the brothers are identical twins may mean that the potential donor brother has a genetic predisposition to develop chronic glomerulonephritis (as indicated by the fact that the ill brother developed it), even though he presently "shows no signs of kidney disease." If the potential donor twin is at risk for developing kidney disease, he may ultimately need both of his kidneys. He may also have some other medical problem that could be affected by the transplant surgery. If the surgery presents a risk to the donor brother's health (other than the minor risk of complications from the surgery), it is unlikely a court would find it to be in the donor brother's "best interests" to give a kidney to his twin.

In sum, in this Case, like in Case 18, not enough information is known to predict with any certainty whether a court would authorize the transplant. As an initial matter, the nephrologist should make her own assessment of whether an immediate transplant is necessary, and discuss with the parents that assessment and any alternatives to a transplant between the twins before judicial assistance is sought.

Ethical Analysis:

The ethical analysis should first consider whether the potential donor brother gives his informed consent to the transplant. The donor brother's right not to undergo a surgical procedure should be paramount. His statement that he wants to help his brother but is afraid of being hurt by the surgeon may not be sufficient to indicate consent. It is unclear whether the brother has been given enough information about the transplant surgery itself, the anesthesia, the recovery period, and all the risks and potential benefits to make a truly informed decision.

Assuming he is given all the relevant information, understands it to a satisfactory extent, and consents to the procedure, the second part of the analysis should be similar to the legal analysis: Would a transplant between the brothers be in the best interests of both brothers? That is, would the potential benefits outweigh the risks and potential burdens? The difficulties in proceeding with the analysis are: 1) as discussed above, certain facts are unknown; and 2) the outcome of the transplant cannot be predicted with certainty.
In addition to the factors considered by the courts (such as whether an immediate transplant is necessary and whether the twin brother is the only suitable donor), the ethical analysis should involve a close examination of the potential benefits and burdens/risks to each brother if the transplant takes place between them.

For the donor twin, the potential *benefits* of the transplant are:
- His brother gets a transplant. For the time the recipient brother has the transplant, he may be healthier and have more energy. He will also have more time available, since he won't have to spend time on CAPD. The donor brother may benefit from the recipient brother's improved health by receiving more companionship, friendship and play time from the recipient brother.
- The recipient brother's access infections and depression related to the infections and/or dialysis will likely end, rendering him more available to provide companionship and happier, and therefore more fun to be with.
- The donor twin may get gratitude and love from the recipient twin for donating his kidney.
- The twin brothers may become closer because of the experience of sharing a kidney.

For the donor twin, the potential *risks* of the transplant are:
- The donor twin dies from the surgery or the anesthesia.
- The donor twin develops complications from the surgery.
- The donor twin develops kidney disease or injures his remaining kidney,

and needs both of his native kidneys.
- The recipient twin rejects the donor twin's kidney. Both twins feel failure, depression, and sadness over the unsuccessful transplant. The recipient twin resents or blames the donor twin for the failure of the transplant. The donor twin blames himself for the failure of the transplant. The twins grow more distant, and lose companionship.
- The recipient twin dies during the transplant surgery. The donor twin loses his brother.
- The recipient twin's depression does not end with the transplant. On the contrary, it is exacerbated by the immunosuppressive drugs. The recipient twin is even less fun to be with, and less close to his twin brother.
- The donor twin feels pain after the surgery, and mistrusts his parents for lying to him that he would feel no pain after the transplant.

For the recipient twin, the potential *benefits* of the transplant are:
- He gets a transplant. For the time he has the transplant, he may be healthier and have more energy to do the activities he wants to do. He will also have more time available to do the activities he wants to do, since he won't have to dialyze.
- His access infections and depression related to dialysis will likely end.
- He will not have to follow the peritoneal dialysis regimen.
- He may become closer with his brother because of the experience of sharing a kidney.

For the recipient twin, the potential *risks* of the transplant are:
- He dies from the surgery or the anesthesia.
- He develops complications from the surgery.
- He rejects the donor twin's kidney.
- His health suffers from having to go through the surgery.
- He feels guilty for having caused the donor twin to go through the operation, to no benefit.
- He feels depressed because the attempted transplant from the one person with the best chance of success, has failed.
- He feels angry with the donor twin for having given him a kidney that did not work.
- The donor twin develops kidney disease or injures his remaining kidney, and needs both of his native kidneys. The recipient feels guilty and loses the companionship and time of his brother.
- The donor twin dies from surgery. The recipient loses a twin brother and feels guilty, sad, depressed.
- The recipient twin's depression does not end with the transplant. On the contrary, it is exacerbated by the immunosuppressive drugs.

Ethically, the parents and the potential donor, with the help of medical professionals to understand the transplant and its ramifications, should reach a decision together about what to do.

Connie Zuckerman, J.D.

Parents are the natural decisionmakers for their children and are given significant, though not unlimited, latitude in determining what medical treatment best serves the interests of their children. In this particular case, the close genetic linkage between the two siblings arguably makes the healthy twin the ideal organ donor, and there is case law to support parental consent in the precise circumstance of one minor twin donating to save the life of the other (*Hart v. Brown. Conn.. 1972*) .In that particular case, the consent was authorized based upon the probable death of the recipient without the transplant, and the attendant psychological trauma to the healthy twin should his sibling die.

In this case, the fear and anxiety of the potential minor donor clearly indicate the need to work with that child prior to any consideration of the appropriateness of the donation. While it could be argued that the child would benefit, given the new lease on life he made available to his twin, there is also the attendant possibility that forcing the child to undergo invasive surgery could as well have longlasting, negative psychological impact on the child. Generally, pediatric practioners do not intervene without at least the assent of a child that age, unless the urgency of the circumstance necessitates immediate action. Given that this intervention does not directly benefit the donor, it would be unethical to proceed without further discussion and counseling of the donor child. Moreover, the authority of the parents to subject their healthy child to this invasive surgery is not certain, and all concerned may be wise to seek legal counsel prior to commencing with the surgery.

Amy L. Friedman, M.D.

From the academic point of view, this transplant must be evaluated on behalf of the potential donor. An 8-year-old child with normal intellectual development is expected to become by his maturity capable of fully comprehending, and perhaps regretting having donated a kidney during his youth. A scar from a surgical procedure, noticeable even when wearing a bathing suit, might adversely effect the development of his self image. The consequences of blood transfusion during a nephrectomy, while extremely uncommon, might even jeopardize his life. The decision to donate a kidney to his identical twin must therefore be made by the donor himself and not by parents serving as his surrogate. Even though he might be predicted to elect to donate his organ (most identical twins are linked in a way the rest of us may not ever fully comprehend), nephrectomy must be postponed until he is able to more fully comprehend such a decision. Consideration of his donation should therefore be postponed until at least the age of 15 or 16.

From the surgical perspective, the risks of nephrectomy in a young child with no need for surgery, are unacceptably high. No indicator is more valuable in guiding my medical or surgical judgements than my heart. After years of caring for patients I have learned to trust the directions it provides. It has alerted me to occult post operative bleeding that required reoperation for control, to explore an abdomen based on physical examination despite an entirely normal

CT scan, and does not fail to assist in my assessment of the veracity of what patients tell me. So when I start heading home but my heart directs me to focus on a previously ignored clinical detail that may well ruin my evening plans, I pay rapt attention.

In this case, my heart is firmly opposed to subjecting an 8 year old child to the risks of a major operation that he does not fully understand and does not need. There is no doubt that he could gain significant benefit from helping his brother. Increased self esteem, preservation of the unique gift of an identical twin brother and recognition as a family hero are by no means trivial. Yet, they do not outweigh the very low, but real risk of death or serious complication in my heart. If I agreed to perform this operation and an untoward event occurred I do not know how I would recover. It is difficult enough to cope with an intraoperative death or technical mistake when there was no doubt that the procedure had been necessary to care for the patient. Each such event in my career has had profound impact on me. Each has required deep soul searching to place in perspective and has prompted sufficiently serious self doubt. Recovery of one's equilibrium after such an event is extraordinarily difficult. As the individual who would actually place the cold steel of the scalpel blade on this child's skin, no legal precedent or court order, no ethicist's supportive argument and no colleague's encouragement could help me feel at peace holding his life unnecessarily in my hands. I would personally decline to participate in this transplant and would encourage others to feel comfortable doing the same.

Carl M. Kjellstrand, M.D.

Resolve as Case 18.

Mildred (Barry) Friedman

Regrettably these parents lie to their well son. There is pain, and sometimes considerable pain, after donating a kidney. Such lies speak poorly for the mental future of both boys. In their favor is the fact of their twinness.

I do believe there is a special relationship between twins. Even prior to birth they have never existed without each other. The donor twin probably *does* want to do what he can for his brother. Fear of pain is normal and the boy would be stupid if he did not entertain worry. That concern can be handled by honestly informing him of the possibilities. His decision would then be based on fact.

Case 19 is presented without a statement concerning the feelings of the ill twin. His thoughts are important because he will spend the rest of his life with guilt or gratitude, blame or understanding.

Without this knowledge I cannot decide on whether or not to operate. I do judge, however, that it cannot go ahead unless the donor is told the truth.

Judith E. Columbo

I feel that the parents are correct in their request that the kidney transplant be performed from one 8-year-old identical twin to another. It is a decision that all parties must take part in. To watch one child go through so much, when a twin could be a healthy alternative is enough to choose the right decision. I do not believe that misinformation about the no pain should be passed onto the donor son by the parents. The procedure can be explained in a child's terms. The discomfort he will experience should be told to the donor. It will be rectified when the recipient child improves over the course of time and they both can share life together.

Editor's Remarks 19

As a renal fellow, I found the saga of identical twin transplants exciting. The court decisions that transformed donor surgery from an assault to a magnanimous humane gesture were profound and exhilarating to read. Now, 50 years later, taking a kidney from a child is not the life or death decision it used to be. Peritoneal dialysis, hemodialysis, and cadaver donor kidney transplantation are available options. Furthermore, it may even be that a monozygotic kidney donor is less desirous because of susceptibility to the same disease that destroyed the twin's native kidneys. The original (Hart versus Brown1972) decision in Connecticut, that a kidney could be removed from a 7 year-old for transplant to a twin is troublesome evoking "bad vibes." Both Attorneys Zuckerman and London believe that further discussion with the potential donor child may ease anxiety and permit the surgery. Patient Columbo has no reservation while patient Mildred Barry Friedman proposes discussions to probe the sick twins deepest feelings before proceeding. Dr. Amy L. Friedman, listening to her "heart" would decline to remove a kidney from a child donor because of the personal trauma she would experience should the child die from "unneeded" surgery.

Having fathered three children, I would not consent to removing any vital organ from one for another. Yes, I am aware of the literature indicating that life with one kidney is no different than with two. I don't believe it. Somewhere down the line, the piper will have to be paid. Whether earlier hypertension, more rapid progression of diabetic nephropathy, or other consequences unforseen, the reason that evolution gave us two kidneys is that there is a survival advantage. Certainly, an adult has the right to trade that advantage for the welfare of another. I would immediately give a kidney to a sibling or a child. That does not mean that I countenance the imposition of painful surgery on a child. I don't.

Response to Study Questions

1. My answer is no. Others have no difficulty accepting parents as surrogates for their children in consenting to organ donation.

2. Here my conviction waivers. With parental consent, donating bone marrow in no way permanently injures the child though Freudians may point to the pain and trauma as formative factors in personality development. I would agree.
3. Even if parents and the court agrees, I would not perform organ extraction on a minor. In fairness, as carefully documented by London, there is legal and moral precedent for using children as donors.
4. In an era when a fast food restaurant can be sued for serving coffee that is too hot and municipalities lose judgments because their children's playgrounds have risky monkey bars, anyone can sue for any reason. As child versus parent suits continue to increase, it is almost a certainty that a minor organ donor will sue (and win) his/her parents for permitting the surgical *assault*.

Case 20

DONOR KIDNEY ALLOCATION TO HIGH RISK PATIENT

Following three successive rejections of cadaver donor transplanted kidneys, a 34 year old woman with end-stage renal disease caused by focal and segmental glomerular sclerosis is returned to maintenance hemodialysis. Review of the record of her transplants shows that they functioned sequentially for five months, three weeks, and four days - in each case, a return of massive proteinuria signaled that the original disease recurred in the transplanted kidney. Responding to the patient's request to "try again," the transplant surgeon vows to use his "influence" to get a repeat cadaver kidney. ***The collaborating nephrologist objects to throwing a good kidney after bad kidneys in a procedure destined to fail.***

Study Questions

1. Recognizing the greater likelihood of transplant failure, should a fourth kidney (from the cadaver pool) be allocated?
2. Can this reasoning be extended to a third kidney? A second kidney?
3. As a generalization, is the probability of failure a variable that should be included when determining kidney allograft allocation?

Monique Janelle London, J.D.

The 34-year old patient has had three kidney transplants, all of which failed. She now wishes to get another transplant. Her transplant surgeon has vowed to use his influence to get her another kidney. The nephrologist objects to offering the patient another kidney. This scenario raises several possible legal issues.

Legal Issues Regarding Transplant Surgeon's Proposed Action:

The transplant surgeon vowed to use his "influence" to get a repeat cadaver kidney for the patient. It is unclear what he means, but he probably will not face any legal liability for doing so. First, as a practical matter, the surgeon cannot unilaterally "get" a kidney for his patient. Kidneys only become available to the transplant center through the UNOS Organ Center, the centralized computer network that links all organ procurement organizations and transplant centers and matches available kidneys with listed patients.

To waitlist a patient with the Organ Center, the transplant hospital must provide detailed information about that patient. The computer system offers specifically matched kidneys to specific patients, based on factors including time accrued on the waitlist and information about blood type, antigen match (HLA mismatch), sensitization (PRA level), geographic location, size and age.

Typically, a transplant center will only list a patient with the Organ Center upon agreement among the transplant team or evaluation committee that the patient is a suitable candidate for a kidney transplant.Footnote 33 In addition to transplant surgeons, the transplant team may include nephrologists, social workers, transplant coordinators, nurses, tissue typing personnel, urologists, nutritionists, immunologists, psychiatrists and psychologists. As this writer understands it, the team typically formulates generalized criteria for waiting list placement, then determines on a case-by-case basis whether individual patients satisfy those criteria. As one member of the transplant team, the surgeon could try to "use his influence" by advocating that the patient be placed on the waitlist even if she does not meet the formulated criteria, or advocating that the existing criteria be modified so as to include this patient. There is nothing illegal about that. Whether the surgeon succeeds in getting the patient waitlisted will depend upon whether he can convince the rest of the transplant team that she should be given another chance at a transplant despite the fact that her last three transplants have rejected in short order.

Once the patient is waitlisted at the transplant center and with UNOS, she is subject to the same allocation rules as everyone else on the waitlist. The UNOS allocation system does not penalize patients for having had prior kidney transplants. On the contrary, if the patient has developed a large number of antibodies from her previous transplants, she may be so sensitized that she receives priority for the next transplant.Footnote 34
Moreover, under the current allocation system, the patient does not lose the waiting time she accrued prior to receiving the third transplant, since that transplant only lasted four days.Footnote 35

Thus, the only other way the surgeon could try to use his "influence" is to get a kidney for the patient sooner than she would ordinarily receive one from the national waitlist. If a kidney is offered to the transplant center for a different patient there, the surgeon could try to divert the kidney to his patient. However, given that she is probably highly sensitized from the last three transplants, it is unlikely that a kidney intended for another patient would be medically suitable for her. The surgeon might try other methods to influence or game the system to obtain a kidney more quickly for the patient. His actions might violate UNOS

[33] Various transplant centers may decide the waitlisting question by majority vote or consensus; some members of the transplant team may have veto power. As this writer understands it, however, whether a patient is listed requires some degree of agreement among the team.

[34] *See* UNOS Policy 3.5.9.3 Panel Reactive Antibody: "A patient will be assigned 4 points if he or she has panel reactive antibody (PRA) level of 80% or greater . . ."

[35] *See* UNOS Policy 3.2.3.2: Waiting Time Reinstatement for Kidney Recipient:

> In those instances where there is immediate and permanent non-function of a transplanted cadaveric or living donor kidney, the patient may be reinstated to the waiting list and retain the previously accumulated waiting time without interruption for that transplant only. For purposes of this policy, immediate and permanent non-function shall be defined as: * * * (2) kidney graft failure from hyperacute rejection in the presence of a current negative crossmatch or non-immunologic causes resulting in removal of the organ within the first two weeks of transplant, or (3) kidney graft failure from non-immunologic causes within the first two weeks of transplant followed by continuous non-function of the organ for three months evidenced by maintenance of the patient on dialysis for the three month period.

policy, but they would not carry legal consequences unless they constituted a separate tort or crime such as fraud, deceit or theft.[Footnote 36]

Legal Issues Regarding Nephrologist's Proposed Action:

The nephrologist objects to the patient getting another kidney transplant, because he believes the procedure is destined to fail. Again, objecting to the patient being allowed to stay on the transplant center's waitlist is not illegal. The transplant team will have to decide, now that the third transplant has failed, whether the patient is an appropriate candidate to be listed for a fourth transplant. The nephrologist is free to argue that the patient should not be listed again.

However, if the nephrologist's argument is successful and the transplant team decides not to waitlist the patient, several legal issues may arise.

Failure to Obtain Informed Consent/Futility:

First, the patient could assert that the transplant center is refusing to provide the "treatment" of waitlisting her (and/or transplanting her), even though she has not "consented" to "discontinue" that "treatment." This writer is not aware of any caselaw discussing whether refusal to waitlist a patient can constitute discontinuation of treatment. If a court did consider such an argument, the hospital could assert the futility doctrine in defense. As noted previously, in many states a physician (or hospital) may refuse to provide treatment which in her best professional judgment would be "futile," "medically inappropriate," "useless" or "unwarranted." *See, e.g., Causey v. St. Francis Medical Center,* 719 So. 2d 1072, 1075 (La. Ct. App. 2d Cir. 1998). It seems clear from the facts presented that a fourth transplant would be futile or useless: the patient would simply reject the kidney after a very short time, and the transplant would serve no benefit.[Footnote 37]

Discrimination:

The patient could also argue that she is being discriminated against based on her "disability" of having focal and segmental glomerular sclerosis (which continues to destroy her kidneys). Disability discrimination in violation of the ADA and the 1973 Rehabilitation Act was discussed in connection with Case 2. The ADA prohibits discrimination based on "disability," which is defined to include any "physiological disorder or condition, cosmetic disfigurement, or anatomical loss affecting one or more... body systems." *See* 42 U.S.C. §§ 12181(7)(F), 12182(a), 28 C.F.R. § 35.104. Section 504 of the 1973 Rehabilitation Act, 29 U.S.C.A. § 794(a),

---

[36] UNOS policies set forth the organ allocation rules, but these rules do not carry the force of law. Theoretically, a transplant center can be denied Medicare and Medicaid reimbursement if it does not comply with the UNOS policies and rules, but this penalty has never yet been imposed on a center.

[37] The wording of the Case suggests that the third transplant failed only recently. On the other hand, if it is now ten years after the third transplant, immunosuppression may have advanced to the stage that a transplant for this patient now has a better chance of being successful for a longer time.

provides: "No otherwise qualified individual with a disability . . . shall, solely by reason of his or her disability, be excluded from the participation in, be denied the benefits of, or be subjected to discrimination under any program or activity receiving Federal financial assistance . . . ." The patient could argue that she is being denied waitlisting solely because of her sclerosis.

However, this argument is unlikely to succeed. The ADA does allow hospitals to engage in traditional risk classification practices. 42 U.S.C. § 12201(c)(1). Denying a patient the ability to waitlist due to sickness the compromises her ability to benefit from a transplant could be justified by such practices. Also, the ADA permits the use of eligibility criteria that are necessary for the operation of the program. 42 U.S.C. § 12182(b)(2)(A)(i). Such criteria could include criteria designed to allocate kidneys where they will do the most good.

Also, as previously noted, one court suggested that cases in which the denied treatment is related to the patient's need for treatment should be immune from judicial scrutiny. *See United States v. University Hospital*, 729 F.2d 144, 156 (2d Cir. 1984). If the *University Hospital* decision were applied to Case 20, the hospital and nephrologist would not be liable for refusing to waitlist and/or transplant a patient with kidney-attacking glomerular sclerosis, since that decision would be directly related to - indeed, based on -- the patient's condition. The apparent justification for this rule is that the denial of treatment is not discrimination against one patient out of many similarly situated. Rather, this patient has a particular condition that makes her *not* similarly situated to patients who are transplant candidates.[Footnote 38] In short, the nephrologist probably will not face liability for discrimination.

Abandonment

The patient might also try to claim that the nephrologist has "abandoned" her by refusing to waitlist her. However, as noted previously, a physician has the right to sever his relationship with a patient, as long as he provides the patient reasonable notice of the severance and gives the patient a chance to find another physician. *See, e.g., Manno v. McIntosh*, 519 N.W. 2d 815 (Iowa Ct. App. 1994). The abandonment doctrine does not seem applicable here, as the requirements to avoid it are met simply by virtue of the situation. There is no indication of urgency in the Case; apparently the patient can remain on maintenance hemodialysis indefinitely until she is able to get another transplant. Thus, the nephrologist could notify the patient that the transplant team intends not to waitlist her, and she would then have ample time to try to find another transplant center that would list her. An abandonment claim thus would fail.

In sum, it seems unlikely that the surgeon or nephrologist (or hospital) would be found legally liable for their actions in this Case. Each member of the transplant team is entitled to a position on whether the patient should be a candidate for transplantation. Neither the individual decisions nor the decision of the

[38] Of course, if the hospital did waitlist other patients with kidney-attacking glomerular sclerosis, the discrimination argument would probably survive, since the hospital would be singling out one patient from among a group of similarly situated patients.

team as a whole have historically been subjected to judicial scrutiny. It would be very difficult as a practical matter to circumvent the UNOS allocation system to gain special treatment for the patient, especially given that the patient is probably highly sensitized and could only receive certain kidneys. The Case does not provide any reason to suspect discrimination or other improper motives for the nephrologist to oppose another transplant. All in all, the potential for legal liability is negligible.

Ethical Analysis:

Although legally simple, this Case poses a difficult ethical question: Should a patient be given the chance to receive a fourth kidney, when her body has already rejected the first three, and many other patients have not yet even received one kidney?

On the one hand, the patient is only 34 years old - relatively young to be on dialysis. Unlike with a 70-year old who is suffering complications of kidney failure and general old age, this patient has the chance to significantly improve her health and live for many more years with a successful transplant. Moreover, unlike a noncompliant patient, this patient has not caused her transplanted kidneys to fail by her behavior. The kidneys have failed due to no fault of the patient, but because her disease has attacked the transplanted kidneys. Thus, she has done nothing to make her undeserving of another chance.

On the other hand, the fact that the patient has already rejected three kidneys indicates that it is highly unlikely that a transplant would be successful for even a short period of time.[Footnote 39] Thus, a 70-year old might gain 10 years of relatively improved health from a kidney transplant, whereas the 34-year old patient might gain nothing. Particularly if the patient is doing well on dialysis, it seems unethical to let her keep "wasting" kidneys that have a much higher chance of benefiting other patients (who might need a transplant more urgently to preserve their lives or health).

Additionally, the facts do not state whether the patient has other health problems besides ESRD and focal and glomerular sclerosis. Even with a successful transplant, she might still be so ill that the transplant would not improve the

[39] However, it is unclear from the facts presented how significant it is that the patient already rejected three kidneys. The Case states that the patient suffered three "successive rejections" of cadaveric kidneys, suggesting that they all occurred over the course of a short period - perhaps a few years. However, it may be that the patient received her first transplant when she was 17, another when she was 20 and the third when she was 24. Immunosuppression has improved greatly over the last ten years, and continues to improve. New drugs are being approved each year. Thus, the patient may have a much better chance of being transplanted successfully now than she had with her third transplant. Moreover, even if the chances of success are slim now, they may be much improved by the time the patient is actually offered another kidney. Given that waiting times have been increasing steadily, and given that the patient is probably highly sensitized, she may have to wait five years or more before she gets another chance at a transplant. By then, she may have a much greater chance at success. If the "destined to fail" element is removed from the equation, it seems much more clearly ethical to waitlist the patient for a fourth attempt.

quality of her health or life. If so, it would be unethical to give her another kidney at the expense of patients who could actually benefit from a transplant. However, if the patient is so sick that she needs a transplant to live, it would be unethical to deny her this chance to save her life. But, offering her a fourth kidney to save her life would be unfair to the other patients who need a kidney to save their lives, but have not yet even received one (or two, or three).
On balance, this writer believes it would be ethical to waitlist the patient for a fourth transplant. Odds are, she is so sensitized that she will have to wait for several years before a suitable kidney becomes available. By then, immunosuppression may have advanced to the point that the graft has a better chance of survival. If not, her nephrologist could discuss this with her and advise that she turn down the offer and continue waiting until her chances of success improve. Assuming the patient has no other major health problems, she is too young to be denied any further opportunities to have a successful transplant.

Connie Zuckerman, J.D.

This case once again raises the issue of equity and fairness in the distribution of an admittedly scarce resource. Because of the nature of her disease, this patient has received three donor organs, with resulting failure in each case. Given the overwhelming likelihood of another failure if transplant is tried again, is it a good use of a scarce resource to once again procure an organ for this patient, and would such use of the resource be fair to others who have yet to receive even one chance at a donated organ?

When distributing a scarce resource, it is appropriate to consider the likelihood and duration of the benefit to be derived by the potential recipient. Given the overwhelming likelihood of almost immediate failure, it is very questionable whether this patient should even resume a place on the list, despite the urgency of her situation. Moreover, it appears that the expectations of both the patient and the transplant surgeon may be out of line with the possibility of any further intervention to benefit this patient. At this point, it would be ethically and legally obligatory upon the patient's physician to realistically assess her circumstances and the range of options available. The likelihood of renewed failure, even with another transplant, necessitates a frank discussion between patient and physician concerning end-of-life decisions to be made.

Amy L. Friedman, M.D.

While a significant shortage of cadaver organs continues, transplant programs are in the unenviable position of performing two simultaneous and often competing roles. As this transplant candidate's advocate, the personal risk benefit ratio of transplantation must be considered. In the setting of repeated and increasingly earlier recurrence of disease leading to failure of all prior engrafted kidneys, there is virtually no likelihood of prolonged graft survival unless a novel approach or different immunosuppressive regimen is available. A literature search and survey of major transplant centers should be undertaken to identify the most current approaches. If a promising strategy, or even an entirely experimental protocol is identified, it should be considered. If not, there does not seem to be any real chance of benefit for her. On the other hand, technical accomplishment of sequential kidney transplantation becomes more challenging with each procedure as sites for vascular and urologic connections become scarred and progressively limited. The operative risk of any renal transplant is real (usually lower than 2-3% mortality) and must not be ignored, but a fourth transplant must be considered even more high risk. Additionally, exposure of the patient's immune system to each new kidney risks the development of antibodies that will preclude a future transplant opportunity. This phenomenon, termed sensitization, is likely to have already occurred to some extent from her three prior transplants. Thus, even if a compatible kidney could be identified, without a significant advance in our ability to prevent recurrence of her primary disease (that has not occurred at the time of this writing) transplantation would afford no significant chance of benefit and very real risk to this patient. Retransplantation under these conditions should not be offered.

As guardian of society's limited organ resources, the transplant team is also responsible to some extent for prioritizing the use of available kidneys. If the risk of transplantation for a specific patient is high, but the benefit unequivocal (as in the case of an elderly patient whose coronary artery and vascular disease make ongoing hemodialysis inadequate, whose peritoneum does not deliver effective dialysis and whose operative risk of suffering a perioperative heart attack is significant), it is still sometimes inappropriate to proceed with transplantation. Use of an organ for one patient deprives another of the chance to benefit. While a reasonable balance between these two roles is often difficult to achieve, the arbiter must continue to be the team directly familiar with the patient. For this reason transplant centers function with a multidisciplinary team composition. Neither the surgeon, nor the nephrologist should be permitted to make an independent decision. When disagreement occurs, team members must collectively determine the most suitable outcome. This approach functions to effectively enforce synthesis of the medical, surgical and ethical issues. It also serves to personally protect team members from shouldering the burden of making these god-like decisions. To do otherwise and permit government, payors or any other third party to usurp this role would dehumanize this process inappropriately.

It should also be noted that even if the transplant surgeon intended to "use his influence" to obtain a kidney, the only available organs would be those declined for use from within the legitimate system. Thus, an organ with excessively long ischemic time (the period of time during which the organ is preserved in ice and has no blood flow, usually limited to a maximum of 32-40 hours) and a significantly diminished chance of ever functioning, or from a donor with excessive risk for the transmission of infectious disease (e.g., from a promiscuous donor whose sexual contacts were unavailable for interview by procurement coordinators) might be available. Further increasing the technical and immunologic risk to this patient through use of such a "marginal" organ would be unjustifiable.

Carl M. Kjellstrand, M.D.

The nephrologist is right. Kidney transplants to patients with focal sclerosis have a high recurrence rate. Similarly kidney transplants into patients who quickly lost a prior transplant from rejection (within a year) are again quickly rejected. It is useless and futile to do a 4th transplant in this situation. It is a waste of scarce resource, it is dangerous to the patient, it is malpractice. Sit down with the transplant surgeon, they can be persuaded by facts.

Mildred (Barry) Friedman

I am opposed to using a cadaver organ to re-, re-, re-transplant any patient. Such use of an organ affords the donor's family neither satisfaction nor pride in their decision to give parts of their loved one to save the life of another person. Donation is called "The Gift of Life". Under these circumstances, it is not.
My heart goes out to the terminally ill woman but her sickness is no one's fault. Unfortunate as it is, she must live or die with what has happened to her. If an endless supply or organs existed, I would say: "Yes, try, try, try again.
The nephrologist has made a wise decision. The transplant surgeon has not.

Judith E. Columbo

I feel that this patient, having received three kidney transplants and rejecting all three because of a pre-existing condition is enough. True the surgical team might have the influence to gain another cadaver kidney, but I agree with the nephrologist, not to transplant for a fourth time on a procedure destined to fail. I strongly believe that the kidney should be offered to a less fragile patient who may have been on the transplant list for a long period of time.

Editor's Remarks20

No legal basis supports my view that a fourth kidney would be wasted in this patient. Dr. Kjellstrand terms the contemplated transplant "useless." How he reaches the conclusion that such a transplant would be "malpractice" eludes my understanding. Patient Mildred Barry Friedman opposes retransplantation on the grounds of organ shortage and Patient Columbo agrees. It may be unfair to expect attorneys to grasp the despair that surrounds repetitive disease recurrence in successive transplants. Thus, Zuckerman sides with the surgeon wanting to perform the fourth transplant because the patient is "too young to be denied," while London after suffering through the pros and cons would waitlist the patient for a fourth transplant noting that she may be too sensitized to accept the organ when she is considered. I guessed wrong in anticipating the judgment of Dr. Amy L. Friedman who would decline a fourth kidney transplant. My perception of intrepid surgeons is that they often are resistant to the pragmatic forces that constrain the rest of us.

I do not reach the intensity of Kjellstrand's negativism though I would strongly side with the nephrologist believing the chances of success for a fourth transplant to be minimal. Complicating my decision is the personal knowledge of a patient in whom the fourth transplant functioned for a decade. Probability, however, lies with the projection that the repeat transplant is doomed from the start.

Response to Study Questions

1. No. I would advise against the nearly certain waste of a limited resource, a cadaver kidney. This decision is now shaky in lieu of Zuckerman and London's legal analysis that waitlisting is both legal and ethical. Were a potential multiple graft recipient to be excluded, I can envision the trial and surrounding media field day when the tabloid press learns that a transplant nephrologist decrees that the requested retransplant not be done.
2. Few data detail the fate of multiple renal grafts. Our program probably would not agree to further surgery though I presently manage two patients with third transplants that have been successful.
3. Absent reliable statistics, any decision about retransplantation is a guess based on impression. For the present, UNOS does not include negative points for prior allograft loss. I would assign a third or fourth transplant only should a cadaver kidney be available in the absence of suitable recipients of a first transplant. This makes sense for distributing a scarce resource.

Case 21

POLITICIAN'S PRIORITY FOR CADAVER DONOR KIDNEYS

A 73 year old state governor, a heavy drinker for 40 years, developed advanced nutritional cirrhosis of the liver, pancreatic cystic disease, and chronic renal failure of undetermined cause. During his initial hospitalization, the patient receives a call of encouragement from the President of the United States. After checking "matches," the director of the transplant program announces that the governor will receive a combined liver and kidney transplant. As media representatives gather in the hospital's conference room, the chief transplant surgeon explains the intended operations to the television news audience, using anatomical charts. A reporter for a conservative magazine asks ***how is it possible for an old man to receive organs while young people continue on an indefinite waiting list?***

Study Questions

1. Although avidly denied, do you believe that important people get kidneys (livers, hearts) faster than ordinary individuals?
2. Should they?
3. If the President of the United States needed a kidney transplant, should the organ be given with a higher than usual priority?

Monique Janelle London, J.D.

This Case does not present any legal issues. It is both possible and legal under the current UNOS allocation system for a 73 year old to get a liver and kidney transplant while young people continue on the waitlist. Individual transplant centers have broad discretion to set their own criteria for whether a person can be waitlisted on the national transplant list. A history of alcohol abuse alone will not generally preclude a patient from ever becoming a transplant candidate. Most centers will allow an alcoholic patient to be waitlisted if the patient can that the problem is under control. For instance, a showing of sobriety for some minimum period, active participation in a treatment program, and a negative blood alcohol test would be sufficient to waitlist the patient at some transplant centers. If the patient's status is sufficiently urgent and a match becomes available, the transplant can occur shortly after the patient is waitlisted. There is no indication from the facts given that any law has been broken.

Ethical Analysis:

Various ethical questions are raised by this Case. Is it ethical to give a liver and kidney to a 73-year old, when young people are waiting for a transplant and may die without one? Is it ethical to give the governor a kidney along with the liver, when other patients have been waiting longer for a kidney alone? Is it ethical to give a liver to an alcoholic patient who has caused or exacerbated his liver failure, when non-alcoholic patients are also waiting for a liver? Each of these questions highlights the difficult balance between fairness and utility in allocation of a scarce, life-saving resource.

Age/Kidney + Liver: From a utility perspective, one issue is whether the liver/kidney transplant has the same potential for benefit in a 73-year old as in a younger person, in terms of graft and patient survival. On the one hand, the 73-year old is quite ill. He has cirrhosis, pancreatic cystic disease, and chronic renal failure. He is hospitalized. His condition may indicate that he will die soon regardless of whether he gets the kidney/liver transplant. On the other hand, these days many people are living well into their 90s. Thus, if his health is improved by the transplant, the patient could live another twenty years. Of course, an otherwise healthy young person has the potential to live for many more years than twenty. However, if a young person has other health problems and complications, a kidney/liver transplant might not significantly improve her chances for survival. This writer is not aware of any statistical evidence that livers do not last as long in alcoholics as in non-alcoholics. Additionally, the graft may have a better chance of survival if a liver and kidney are transplanted at the same time from the same donor. The facts give no other indication that the chance of graft survival would be different for the subject patient and a younger patient. In sum, there is no clear basis for concluding that the kidney/liver transplant would have more utility for a young person than for the governor.

From a fairness perspective, the issue is whether it is fair to offer the kidney and liver to a 73-year old when younger people are waiting. Assuming the patient was offered the transplant under the UNOS allocation system, he was offered it because he is the patient with the most urgent need for the transplant in his area, who also had sufficient matching characteristics with the organs. Younger patients should be, and generally are, given priority for transplants. However, if the governor is the person in most urgent need of the transplant, it is fair for him to receive it ahead of others. On the other hand, if there are other people on the waitlist who are suitable candidates for the liver and need it more urgently, the liver should be offered to those patients first.

Ordinarily, kidneys are offered first to patients who have been waiting the longest (assuming they are otherwise suitable candidates). Thus it may be unfair to offer the kidney to the governor over a patient on the waitlist who has been waiting much longer for a kidney transplant. However, the utility of transplanting a kidney and liver together in a patient who urgently needs a liver to live may outweigh the fairness of offering the kidney separately to a patient who has been waiting longer, but can continue to live on dialysis.

Alcoholism: The governor was a heavy drinker for 40 years.[Footnote 40] The Case suggests that his alcohol use caused cirrhosis of the liver and necessitated the liver transplant. Thus, another issue is whether it is ethical to give the governor a liver/kidney transplant when other patients are waiting for livers who did not cause their liver failure by abusing alcohol.

From a utility perspective, the answer depends on whether the governor will continue drinking heavily after the transplant. It is unclear from the facts pre-

[40] This writer assumes the governor was an alcoholic during that period.

sented whether and when the governor stopped drinking heavily. He may have quit drinking years ago, or he may still be alcoholic. If he has quit drinking, the utility of the kidney/liver transplant will not be compromised. As this writer understands it, no connection has been established between past alcohol abuse and liver or kidney graft survival. All else being equal and assuming no future alcohol abuse, the chance of graft survival would be the same for the governor as for a non-alcoholic patient. Thus it would be ethical for him to receive the transplant.

On the other hand, if the governor has never quit drinking, he might drink after the transplant and cause the cirrhosis to return and damage the transplanted liver. He should not be given the transplant if there is a significant risk he will waste the liver. It should be up to the governor to show that he will not abuse alcohol after the transplant. However, this may be difficult given the apparent imminence of the transplant. The governor probably will not have a period of months to prove he can stop drinking. In his case, it might suffice for him to promise publicly to stop drinking. Hopefully, his status as a public figure (and constant monitoring by the press and media) would ensure that he would keep that promise. If the governor can make a sufficient showing that he will not continue drinking after the transplant, it will still serve utility to transplant him.

From a fairness perspective, it seems unethical for the governor to get a liver transplant ahead of others who did not cause their liver failure by abusing alcohol. The governor drank heavily for 40 years. During his tenure as governor, he was probably exposed to a variety of issues surrounding alcohol abuse. He must have been sufficiently educated about drinking to know that so much drinking could damage his liver. This writer assumes that the governor voluntarily brought about his illness by his own intentional behavior.[Footnote 41] For that reason, he does not deserve to get a liver ahead of other patients who did not cause their illness. Thus, if a non-alcoholic patient on the waitlist needs a liver as urgently as the governor (and is an equally suitable candidate), that person should get the liver rather than the governor. However, if the governor has the more urgent need, he should still be given the transplant ahead of a non-alcoholic patient. It is more important to be fair in the matter of urgency of need - which has life and death consequences - than it is to be fair in the matter of rewarding and punishing past behavior.

In sum, if the governor is the transplant candidate most urgently in need of the liver, it is ethical to give it to him even if there are other, equally suitable candidates who need the liver less urgently. If the liver/kidney combination has a better chance of success than a liver transplant alone, it is ethical for the governor to receive both organs. However, if other suitable, non-alcoholic candidates on the waitlist need the liver with equal or more urgency than the governor, those candidates should receive the liver instead of the governor.

[41] However, many in the medical field would take a different position. They would contend that alcoholism is a disease, and an alcoholic is unable to control his drinking. If alcoholism were viewed as a disease on par with other diseases that cause liver failure (such that the patient did not cause the liver failure through voluntary behavior), then it would seem fair for the governor to receive a liver transplant ahead of other suitable candidates whose livers failed due to other diseases.

Connie Zuckerman, J.D.

As in the case of continuous retransplants, so, too, does this case raise the question of equity and fairness in organ distribution. That is, is it fair that one individual receive two donor organs while thousands of others await their opportunity to receive a single organ for lifesaving purposes? Moreover, given the possible connection between this potential recipient's history of heavy drinking and his deteriorated current condition, the question of fairness reemerges: Should he in some way receive less priority on the queue than those who in no way contributed to their illness? Finally, his celebrity status appears to have allowed him to jump the wait list, a patently unfair result to the thousands of others who must patiently wait in the hopes of surviving until their turn is called.

While legitimate debate can be had whether two donor organs should go to one recipient when the possibility exists to instead save two individuals, the more difficult aspect of this case concerns the governor's "contribution" to his current situation. While some would argue that alcoholism is a disease for which individuals cannot be held accountable, and, further, that one cannot always be certain of the connection between previous behavior and current illness, others may view his drinking history with at least some taint of moral failing, and justify its inclusion as a criteria to disqualify him as a potential recipient. This debate raises the more fundamental questions as to the justification to include "non-medical" factors as part of the distribution criteria. The fact that clout and connection, however, appear to have elevated this candidate to the top of the list may work to the deteriment of the overall procurement program, which continously struggles with the public's concern about an equitable system in its attempt to recruit potential organ donors.

Finally, in this country, age in and of itself does not automatically disqualify a potential organ recipient from access to the wait list. The fact that this potential recipient is 73 years old would not negate his potential consideration as a candidate. What should instead be considered is his personal medical situation, including such factors as the likelihood and duration of the benefit to be achieved, the improvement in the patient's quality of life and the urgency of the patient's condition.

Amy L. Friedman, M.D.

This case involves an individual some might consider to have relatively high worth to society. He is also old and has participated in causing his own disease. Whether his life should be considered constructive or destructive is open to interpretation. For example, this apparently successful politician must by definition, have excelled in the practice of politics. Many would assume such an individual is skilled at lying and hiding his own flaws and thoughts. He has probably put his own self interest above those of his family. The typical politician might thus be considered a prime example of the evil in humanity. Perhaps he would be assigned a relatively low score on a scale of integrity. Yet, serving as a leader to others and making judgements (whether right or wrong) which move his state forward certainly demands a profound personal commitment and dedication unequaled in most roles. Just as this politician might be viewed as an idol or a representative of the devil by some, so might the weaknesses of each transplant candidate be open to subjective judgement. Consideration of the individual's value to society, therefore, must not be included in assessment of his(her) right or priority for organ allocation. For this reason allocation do not incorporate patient "worth" or merit in any manner.

This case also raises the important issue of whether or not youth with the accompanying likelihood of prolonged survival of both patient and organ is an appropriate factor upon which to base organ allocation. In fact, age discrimination is illegal in the United States. Yet it is clear that as age rises, the likelihood of significant, co-morbid medical conditions also climbs. Thus, for example a 65-year-old is far more likely to have significant coronary artery disease than a 25-year-old. We all have encountered, however, 35 year old individuals who seem far older than their chronologic age. Thus, one might anticipate that the best host for a specific organ would be youthful. Paradoxically, however, the very youth and vigor of that host's immune system makes acute rejection more likely than in an individual whose immune response has aged. While most would argue that the greatest likelihood of long-term graft survival undoubtedly lies with a young versus. an old recipient, individual outcomes can never be predicted. For this reason, careful consideration of each transplant candidate's physiologic age is made by the transplant team and the patient himself (herself). If the decision is reached that transplantation remains desirable, than age should not be factored in to the allocation of organs to adult candidates. The unique exception should continue to be the appropriate, positive weighting of organ allocation for pediatric recipients. This current bias has been widely agreed on because of the developmental delays such as growth failure, which result from organ failure and cannot be reversed later in life even with successful transplantation.

Although few details are available from this patient's description, the issue of substance abuse is an important one. Since ongoing alcohol use in an alcoholic often leads to non-compliance with medications and other medical advice, it is generally agreed on as an absolute contraindication to organ transplantations. To maximize the likelihood of successful transplantation from the psychosocial perspective, the governor should be fully accepting of the role of alcohol in causing his disease. He should be fully abstinent from its use for six months prior to transplantation and must be willing to make a full commitment to lifelong abstinence. Unless he stopped drinking long before this acute hospitalization, ongoing alcohol use must be considered an absolute contraindication to active transplantation.

Finally comes the important discussion of whether an individual surgeon or transplant program is able to simply bypass the national allocation system. Certainly, there is no security mechanism that functions in the middle of the night to physically guard the organs that rest in the ice coolers in operating rooms. Although the individual surgeon might actually perform a transplant operation using organs which should by all rights have been allocated to a different recipient, such an action cannot occur without notice. The transplant would be immediately recognized as having occurred outside of the nationally active transplant network with immediate and public censure of the transplant program involved. Means of addressing such abhorrent behavior, albeit bureaucratic, would have profound consequences for the future activities of that surgeon and transplant center.

In summary, while a 73-year-old individual with alcohol induced liver and kidney failure might ultimately be considered a suitable candidate for combined liver and kidney transplantation. Organ allocation must depend on compliance with six months of abstinence associated with predictors of long term abstinence, and organ allocation according to the nationally generated, computerized list which does not include celebrities or patient merit as a weighting factor.

Carl M. Kjellstrand, M.D.

The reporter is right. Organs are scarce and a common national good. "The bastards in Washington now not only take our money and squander it, now their physicians (the dogs in "Animal Farm") are taking our organs too. I am damned if I am going to fill out a donation card". Organs should strictly go to those where they will last the longest. A 73 year old man in USA, even without being on immunosuppression, has a life expectancy of only 9 years. A 30 year old can expect to live 44 years. This exact scenario was played out in Canada where a 72 year old politically influential columnist received a heart transplant from a surgeon who was also an appointed senator. Till then, the oldest heart transplant recipient in Canada was 62 years. The cadaver transplant rate in Canada is constantly falling. The estimate in which physicians are held is also constantly falling in the USA. The public more and more, I believe, regard physicians as the whores of the rich, powerful and brutal. We are reaping the dragon's harvest of sowing such dragon's teeth.

Mildred (Barry) Friedman

Lacking in the summary of Case 21 is information concerning the prognosis of the patient. Organs are normally allocated on a point system which takes into account age and prognosis among other things. There is no reason for this man to be treated differently from other potential recipients. If the usual procedure was followed, arguments about favoritism would be negated.
He is not special. Even if *he* were the president no valid reason for placing him first on the list would exist. Indeed, a sick president, recovering from major surgery, might well be expected to resign. Our ill state governor should keep the well-being of his state in mind and leave his post with or without surgery.
The reporter's question is a good one and deserves an answer.

Judith E. Columbo

In this case it is possible for an old man who happens to be a state governor to receive an organ transplant while young people wait an indefinite time on a transplant list. I doubt whether a 73-year-old average man would be considered for a liver and kidney transplant. Age is a factor that should be considered and the governor 40-year drinking problem did not help. I believe the magazine reporter is asking a reasonable question. A question he will not get a reasonable answer because unfortunately, who you know is more important than what you know

---

Editor's Remarks21

George Orwell in "Animal Farm" commented that "some animals are more equal than others."[Endnote 38] His prescient projections of a "Big Brother" world in 1984 though not as yet confirmed contain sufficient truth to be bothersome. My own observation leaves no doubt that the famous and wealthy receive a different class of medicine than the poor. It may not be better. Hitler's doctor made him a drug addict as was also the case for Elvis Presley. Transplant surgeons speak of "gaming the system" as a means to beat the strict order of UNOS allocation of organs. As an example, individuals with sufficient funds to travel widely can gain listing in multiple transplant regions thereby increasing their chance of being selected somewhere. The poor cannot compete.

Alcoholism as a cause of liver failure does not preclude acceptance for a liver transplant[Endnote 39] providing that there has been abstinence from alcohol for varying times - usually six months. Validation of this policy is provided by the fully satisfactory graft and patient survival for at least three years.[Endnote 40] The Governor in this case, however, presumably continued his substance abuse through the destruction of his liver and kidney. Lacking evidence of personal redemption, the Governor should not receive either a liver or kidney. But, the President called focusing the spotlight is on the transplant team and their hospital for front page attention. As a concsequence, the transplant will be performed, for the wrong reason.

Age, per se, is not a valid concern in organ allocation according to Glover and Moss: "Rationing according to social worth, ability to pay, or age is not ethically justifiable."[Endnote 41] Obviously, medical benefit, and the duration of extended life, from a kidney transplant is greater for a thirty-year old than a ninety-year old, all other factors being equivalent? Nevertheless, Nilstun and Ohlsson suffer the question: "Health care rationing by age is inconsistent with the principles of equality and liberty. But in some situations such rationing has support from the principles of solidarity and efficiency. The compromise suggested is that, as a rule, rationing by age should not be permitted, except in situations with intrinsic scarcity (as is the case with transplantation) and in situations with temporary extrinsic scarcity (as was the case with dialysis for a period of time)."[Endnote 42] This mumbo jumbo would provide an orthodox rabbi with sufficient substrate for weeks of interpretation.

Intrepid surgeons have performed kidney transplants in recipients in their eighth decade, but consensus thinking holds that a high mortality and aggravated morbidity accompany the stress of surgery and immunosuppression in those older than 60 years.[Endnote 43, Endnote 44] In my view, cadaveric renal transplantation in the elderly requires careful selection, excluding serious cardiovascular disease while giving truthful counseling as to the greater risk of death - approximately one-third of recipients likely to die within three years. As a generalization, I advise that kidney transplantation using the common pool of cadaver kidneys not be applied in recipients older than 60 years. Establishing an upper age limit for initiating dialytic therapy is less supportable by outcome-based trials though few individuals older than 80 will achieve even marginal rehabilitation.

Response to Study Questions

1. Without question, in my mind, politicians, actors, high ranking clergy, and sports figures jump the queue getting a faster turn at cadaver organs than do the rest of us. To support this allegation is nearly impossible though I have watched it happen repeatedly.
2. In the real world, the Pope ranks higher as a person than does a prisoner and would get an organ transplant in an eye blink. No this should not be so but neither is there justice in starvation in Russia or Chad but it happens daily.
3. For a US President, there would be so many "emotionally related donors" that resort to a cadaver kidney would be unnecessary. If the President was judged a candidate for a heart transplant, a way would be designed to prioritize an organ immediately. That is the way the world turns though it should not.

Case 22

CADAVER DONOR KIDNEY FOR NON-COMPLIANT DIALYSIS PATIENT

A 32 year old postman had progressive diabetic nephropathy due to insulin-dependent (type 1) diabetes with onset at the age of 17 years, disrupting the patient's plans for a career in professional football. Despite counseling at school, the patient followed a consistent pattern of minimal compliance with his medical regimen. He had two or more episodes of ketoacidosis per year for the past decade but failed to perform finger stick blood glucose tests. Although he sustained a "minor stroke" due to uncontrolled hypertension, the patient rarely took antihypertensive or diuretic medications. He is blind in the right eye because of retinal hemorrhages but missed several recent appointments for laser surgery of the left eye - a vital step to preserve vision. While the right great toe has been amputated because of an nonhealing ulcer, the patient has not accepted a prescription for orthopedically correct "old ladies" shoes. Currently, the patient is consistently late for hemodialysis appointments, gains more than five kgs between treatments because of dietary indiscretion, and does not test his blood glucose level. Requesting a place on the transplant recipient list, the patient states that should he be given a new kidney, "I will try to do what the doctors say." In the opinion of the patient's nephrologist, ***a kidney transplant for this patient is a wasted organ, a past pattern of noncompliance is sufficient to presume future noncompliance.***

Study Questions

1. Is noncompliance with a dialysis regimen reason to presume noncompliance with a proposed kidney transplant?
2. How can the patient's vow to adhere to a transplant regimen be accepted or denied before the fact?
3. Should speculated noncompliance be sufficient reason to exclude individuals from a possible organ transplant?

Monique Janelle London, J.D.

This Case does not appear to raise any sustainable legal claims. First, it does not lend itself to a claim of lack of informed consent. Like in Case 20, here the patient could try to assert that the nephrologist is "withholding" the patient's "treatment" of waitlisting him for a transplant without the patient's consent. However, the act of waitlisting a patient for transplant is not a "treatment" requiring a patient's consent to administer or withhold. Rather, nephrologists and other members of the transplant team or evaluation committee generally have broad discretion (usually limited only by criteria they develop themselves) to evaluate whether the patient is a suitable candidate for transplantation. Transplant teams generally screen for candidates who are likely to lose their

grafts due to noncompliance as part of their standard evaluation.[Footnote 42] Thus, on the facts given, a decision not to waitlist the patient would be well within the nephrologist's discretion. There is no consent issue.
Nor would the patient be able to maintain a claim for discrimination under the Americans With Disabilities Act or the Rehabilitation Act. The nephrologist's opposition to waitlisting the patient is unrelated to any disability the patient may have. Rather, the opposition is based on the patient's past pattern of non-compliance with his medical regimen, which does not appear to stem from any disability.[Footnote 43]

In short, the nephrologist is unlikely to suffer any legal consequences for objecting to listing or refusing to list the patient for a kidney transplant.

Ethical Analysis:

The ethical analysis is more complicated. The primary relevant inquiry, in this writer's view, is a utilitarian one: whether the patient's past behavior is a sufficiently reliable indicator that he will engage in future behavior that will significantly increase the risk of rejecting a transplanted kidney. For instance, if the patient's past behavior were a 100% guarantee of noncompliance with the post-transplant regimen, and that noncompliance were a 100% guarantee of graft rejection, it would be ethical to deny the patient a place on the kidney transplant waitlist. Kidneys are a scarce lifesaving resource that should only be allocated where they have at least a certain threshold chance of success. Regardless of what this threshold is, a zero percent chance of success does not meet it. On the other hand, if the patient's past noncompliance has *no* bearing on whether he will comply with the post-transplant regimen, he should not be denied a place on the waitlist due to past noncompliance.

Utility:

For the reasons that follow, this writer believes that the significance of the patient's past behavior is somewhere in between a guarantee of future non-compliance and irrelevant to future noncompliance. That is, the patient's past behavior does increase the risk, but does not merit the presumption, of non-compliance post-transplant.

First, the patient may not understand that his behavior has had a detrimental effect on his health. For instance, he may not know that finger stick blood glu-

---

[42] A 1991 survey of kidney transplant centers across the country disclosed that the vast majority considered compliance issues in evaluating whether a patient should be wait-listed for a transplant. *See* Eleanor L. Ramos et al., The Evaluation of Candidates for Renal Transplantation: The Current Practice of U.S. Transplant Centers, 57 Transplantation 490, 490 (1994). Eighty-three percent of the centers responding stated that they consider the patient's attendance at dialysis in assessing compliance. *Id.* at 493.

[43] If the patient has a psychiatric disorder that causes him to be noncompliant, he could argue that he is being discriminated against based on that "disability." *See* 28 C.F.R. § 36.104 (1994); 29 C.F.R. § 1630.2 (1994). Although the patient may be statistically more inclined to have a psychiatric disorder by virtue of the fact that he works for the Postal Service, the facts given do not indicate that he has any such disorder.

cose tests are necessary to detect and/or prevent ketoacidosis. He may not have realized that failure to take antihypertensive and diuretic medications could cause a minor stroke. He may not understand that laser surgery is necessary to preserve the vision in his left eye. He may think that now that his toe is amputated, it doesn't matter whether he wears orthopedic shoes or not. Given that his job as a postman requires him to walk in public, he may think it more important to look "normal" than to wear corrective shoes.

The patient may not see a connection between being late for dialysis treatments or getting shorter treatments and his health. He may not understand that water weight gain between treatments can damage his heart. Or, he may not know how to control his sodium intake so that he doesn't get so thirsty and drink so much fluid between treatments. He may be a very large person (as indicated by the fact that he had plans to play professional football) who can tolerate removing over five kilograms of fluid in one dialysis session. Therefore, he may believe that he suffers no medical consequence from gaining so much weight between dialysis treatments. The patient's intellectual capacity (perhaps worsened by the "minor stroke") may further affect his ability to understand his current medical regimen.
The patient may not understand all of the above, yet still be very capable of understanding that he must take his immunosuppressive drugs and follow his doctor's orders to keep a transplanted kidney. In that case, his prior noncompliance regarding other areas of his health would not necessarily indicate future noncompliance regarding a transplant. If his problem is related to a lack of understanding, he should be aggressively educated until he understands what he must do to keep the transplant.

Second, the patient's financial, employment or family circumstances may be hindering his ability to attend his medical appointments. For instance, he may not be able to afford the type of transportation he needs to get from work to dialysis on time. His job may require that he be at work during certain times when medical treatments are scheduled. His time may be constrained by responsibility to family members. In the future, it will be easier for the patient to comply with scheduled appointments. He will not have to get to dialysis treatments three times a week; he will only have to attend occasional follow-up doctors' appointments. The facts imply that the patient does actually show up for every dialysis treatment, even if he is late - showing that he is compliant to a degree regarding his dialysis appointments. Thus, the patient's past problems with attendance may not be an indicator of future noncompliance, but only of possible circumstances to be addressed to ensure the patient attends post-transplant appointments.

Third, the patient's past noncompliance may have been intentional, but still not a reliable predictor of future noncompliance. On the one hand, intentional noncompliance in the past may indicate that the patient intends not to comply with his medical regimen in the future. But his own statements belie this conclusion. He requested a place on the transplant waitlist. This suggests he cares enough about his health to want the transplant to be successful - otherwise, he would not undergo the surgery in the first place. The patient also said that he would try to do what the doctors say after the transplant. This statement may indicate a commitment to make a change from his past behavior.[Footnote 44] Even if the patient was intentionally noncompliant in the past, he may have a totally different attitude about transplantation than he has about his current medical regimen. The nephrologist (or a social worker) should discuss with the patient his view about getting a transplant. If the patient indicates that he considers it a new lease on life, and intends to do whatever it takes to keep the graft, that attitude should be taken into account in deciding whether the patient should be waitlisted.[Footnote 45] Intentional noncompliance also suggests that the patient would have the ability to change his behavior to compliant behavior simply by changing his attitude. Indeed, it might more difficult for the patient to become compliant if his noncompliance were due to failure to understand what his medical regimen was or why he should follow it.

In sum, the facts presented about the patient's past behavior are not a sufficiently reliable indicator that he will be noncompliant post-transplant. Those facts only indicate an elevated risk of noncompliance. *Some* risk of noncompliance exists for every transplant recipient -- even those who have been compliant with their pre-transplant regimen. The post-transplant medication regimen can be more demanding than the pre-transplant one, and patients may become unwilling over time to continue to suffer the side effects of the immunosuppressive drugs. Thus the risk alone is not enough to deny the patient a place on the waitlist.

And even if the subject patient has an increased risk of non-compliance, that does not guarantee that he will reject his graft. Graft survival can also be affected by a patient's age, overall health, the quality of the match, whether the patient has already had one or more transplants, the patient's financial status, health insurance coverage, sources of income and job status, any support system of family or friends, mental health, and any past or present substance abuse. The subject patient has diabetes, which may weigh against graft survival. However, he is young and this is his first transplant - two factors that favor graft survival. The quality of the match will not be known until a kidney becomes available. Presumably the patient has good health insurance coverage and steady income for the time being through the postal service. Whether the other factors are present is not known. All known factors combined, the subject patient probably has a chance of a successful transplant on par with other patients who have been waitlisted. Thus, from a utilitarian perspective, it would be unethical to exclude the patient from the waitlist solely on the basis of the facts provided.

Fairness:

Another potential ethical consideration is the *fairness* of allowing the subject patient to be waitlisted and get a transplant at the expense of another patient with a similar chance of a successful transplant who *has* been compliant with the pre-transplant regimen. On the one hand, it seems unfair to "reward" a patient who has not complied with his pre-transplant regimen, especially when there

[44] On the other hand, he could have expressed stronger commitment by stating, "I *will* do what the doctors say."

[45] To ensure that the patient is willing to comply with the post-transplant regimen, the nephrologist could require him to be compliant with his dialysis regimen for six months.

are other patients on the waitlist whose behavior makes them more "deserving" of a transplant. A "bad" patient who is flouting doctors' orders seems less deserving of a kidney transplant than a "good" patient who complies with his medical regimen.[Footnote 46] However, it is unclear that the patient intended to be noncompliant or disobedient. He may have believed his behavior was justified, not forbidden or not important to his health.
Moreover, awarding transplants only to obedient patients because those patients are "good"- regardless of what effect their past behavior has on post-transplant compliance issues - could lead down a slippery slope. If transplants are awarded on merit or goodness, patients might receive priority based on their contributions to society, the tax base, charities, the hospital, etc. Such a system would create a perception of great unfairness and dissuade people from supporting organ donation - a net bad result for everyone.

In conclusion, this writer believes that the ethical considerations regarding a patient's behavior should be limited to the utility of giving the patient a transplant. That is, the only relevance of the patient's past behavior should be as a future predictor of graft (and patient) survival - not as a basis on which to now "punish" the patient for his past behavior. Under a utility analysis, on the facts given, the patient should be waitlisted.

Connie Zuckerman, J.D.

This patient's previous pattern of compliance in and of itself should not automatically disqualify him from consideration as an organ recipient, but it must be considered in the evaluation of his current medical condition and in the prospects for success should the transplant actually occur.

First, it must be clear that given all of the patient's other conditions, he is medically suitable for the transplant. That is, given his current condition, is it likely that the transplant will be successful and of lasting duration, and that it will provide measurable improvement in the quality of life he perceives for himself? Moreover, the success and duration of benefit of the transplant may be highly dependant on such "non-medical" factors as his social support system and psychological make-up. His previous history seems to indicate that he lacks sufficient support to maintain a strict adherance to a medically beneficial routine of personal care. Such a factor might well bode poorly for the success of such an aggressive intervention as an organ transplantation. Before giving inappropriate weight to these factors, it would be incumbent upon this patient's treating physicians to thoroughly address and attempt to ameliorate the reasons for this patient's previous history of non-compliance. Such past behavior may not indicate any will or intent on the part of the patient to be non-compliant but may instead result from factors beyond the control of the patient for which assistance might be very valuable. It would be unfortunate if behavior for which he

[46] This perspective assumes that the subject patient was intentionally noncompliant. He would not be considered "bad" for behavior over which he had no control or understanding.

lacked control led to the denial of medically beneficial treatment for him, particularly if efforts were not conducted to assist him.

Amy L. Friedman, M.D.

Our role as providers of health care is to inform patients about their state of health, therapeutic options and the associated risks, benefits and prognoses. We neither can nor should attempt to impose our preferences on them. When a competent patient chooses to disregard even the most obviously appropriate advice although I feel regret, as long as I have done my best to provide counsel, I must respect and accept his right of independent choice. Certainly as a surgeon I would feel uncomfortable invading the very physical being of someone who did not sincerely believe I should. Although I am unaware of scientific proof, most surgeons have been in the unenviable position of having proceeded with an invasive procedure in such a patient that had an untoward outcome. Bearing the sense of responsibility even if the outcome was not caused by any error or misjudgements, is tremendously difficult.

However, while I accept the patient's right to decline part or all of the prescribed medical prescription, I cannot participate in the initiation of a therapy associated with significant danger unless I believe he will permit me to care safely for him. Although not entirely elective, organ transplantation is not suitable therapy for all candidates. Organ transplantation requires modulation of the immune response through the use of pharmacologic immunosuppression. The balance between too much and too little suppression may be difficult to achieve and routinely requires a high level of patient participation. Frequent clinic visits, blood draws, and accurate use of prescribed medications determine success or failure. In my opinion, a noncompliant patient or one incapable of compliance cannot be safely managed through this process and should not be offered transplantation.

On the other hand, people may make and learn from their mistakes. A prior history of noncompliance is not absolutely predictive of future failure to properly follow medical directions and should not necessarily preclude a candidate's acceptance for transplantation. Following thorough discussion the patient expressing an earnest intention to maintain compliance and qualify for transplantation should be given a solid opportunity to do so. Together with the dialysis professionals a series of specific therapeutic goals are developed to reflect the patient's ability to function cooperatively with the healthcare team. It is agreed prospectively that satisfactory completion of these steps as well as ongoing agreement by the dialysis team that the patient remains a suitable candidate is a prerequisite for transplantation. While this approach does not work for all, I have seen some remarkable success stories. Not only does the patient develop respect for the fairness of the system, but he achieves a significant improvement in self esteem!

Carl M. Kjellstrand, M.D.

As stated in the previous case, kidneys for transplantation are a national scarce resource and should go to where they last the longest. Therefore, the reasoning of the nephrologist is correct. On the other hand, I worry about non-conformity as a subterfuge for discrimination. We will relentlessly pursue the question of alcoholism in a poor Indian as a contraindication for liver transplant, but we will be much more circumspect if it is a powerful, white attorney or senator.
I suggest heart to heart talks with the patient and that he signs a witnessed agreement setting some realistic compliance goals for the next 6 months and see how compliance is going during that time. If good, go ahead with a transplant, if not - sorry. Realistic goals include some reasonable blood glucose control, a limit of weight gains to less than 3 Kg (that is 50% above the mean) between dialyses and the use of good foot care.

Mildred (Barry) Friedman

"Another chance" should be allocated to the postman if he proves that he means what he says. Reaching an agreement with him that would make him responsible for reasonable compliance (total compliance would be too much to ask) over a stated period, perhaps six months, would allow him to prove the sincerity of his statement. Encouragement and education should help him but the behavior is up to him. Somehow, I think humor might help. Certainly leaning heavily on him won't help. A little extra attention to his positive attempts, might.
If he does not become much more compliant, I would agree with the nephrologist and vote against transplanting him.

Judith E. Columbo

In this case a 32 year old man has carried his anger to a self-destroying point. It is true that life is not fair but one must grow and learn from each experience. This patient continues on the same path of non-compliance. His refusal to learn the effects of diabetes, like hypertension, stroke, kidney disease, amputation and blindness caused each of these side effects to take place. Furthermore, the patient's conduct continues by missing hemodialysis appointments and by fluid overload between treatments. I feel the nephrologist was just in feeling that a kidney transplant was a wasted organ for this patient.

Editor's Remarks22

The many faces of noncompliance with a medical regimen can position physician and patient at opposite ends of a tug of war. Before labeling a patient as a problem in adherence to a program, the following questions should be considered:
a. Does the patient realize the genesis of his/her kidney failure?

b. Have goals and objectives of treatment program been explained in terms comprehensible to the patient?
c. Does the patient have the necessary intellect and motor skills to comply with the treatment program?
d. Are there family members, partners, clergy, or other support figures who might assist in reasoning with the patient?
e. Does the patient have a psychiatric or organic brain disorder that prevents participation in and compliance with the treatment regimen?
f. Is the patient gaining benefits (disability, family attention) from the non-compliant behavior?

After analysis of patient specific aspects of undesired conduct, resolution should be attempted following a prepared and rehearsed rational program:
g. Remove "communication spoilers," such as criticizing, name-calling, moralizing, threatening, ordering and psychologic diagnosing.
h. Employ "reflective listening," (a technique that signals having "heard" what another has said.) to signal that the patient's complaint is being "adjudicated."
i. Deal directly with problem behaviors: small steps, involve the patient, build on patient's strengths, be clear on who is to do what when.
j. Devise new approaches to "old problems," such as lateness and complaints.,
k. Detail the consequences of aberrant behavior in terms that are comprehensible.
l. Prepare a behavior contract that specifies what is to be done by patient and renal team.
m. Prepare in advance to manage anger.
n. Anticipate for the staff a step-by-step coping with agitated and disruptive patients.
o. Establish and publicize a grievance procedure.
p. Appoint a patient representative to serve as an advocate when dealing with the "establishment".

Both attorneys, Dr. Kjellstrand, Dr. Amy L. Friedman, and Patient Mildred Barry Friedman would not penalize the patient for his past behavior by denying listing for a kidney transplant. I concur. Patient Columbo is less forgiving indeed, she assigns the major diabetic complications as the result of noncompliance to routine diabetic care.

Response to Study Questions

1. No evidence supports a positive or negative answer. I tend to believe that a kidney transplant will not stimulate conduct reform in a patient that has had little regard for the rules and treatment components of dialysis.
2. It can't. But, the satisfactory post-transplant conduct of alcoholic liver recipients is encouraging.
3. Redundant. No.

Case 23

ORGAN DONATION/ACCEPTANCE BY ORTHODOX JEWS

A 47 year old attorney manifests life threatening congestive heart failure due to idiopathic cardiomyopathy. Conservative management is able to sustain a bed and chair existence but constant oxygen administration is required and the patient is obviously agonal. An urgent heart transplant is advised and the patient, an orthodox Jew agrees. The cardiac surgeon recalls that the patient refused permission to use his son's organs following a fatal automobile accident three years earlier on the grounds that "Jewish law requires that a body be intact to be acceptable to God." Annoyed at the refusal to permit organ donation, the surgeon declines to list the patient for a heart transplant. ***"You can't have it both ways," the surgeon states.***

Study Questions

1. Is the cardiac surgeon expressing antisemitism?
2. Does a person have the right to refuse to donate organs while being willing to accept organs?
9. Does the heart surgeon have the right to decline placement on a potential recipient list?

Monique Janelle London, J.D.

The patient's decision does not raise any legal issues. There is nothing illegal or impermissible under the current organ allocation system about the patient refusing permission to procure his son's organs, but then seeking to receive or receiving a heart transplant himself.
Nor is there anything illegal about the surgeon declining to list the patient for transplant. Surgeons, as members of the transplant team, can advocate for or against a patient getting waitlisted during the candidate's evaluation process. The transplant surgeon may have veto power (particularly since he is the person who would be performing the transplant), in which case his refusal to list the patient would be decisive. Although the surgeon might be held to answer to the rest of the transplant team for his refusal to list the patient, he would not be subject to legal liability.

The only possible claim the patient could make is one for the surgeon's "abandonment" of his relationship with the patient. However, it does not appear that the surgeon is yet even in a relationship with the patient. Even if he is, the surgeon is entitled to end that relationship if he provides reasonable notice of the termination of treatment and sufficient opportunity for the patient to secure alternative medical attention. Here, unless the patient requires an immediate heart transplant (i.e., within a matter of hours or days), the surgeon will be able to satisfy the requirements for terminating the relationship. Given that the patient is "able to sustain a bed and chair existence" (as opposed to an intensive care unit existence), the situation is not so urgent as to subject the surgeon to abandonment liability for refusing to waitlist the patient for a heart transplant.

In short, this Case presents no sustainable legal claims.

Ethical Analysis:

The ethical issue is whether the patient should be allowed to receive a heart transplant, given that he refused to donate his son's organs.

The patient has a religious belief that a body must be intact (apparently only *after* death) to be acceptable to God. He refused consent to procure his son's organs because he believed that if the son's body were desecrated after death, it would not be acceptable to God. There is nothing unethical about the patient having and following this religious belief. However, he should apply it consistently to all people - not only his son. If the patient's belief prevents him from donating organs, he also should not receive organs. If he were to receive a heart transplant, he would be promoting desecration of someone else's body after death, which would render that body unacceptable to God.

On the other hand, the view could taken that receiving a transplant is still consistent with the patient's belief, because the donor's body will be desecrated whether the patient accepts the heart or not.

Regardless of the possible unfairness of the situation, this writer believes that it would be unethical to deny the patient a heart transplant. Despite the decision the patient made about his son and the religious beliefs underlying that decision, the fact is that the patient's own life is now at stake. From a utilitarian perspective, what he did in the past has no bearing on the chance of the transplant being successful. From a fairness perspective, the patient should not now be deprived of a chance at life as "punishment" for following his religious convictions in connection with his son's death. Thus, there is no ethical basis for denying the patient a chance at a heart transplant.

Connie Zuckerman, J.D.

Donor organs available for transplantation are one of the truly *scarce* resources in our current health care system. While many diagnostic and treatment options are sometimes inaccessible to patients because of their expense, donor organs represent a situation of not only high cost, but also of genuine scarcity, such that true rationing must take place, i.e., determining which members of an otherwise qualified group will gain access to the medical resource. Simply put, there are too few organs available to meet the growing number of medically eligible transplant recipients. Therefore, considerations of distributive justice and proper stewardship of this scarce resource naturally arise when the possibility of organ transplantation is raised for a particular patient. These concerns also play a prominent part in policy determinations related to the distribution of donor organs across the United States.

This patient has been medically evaluated as being a potential candidate for a heart transplant, and the patient agrees with this medical plan. Being placed on the wait list for a donor organ does not automatically mean that the patient will receive a heart transplant, but it does mean that the patient has likely been evaluated according to well established criteria as being a medically appropriate candidate to receive a new organ. This determination is primarily based on an objective medical evaluation of the patient's current condition and prognosis, as well as his potential to benefit from the new organ and his ability to sustain the rigorous post-transplant regimen necessary to avoid rejection of the donor heart. In this particular case, the surgeon declines to place the patient on the wait list not because of the patient's failure to meet these criteria, but rather due to his personal disdain for the patient's previous unwillingness to donate the organs of a loved one. In essence, this surgeon has made a moral judgment of the patient's prior behavior and on that basis, chooses not the list the patient. While the surgeon's actions may be comprehensible, and his frustration explainable, his actions are not ethically justifiable.

Understandably, the surgeon finds it morally untenable that a person would be willing to accept a donor organ for himself, but be unwilling to donate an organ to another in need. Such behavior seems selfish and self-serving, and appears to violate fundamental notions of distributive justice, such that benefits and burdens should be equitably shared. Frustrated by the shortage of available organs and dismayed by the seemingly unfair behavior of this patient, the surgeon makes a moral judgment not to refer the patient to the transplant list, even though the patient is medically eligible. Such a judgment may not constitute anti-Semitism (that is, the surgeon's bias does not appear to be based on the patient's Jewish heritage per se), as presumably this surgeon would act similarly regardless of the patient's religious identity. However, it does, in essence, punish the patient and deny him access to a potential resource for which he is otherwise qualified, based on the patient's previous decision to decline to voluntarily donate a loved one's organ. Further consideration of this quandary is in order.
We do not know the precise circumstances under which this patient previously refused to grant permission to donate his son's organs following the boy's tragic and sudden death several years earlier. One can posit many possible reasons for this refusal which may further explain his actions. Our system of organ donation is one that relies on the voluntary decisions of donors and their families. It is a fragile system that of necessity must respect the individual values and autonomy of donors and their families. Given the shortage of available donor organs, it may be unfortunate that a family would be unwilling to donate the organs of a potential donor, but they clearly have the right to decline to donate, and they cannot be forced, pressured or coerced into doing so. Such manipulation would undermine the integrity of the voluntary system currently in place and potentially discourage other possible donors from altruistically coming forward.

It is unclear how old the son was when he died, but it is possible that the son was old enough to have his own established religious beliefs, such that the father's decision not to donate was done out of respect for his son's faith rather than due to his own personal religious beliefs. As well, up until a few years ago, most Jewish religious leaders considered organ donation a violation of several fundamental tenets of Jewish law: that the body should not be desecrated upon death, that delay of burial was impermissible, and that the brain death criteria necessary for organ donation violated traditional Jewish teachings of when death occurred. Such teachings, however, did not per se bar Jews from *receiving* an organ donation, thus causing significant ethical tension within the Jewish and medical communities. However, within the last several years, leaders from all the major movements of American Judaism (Reform, Conservative and Orthodox) have re-examined the issue of organ donation, in light of the growing disparity between supply and demand, improvements in transplant technology, and in light of the broader context of Torah teachings. As a result, leaders from these movements have now publicly articulated their support for organ donation, consistent with the Torah teaching of "pikuach nefesh," which is the obligation to save a human life if it is within one's power to do so, even overriding other Torah teachings that may appear to be in conflict. While a small minority of Orthodox leaders have not joined this consensus, this attitude represents a new and important obligation on the part of Jewish patients to donate their own or their loved one's organs when they are in a position to do so. It is thus possible that given this new articulation of Jewish teaching, this patient would now voluntarily donate a loved one's organs were he ever to face a situation as he previously did with his son.

Ultimately, while the surgeon may be frustrated by what he considers an unfair situation, his individual moral judgment should not stand in the way of denying this patient access to a wait list for which he is otherwise medically eligible. Moreover, to deny access would be to punish this patient for his expression of his own individual autonomy, or for his advocacy of the wishes of his deceased son. While the surgeon may not agree within the patient's prior actions, using his own individual moral judgment to make medical decisions or limit medical options sets a dangerous precedent and is ethically indefensible in this clinical situation. If he continues to be unable to offer this patient the medically indicated option of placement on a transplant wait list, then he should withdraw from the case and transfer this patient's care to another qualified physician who will be able to treat this patient without interference from individual moral judgments.[Footnote 47, Footnote 48]

Amy L. Friedman, M.D.

It is extremely unfortunate that many are eager to receive organs but unwilling to donate. Far from a rare occurrence, or one isolated to Orthodox Jews, in practice we find that even those who have directly benefited from the donation of organs and have undergone transplantation are often opposed to participating as tissue or organ donors to others upon death. While difficult for the transplant professional to comprehend, the reluctance to donate is so prevalent in

[47] Caplan, AL and Coelho, DH. *The Ethics of Organ Transplants: The Current Debate.* Amherst, NY: Prometheus Books (1998).
[48] Ahronheim, JA, Moreno, JD, and Zuckerman, C. *Ethics in Clinical Practice.* Gaithersburg, Maryland: Aspen Publishers, Inc. (2000).

American (and most other developed countries) society that it would be unreasonable to link to acceptance or denial of entry to the transplant waiting list. In addition, a practical solution to the logistic challenge of tracking attitudes would require an inappropriately high utilization of resources. In this circumstance, it would be inappropriate to deny access to a new heart to this patient. It would also seem unlikely that an entire transplant team would agree to decline listing him. The transplant surgeon, (whose anger is certainly born of frustration) should acknowledge that his own subjective feelings should not be permitted to bias the group's decision. On the other hand, this situation raises a perfect opportunity to engage in open dialogue about the issue of organ donation with the religious community to which this patient belongs. The clerical leaders should be invited to reassess the reasonableness of inconsistent interpretations of how intact a body must be to be acceptable to God. It would certainly seem apparent that the Jewish belief in the obligation to save life takes precedence over the need to simultaneously return all body parts. What can be so wrong with delaying the return of a heart or kidney by a few years?

Carl M. Kjellstrand, M.D.

Transplant surgeons - like all - enjoy being morally indignant, and will fly off the handle while enjoying their bogus morality. Transplant teams overall make their decisions based on racist, sexist and ageist considerations. The situation has not improved in spite of declamations following repeated articles of empirical data showing this unjustice. In 1999 the distribution of renal transplants is as unfair as it was in 1986 when the first paper pointed this out. Men, white, rich and young are the common recipients while the women and the poor donate. Although the recipient in this case is a white, powerful male, I have all reason to believe that this decision has bigotry, and furor of those different, as its mainspring.

Cadaver organs are a national resource not to be distributed by whims or brutal power. Scandals all over the world: selling kidneys in India, letting base-ball stars and politicians jump the liver queue in USA, a heart transplant to an influential person in Canada suddenly extending the age-limit by a decade and CEO's in Sweden buying hearts are sorry proofs that the medical establishment is in a sad shape.

Two thousand years ago a Chinese Medical Code stated:

Rich or poor
Foreigner or Countryman
Intelligent or dumb
Men or Women
Friend or Foe.
All should be treated equal

The distribution of cadaver organs should follow established just protocol and we have a long way to go.

Ad hoc decisions about distributive justice are always wrong as they tend to be based on emotions and not carefully considered thoughts about fairness. Transplant organs are now preferentially given to the rich and powerful. The medical establishment is abusing and selling peoples altruism. The public is aware of this. The decreasing willingness to donate organs proves it.

Some communitarians have suggested that you have to agree to donate in order to go on a recipient list. If the transplant team had established this, together with other considerations, as a pre-requisite, then I would have no quarrel with the decision to exclude non-donors.
The rules should also be based on the law that specifically prohibits discrimination based on sex, age, religion, and so on.
One consideration that does conflict with this is based on utilitarian grounds. Renal transplants always have to be rationed. Only 10% of people starting dialysis will ever have a renal transplant. Transplant organs are a national recourse and for the greatest good they should be distributed to where they will last the longest. It would be insane to let an old woman or man dying of cancer on dialysis to compete equally with a healthy young person. Age will inevitably come into play because it brings with it factors that limit longevity. However age itself is not what should prohibit a person from going on the list, comorbidity is the determining factor. Some 70-year-olds are better candidates than some 40-year-olds.

1. Anti-semitism cannot be deterrnined, only that the transplant surgeon is out of bounds.
2. Yes-, you can accept an organ while refusing to donate - see caveat.
3. No-, he has not, this is a decision beyond personal whims.

Judith E. Columbo

Religion plays an important part in the life of many patients. In this case the 47 year old man is willing to accept the urgent heart transplant while on the other hand refused to allow his son's organs, after a fatal accident, to be donated. The patient in this case chose not to use the son's organs for donation for religious reasons. The patient's willingness to accept an organ does not go against his religious beliefs. I feel the surgeon is wrong in allowing his personal opinion to affect his medical judgement.

Editor's Remarks23

Donating an organ from a family member is not a condition for receiving an organ from the national pool. The surgeon is petty and vindictive. Religion does not have to follow logic. The attorney broke no laws when he declined permission to use his son's organs. There is no reason for punishment. Dr. Kjellstrand correctly nails the transplant surgeon as a bigot. A gentler Dr. Amy L. Friedman cautions the surgeon not to permit "his own subjective feelings to bias the group's decision." Zuckerman is kinder holding that: "using his own individual moral judgment to make medical decisions or limit medical options sets a dangerous precedent and is ethically indefensible." Patient Columbo concurs as do I.

Response to Study Questions

1. Why raise the specter of antisemitism? Transplant surgeons are frequently excessively opinionated and prone to issue thunderbolt judgments with or without justification. The surgeon in this instance is wrong and may in no way be expressing religious bias.
2. Yes. Orthodox Jews really believe that the body must be buried intact for acceptance by their God. Even an amputated limb must be reclaimed for inclusion in the coffin.
3. Not out of personal pique or spite. Absent other evidence of non-suitability, the patient must be given his chance to receive the precious resource of a cadaver heart.

Case 24

HOPELESS PROGNOSIS

A 38 year old hospital clerk develops renal failure due to bilateral ureteric obstruction by carcinoma of the uterine cervix. Previous therapy over the past year included three operations for tumor resection, four courses of chemotherapy, bone marrow transplantation and a course of local radiation. There are extensive liver, lung, and bone metastases. Both consulting oncologist and radiologist state that neither further chemotherapy nor radiation is indicated. The collaborating urologist, unable to catheterize either ureter states that he will perform cutaneous ureterostomies providing that dialytic therapy is initiated. The patient is weak, frail, depressed, and barely communicative. Her family states that she has been withdrawn and disinterested in family matters for four months. An on call nephrologist noting advanced hyperkalemia and a serum creatinine of 21 mg/dl declines dialysis on the grounds that ***"death in uremia is kinder than death from cancer."***

Study Questions

1. Echoing the question pertaining to "futility" in initiating long-term dialysis for a patient with established ESRD, the issue here is whether or not perform what amounts to a rescue in reversible obstructive uropathy. Should the catheter be passed?
2. Is it appropriate (a precondition) to advise the patient of her condition and the options open?
3. Has the nephrologist gone beyond his purview in declining dialysis that is a precondition to placement of ureteral catheters?

Monique Janelle London, J.D.

The patient is dying of cervical cancer. The facts do not give an estimate of how much longer she is expected to live. The cancer has caused an obstruction of the patient's ureters, such that she is currently in renal failure. If untreated, the renal failure will probably cause her death within a matter of days; if dialysis is initiated, apparently the patient would still die of cancer, although it is unclear how much longer she could live. The nephrologist believes that death from uremia sooner will be less painful to the patient than death from cancer later, so he decides not to initiate dialysis.

Right to Self Determination and Informed Consent:

As explained previously, under the doctrine of informed consent, a physician has a duty to disclose to a competent patient (or an incompetent patient's surrogate) enough information so that the patient can make an informed judgment about whether to undergo medical treatment. It is "for the individual to decide whether a particular medical treatment is in [her] best interests, whether that decision is wise or unwise." *Shine v. Vega*, 429 Mass. 456, 463-464, 709 N.E.2d 58 (Mass. 1999), quoting *Norwood Hosp. v. Munoz*, 409 Mass. 116, 123 (Mass. 1991); *see also In the Matter of R.H.*, 35 Mass. App. Ct. 478, 622 N.E. 2d 1071, 1072 (Mass. 1993).

Thus, if the patient is competent, she is entitled to make the choice whether to initiate dialysis. However, the facts state that the patient is "depressed and barely communicative," and has been "withdrawn and disinterested in family matters for months." Thus the patient may be incompetent to make decisions about her medical treatment. If so, the nephrologist should find out if the patient made any sort of advanced directive when competent, expressing her wishes regarding medical treatment in the present situation, and he should honor those wishes. If the patient did not clearly indicate her wishes when competent, her right to make medical decisions now can still be exercised on her behalf by her family or other surrogate. *See, e.g., In re Doe*, 262 Ga. 389, 418 S.E.2d 3, 6 (Ga. 1992).

If anyone in the patient's family or her other legal representatives oppose withholding dialysis, the nephrologist should initiate dialysis unless he can obtain a court order authorizing him not to do so. *See John F. Kennedy Memorial Hosp. v. Bludworth*, 452 So. 2d 921, 926-927 (Fla. 1984). Even if all parties involved agree that dialysis should not be initiated, the nephrologist may still need court authorization to withhold treatments to avoid legal liability. As explained in Case 2, the courts are split on this issue. *Compare Rasmussen v. Fleming*, 154 Ariz. 207, 741 P.2d 674, 692 (Ariz. 1987) (Feldman, Vice C.J., concurring) ("Even where there is unanimity of opinion between the guardian, the family, and the doctors . . . 'substituted judgment' and 'best interest' decisions should be validated by court order.") with *In re Longeway*, 133 Ill. 2d 33, 549 N.E.2d 292, 295 (Ill. 1989) ("For many years, members of a patient's family, together with doctors and clergy, have made decisions to withdraw life-sustaining equipment from incompetent, hopelessly ill patients without seeking judicial approval.").

In short, if the nephrologist declines to initiate dialysis without informed consent from a competent patient, he risks being sued. As discussed in connection with previous Cases, in certain states a physician may refuse to provide treatment if in his best professional judgment it would be "futile" or "useless." *See, e.g., Causey v. St. Francis Medical Center*, 719 So. 2d 1072, 1075 (La. Ct. App. 2d Cir. 1998). However, it is unclear that the futility doctrine would be a successful defense under the facts. First and most importantly, the patient is conscious. In some courts this will negate a claim of futility. *See, e.g., Drabick v. Drabick*, 200 Cal. App. 3d 185, 245 Cal. Rptr. 840, 852 (Cal. App. 6th Dist. 1988), *cert. denied*, 488 U.S. 958 (1988) (holding that the medical advice that would support a decision to terminate life support "must include the prognosis that there is no reasonable possibility of returning to cognitive and sapient life"). The reasoning is that a conscious patient may get value from the extra time provided by the lifesaving treatment, as opposed to the permanently unconscious patient for whom the treatment "merely prolongs the dying process" with no other benefit. *See Causey v. St. Francis Medical Center*, 719 So. 2d 1072 (La. Ct. App. 2d Cir. 1998).

Second, the facts give no indication of how long the patient could be expected to live on dialysis given the stage of her cervical cancer. It may be that, with dialysis, the patient could continue living for months or even years, again calling into question the idea that initiating dialysis would be "futile."[Footnote 49]

Discrimination Under the ADA and the Rehabilitation Act:

The nephrologist also risks being sued for discrimination against the patient based on her "disability" of having cervical cancer. The potential applicability of the ADA and Rehabilitation Act to withholding of lifesaving medical treatment has been discussed in detail in connection with previous Cases and will not be repeated here. In short, the nephrologist might be liable for discrimination in the Fourth Circuit, see *In re Baby K*, 832 F. Supp. 1022 (E.D. Va. 1993), *aff'd on other grounds*, 16 F.3d 590 (4th Cir.), *cert. denied*, 115 S. Ct. 91 (1994)), but probably would not be liable for discrimination in the Second Circuit, *see United States v. University Hospital*, 729 F.2d 144 (2d Cir. 1984).

On balance, to avoid liability, the nephrologist should initiate dialysis unless he obtains informed consent from the patient (or her legal representatives and the court) to withhold treatment.

Ethical Analysis:

It is unethical for the nephrologist to decide unilaterally when and how the patient's life will end. The nephrologist may have the best intentions, but he has no right to impose his values on the patient's own life. The nephrologist may be correct that death in uremia is less painful than death from cancer. However, the patient may place more importance on values other than pain avoidance. She may be willing to endure the pain of cancer in order to gain the time to reflect, to write, to hear music, to see a sunset, a full moon or the faces of loved ones, to say final words to various people, to give others a chance to say final words to her, to pray, to make final arrangements, or just to experience life. It should be up to the patient whether she endures more pain for a chance to have more time to do these things.
Moreover, miracles can happen. The patient's cancer could go into remission for a period, or even disappear. The patient should have the right to that chance if she wants it. However, if dialysis is not initiated, she will die unquestionably within a few days.

The patient has been "withdrawn and disinterested in family matters for four months." She is weak, depressed and uncommunicative. This seems like a natural condition for a person who is in advanced stages of cervical cancer. It does not necessarily mean that the patient wants to hasten her death by not treating her renal failure. Unless the patient herself gives competent, informed consent to withholding dialysis, the dialysis treatments should be initiated. If the patient decides thereafter that she is ready to die, she can ask that the dialysis treatments be discontinued.

[49] On the other hand, as pointed out in the discussion of Case 5, if the patient is deemed "terminally ill" based on the predicted life span of less than six months, the nephrologist may not be liable for withholding dialysis. *See* LA. REV. STAT. ANN. § 40:1299.58.8(A)(1) (immunizing from liability medical personnel who withhold or withdraw life support from a qualified patient who has a terminal and irreversible condition).

Connie Zuckerman, J.D.

This patient's tragic circumstance reflects the ethical dilemmas which often arise when a patient's condition deteriorates to a terminal phase of the illnesses, and the goals of care have neither been articulated or reconsidered in light of this deterioration.

Until now, an aggressive array of medical treatments and interventions have been utilized for this patient. While the case scenario does not expressly address the goals of care when the patient was first diagnosed, nor the patient's wishes and values regarding medical treatments, it is fair to presume that this patient and her involved physicians agreed that the initial goal of treatment was to try to eradicate the carcinoma, or at least halt the spread of the disease in order to allow the patient to maintain some level of functional existence, despite her advancing illness. Given the aggressive nature of the treatments, and the significant burdens that the patient endured as a result, presumably there was at least an initial determination that the benefits to be achieved from the treatments outweighed the burdens that would afflict this patient. While the patient's physicians could articulate to her what medical options were available to address her cancer, only the patient, according to her own personal values, could determine what benefits were worth what risks to her. Patients with decisional capacity have the ethical and legal right to make this determination of their own best interests. Physicians' medical expertise and experience are often critical to patients in arriving at a decision, but ultimately the choice is the patient's to be made.
It is unfortunate but necessary to confront the reality that despite these aggressive measures (and perhaps in some way as a result of these invasive procedures), this patient will inevitably die in the near future. In a sense, as the nephrologist has framed the issue, the question in this case at this time is not whether this patient will die but rather due to what complications and under what circumstances.

Currently, it appears that the patient can no longer participate in the decision making process, though this does not seem to have been formally evaluated, nor is it clear that any measures have been taken to address the patient's apparent depression or other conditions that may be impairing her ability to be engaged in a discussion about her care. Before any further determinations can be made about what treatment options are appropriate for this patient at this time, it is necessary to ascertain whether the patient has the capacity to participate in this decision making process and if not, whether there is a designated surrogate decision maker who can represent the wishes and interests of the patient if she can no longer speak for herself. For example, if would be important to determine whether, during her previously arduous treatments, the patient articulated any wishes regarding treatments should her condition continue to deteriorate (an oral advance directive) or whether the patient left written instructions about her wishes (a living will) or designated a loved one to be her health care proxy should she no longer be able to speak for herself. Given the patient's disease and the real potential that she might lose decisional capacity, it would have been ethically mandatory for her physicians to educate and assist her in the execution of some form of advance directive.

At this point, many possible treatment options may exist, including efforts to reverse the patient's obstructive uropathy. While such efforts may not be technically futile in that they may address the immediate circumstances of the patient, they will not address the underlaying terminal condition of this patient. Thus, more than ever, at this point it would be critical to determine the benefits to be gained by further treatments versus the burdens to be borne by the patient in light of the treatment. Such balancing must inevitably take place in the broader context of the goals of care at this point, a determination that of necessity must take into account the individual values of this patient, to the extent they can be determined. While a particular intervention may be technically feasible, it might do little to benefit the patient while imposing undue harm. Clearly, the consulting oncologist and radiologist believed that their treatment options no longer held out any benefit for the patient, and the nephrologist is as well is clearly weighing the benefits and burdens of dialysis for this patient. Dialysis may be technically feasible, but will it only prolong her dying and suffering from the underlying carcinoma? What is missing, however, is the patient's voice in this weighing process. If at all possible, it would be valuable to ascertain what goals the patient might have at this late stage in her illness.

Often physicians have difficulty re-evaluating and re-focusing the goals of care from cure to comfort as patients gradually decline to a terminal phase of illness and curative measures prove to be of little medical benefit to patients at this stage. In this particular patient's circumstance, there appears to have been no discussion yet about a palliative approach to care, whose highest goal would be to maximize the patient's comfort, even if that meant a shortened life span. Palliative care focuses on aggressive pain management, enhancing patient functioning to the extent possible, and addressing the psychosocial, emotional and spiritual interests of the patient as death approaches. The goal of palliative care is not to hasten death but not to unnecessarily prolong the dying process either. It also explicitly addresses the needs and concerns of the patient's family as they accompany the patient toward death and then into bereavement. Often, this palliative care is obtained through enrolling the patient in a home hospice program, though many hospitals and long term care facilities also now have palliative care measures available to patients and their families. The tragedy, however, is that such decisions to evolve to a palliative approach to care often come very late in the patient's illness, so that neither patient nor family receive the full benefit available through such programs as hospice. In this particular case, it would be imperative for palliative care and hospice enrollment to be considered legitimate medical options at this point in time. Often, patients and their families feel a sense of abandonment from their physicians when curative measures are no longer beneficial. Palliative care offers an alternative for physicians to be actively involved and engaged with the patient, even while recognizing and accepting that the patient's death will be the inevitable outcome. Helping patients have a comfortable and pain free death is an essential ethical obligation for any physician caring for a terminally ill patient.

Thus, the instincts of this nephrologist to spare the patient a prolonged and painful death may be admirable, given that the patient's death is imminent and inevitable. However, the decision to work toward the goal of a peaceful death is one that of necessity must involve either the patient or the patient's surrogate decision makers to ensure that patient's own values are at the core of the decision making process.[Footnote 50, Footnote 51]

Amy L. Friedman, M.D.

Without fail, life will end for each of us. The physician's role is to lengthen life when feasible and desired by the patient whose quality of life justifies the means of prolongation. The essence of compassionate care is identification and fulfillment of realistic patient wishes. This patient, though fairly young, has virtually no hope of substantial survival even under the best of circumstances. Most of us, given the likelihood of significant suffering would in her place, choose to avoid futile therapy. Many might even actively seek a manner of hastening death, though that is currently considered unacceptable in our society. If she is currently unable or unwilling to express her own choice to avoid or pursue dialysis, then her family must be asked to participate. It is precisely these types of situations that health care proxies and living wills should cover. The family is likely to be at least familiar, through prior discussions, with the patient's general preferences regarding termination or prolongation of life. It would also have been appropriate for her oncologist to have held an anticipatory discussion directly with the patient covering these general issues. Though the position held by the nephrologist is entirely reasonable, unilateral determination to withhold dialysis, particularly by a physician not previously involved with her care, when either the patient herself or her representatives are available, would be inappropriate. However, in holding the discussion regarding therapeutic options (that include the withdrawal of care) it would be entirely suitable for the nephrologist to share his(her) opinion that uremia is a kind way of dying.

If, however, this dying woman were to determine that her quality of life continued to be acceptable, dialysis should be made available to her. Her wish to live until her child's next birthday party, or to complete a life goal (perhaps she is writing a book or knitting an afghan for her husband) would be sufficient justification for the use of this therapy. While some would consider this an extravagant use of healthcare resources, we have not yet developed a uniform approach to limiting expense. It would seem wholly unreasonable to deny such an unselfish request while continuing to offer expensive coronary bypass operations to individuals who continue to smoke.

Carl M. Kjellstrand, M.D.

The decision to withhold life-prolonging treatment is exceeded in difficulty, guilt and angst only by the decision to stop life-support and let patients die. Still, giving up is often the best option among a group of exceedingly poor choices.

Two considerations are needed in this case; the doctrine of gain vs. burden best formulated in the Catholic "Doctrine of the Faith" and autonomy, respect for

[50] Institute of Medicine, *Approaching Death: Improving Care at the End of Life*. Washington, D.C.: National Academy Press (1997).

[51] Doyle, D, Hanks, GWC and MacDonald, N. *Oxford Textbook of Palliative Medicine*. Oxford, England: Oxford University Press (1998).

our differences. Burden vs. gain needs to be used in the two decisions that are independent, but artificially connected by the urologist. Should one:
a) Do percutaneous urterostomy?
b) Dialyze the patient?

How to act, depends almost entirely on the patients wishes and only secondarily on your perception of the prognosis. Although the latter should not be, it is invariably, influenced by your personality and dangerously on your mood and prejudice. The two last changes and changes...
To believe that these decisions can be logically pre-determined or codified simply shows that you do not have the sophistication or personality to deal with the most uncertain of clinical situations. These situations are, by their nature, always fluent, constantly changing, messy and contain an inordinate amount of unknowns.

At one extreme, if the patient is an orthodox Jew, whose religion virtually demands any life-prolonging procedure, and the renogram shows near normal uptake - do a ureterostomy and use dialysis as a back-up, preferably for an agreed to, limited time, if renal function does not pick up immediately.
If the patient has expressly stated, or as appears to be the case with this woman, indirectly - no more invasive or difficult treatments - or if the renogram shows no uptake - just stand there -do not throw technical futility trying to avoid making the tough but right decision.

In between these extreme decisions we will all fumble as best as we can with the impossible metaphysical difficulties and hope that whatever Gods maybe will be on our side.
These decisions always leave a terror of panic and a special rumbling of doubt. So much in clinical medicine is trial and error - these decisions with their absolute conclusion, leave no room for the consolation of going back to do it differently. Finis!
Whatever the decision, someone will think it evil and morally detestable and happy to climb some awful, religious horse to do damage even to the most saintly doctor.

Knowing next to nothing of the case my interpretation is that the patient has long ago given up. To do technical stupidities with futile and painful consequences instead of letting the patient take farewell and solve some remaining questions and conflict with her family strikes me as inhumane. Let nature take its course and smooth the avenues of death.
In a similar situation, an old man with sudden onset of uric acid nephropathy from a most malignant leukemia, with at best only a few weeks to death, asked me to dialyze for two weeks. This would allow him to see an Australian grandchild before he died. We did, the grandchild arrived and then the old man died in peace and contentment. Perhaps this case-patient also needs some time for re-conciliation. How about sitting down and converse with the patient, she seems neglected. This is a most difficult conversation, as it is carried out at the bedside in the frightening company of death.

Judith E. Columbo

Death in any terms is death. The sentence death from uremia is kinder than death from cancer is hard for me to understand. I am troubled with the word kinder and death in the same sentence. This 37 year old hospital clerk is remarkable she has come this far. Renal failure, extensive lung, liver and bone metastases, courses of chemotherapy, bone marrow transplant, local radiation are some of the procedures the patient has had to endure. Even though I agree with the nephrologist to withhold dialysis, the grounds for the decision should be stated as that death in uremia is more humane (not kinder) than death from cancer.

Editor's Remarks24

At the end of patients' lives, physicians are conflicted caring for a terminally ill patient. Yet, when caring for a terminal patient, as pointed out by Zuckerman: "Helping patients have a comfortable and pain free death is an essential ethical obligation for any physician." Their self-image as omnipotent is about to be unmasked as a facade. Surely, there must be one more trick, a further procedure, a newly discovered drug that will hold back the inexorable force of nature. So, we apply intervention after intervention pretending they will succeed when we know they won't in the elderly and others with no hope.[Endnote 45] Our inability to permit a restful death in children stricken with cancer who have no chance of recovery is lamentable.[Endnote 46] Perhaps, saddest of all aspects of medically controlled dying is the reluctance to administer sufficient sedation and palliation to permit a peaceful exit.[Endnote 47] Clouding the conduct of physicians tending the dying are ethicists' pronouncements that can amount to jibberish[Endnote 48] coupled with threats of litigation as noted by London: "If the nephrologist declines to initiate dialysis without informed consent from a competent patient, he risks being sued." "It is unethical," London asserts, "for the nephrologist to decide unilaterally when and how the patient's life will end." But, we do just that all of the time! On the other side, Kjellstrand pronounces: "To do technical stupidities with futile and painful consequences instead of letting the patietn take farewell and solve remaining questions and conflict with her family strikes me as inhumane." Me too.

Still, might there be yet one more rabbit to be pulled out of the hat, the pre-grieving family queries? Isn't it worth one more course of radiation? Confronting and reacting to these questions is an unavoidable component of the difficult art of medicine. At least four times a year, I urge that young women with advanced uterine cancer and uremia induced by obstructive uropathy not be dialyzed. Each time, I explain to the patient that weeks and perhaps months may be gained by reversing the renal failure but the malignancy will not be ablated or eradicated. Only rarely do I recall the stricken woman asking to begin dialysis - when a spouse or parent insists that she go on. Physicians earn their fees, in part, for addressing the tough aspects of life. This is one of them. I agree with the on call nephrologist and would not start dialysis. I am made uneasy, however, by Dr. Amy L. Friedman's legitimate point that life quality may be acceptable to the patient even though abysmal to others including the responsible physician.

One does not need informed consent to do nothing further. Deciding not to amputate a limb, replace a heart valve, withhold an antibiotic, or decline dialysis is a medical judgment - that may have to be defended when lawyers catch the scent - but nevertheless, resides in the provenance of the physician and patient without interlopers.

Response to Study Questions

1. Contingent on the accuracy of appraisals by oncologist and radiologist that all options in cancer management are exhausted, dialysis should not be initiated. Now catabolic and depressed, the long suffering patient is entitled to dignity as she dies. Enough is really enough.
2. Absolutely. No individual, family member, or agency has the legal authority or moral imperative to make life or death decisions for another mentally competent adult. It is even possible that for some unsuspected purpose the patient wishes weeks of life prolongation that might easily be enabled by dialysis. I recall the world famous economist dying of polycystic kidney disease - before introduction of chronic dialysis (1960) - who begged for three weeks to finish his latest textbook. My mentor, Dr. John P. Merrill arranged what then (1959) was extraordinary, a series of linked acute hemodialyses permitting completion of the project. Should the patient under consideration request attendance at her daughter's wedding two months hence, I would relent and try to meet that goal by maintenance hemodialysis.
3. No. By taking a position, the nephrologist fulfills an obligation to the patient. That I agree with the decision not to dialyze is secondary to my appreciation for the straightforward and clear opinion expounded.

EDITOR'S EPILOGUE

All of the foregoing can be distilled down to three themes:

1. Must every uremic patient be treated with dialysis or a kidney transplant irrespective of mitigating circumstance such as citizenship, age, mental incapacity, or severity of illness?
2. Are some patients "more equal than others" (rich, politically well positioned, religious consideration) in terms of priority for a solid organ allograft or acceptance for dialytic therapy?
3. Are there conditions that permit the renal team to disengage from therapy once begun (noncompliance, vegetative state, futile prognosis, irreversible psychosis)?

Each of these questions could be selected for substantive deliberation. Debate surrounding the issues comprises the substance of this work. What is intended in sharing our experience is that the reader will be provoked to address the disturbing and often distressing front line decisions that arise in the practice of nephrology and transplant medicine. Feel free to contact the editor to convey your feelings whether they be outrage or concurrence. There are neither simple nor easy answers. Good luck!

REFERENCES

1. Brown v Bower, No. J86-0759(B) (SD Miss Dec 21, 1987).
2. Bower, John D., The Yangtze Syndrome: "Pull Man From Yangtze, Responsible for Man's Life", Contemporary Dialysis and Nephrology, February, Pages 30 & 37, 1989.
3. Orentlicher, David, Denying Treatment To The Noncompliant Patient. JAMA 1991:265: 1579-1582.
4. Bender W. Abraham Flexner--a crusader against medical maleducation. J Cancer Educ 1993;8:183-189.
5. Channel 4000, 1997 James Michener Dies at 90 Internet Broadcasting Systems, Inc.
6. Neumann ME. Novelist Michener dies after withdrawing from dialysis. Nephrol News Issues 1997;11:60-62.
7. Orenlicher D.1991 Denying treatment to the noncompliant patient. JAMA;266: 1579-1582.
8. Williams DI, Williams DJ, Williams IG, Unwin RJ, Griffiths MH, Miller RF. Presentation, pathology, and outcome of HIV associated renal disease in a specialist centre for HIV/AIDS. Sex Transm Infect 1998;74:179-184.
9. Rao TKS, Manis T, Friedman EA. Dismal prognosis despite maintenance hemodialysis in AIDS nephropathy and chronic uremia. Trans Amer Soc Artif Internal Organs 31:160-3, 1985.
10. Ahuja TS, Borucki M, Funtanilla M, Shahinian V, Hollander M, Rajaraman S. Is the prevalence of HIV-associated nephropathy decreasing? Am J Nephrol 1999;19:655-659.
11. Schneiderman LJ, Jecker NS, Jonsen AR. Medical futility: response to critiques. Ann Intern Med 1996;125:669-674.
12. Brody BA, Halevy A. Is futility a futile concept? J Med Philos 1995;20:123-144.
13. Caesar N. It's OK to ignore referral bans in certain cases, HCFA indicates.anag Care 1999 Feb;8:55-56.
14. Davis JP. Fraud and abuse. Understanding the Stark II proposed regulations. Healthc Financ Manage. 1998 Apr;52:65-69.
15. Garg PP, Frick KD, Diener-West M, Powe NR. Effect of the ownership of dialysis facilities on patients' survival and referral for transplantation. N Engl J Med 1999;341: 1653-1660.
16. Agodoa LY, Wolfe RA, Port FK. Reuse of dialyzers and clinical outcomes: fact or fiction. Am J Kidney Dis 1998;32(6 Suppl 4):S88-S92.
17. Collins AJ, Ma JZ, Constantini EG, Everson SE. Dialysis unit and patient characteristics associated with reuse practices and mortality: 1989-1993. J Am Soc Nephrol 1998; 9:2108-2117.
18. Friedman EA. ESRD therapy: An American success story. JAMA 1996, 275:1118-1122.
19. El Sayed NM, Gomatos PJ, Beck-Sague CM, Dietrich U, von Briesen H, Osmanov S, Esparza J, Arthur RR, Wahdan MH, Jarvis WR. Epidemic transmission of human immunodeficiency virus in renal dialysis centers in Egypt. J Infect Dis 2000;181:91-97.
20. Wreghitt TG. Blood-borne virus infections in dialysis units--a review. Rev Med Virol 1999;9(2):101-109
21. Purgus R, Tamalet C, Poignard P, Spire B, George F, Robert A, Olmer M. Long-term

nonprogressive human immunodeficiency virus-1 infection in a kidney allograft recipient. Transplantation 1998;66:1384-1386.

22. Hooi LS. Human immunodeficiency virus infection in recipients of living unrelated donor renal transplants--a report of 4 cases. Med J Malaysia 1993;48:232-235.

23. Simonds RJ, Holmberg SD, Hurwitz RL, Coleman TR, Bottenfield S, Conley LJ, Kohlenberg SH, Castro KG, Dahan BA, Schable CA, et al. Transmission of human immunodeficiency virus type 1 from a seronegative organ and tissue donor. N Engl J Med 1992;326:726-732.

24. Fellner CH, Schwartz SH.. Altruism in disrepute. Medical versus public attitudes toward the living organ donor. N Engl J Med. 1971;284:582-585.

25. Thiel G. Emotionally related living kidney donation: pro and contra.Nephrol Dial Transplant 1997;12(9):1820-1824.

26. Said MR, Curtis JJ. Living unrelated renal transplantation: progress and potential. J Am Soc Nephrol 1998;9:2148-2152.

27. Binet I, Bock AH, Vogelbach P, Gasser T, Kiss A, Brunner F, Thiel G. Outcome in emotionally related living kidney donor transplantation. Nephrol Dial Transplant 1997; 12:1940-1948.

28. Kjellstrand CM., Logan G: Racial, sexual and age inequalities in chronic dialysis. Nephron 1987;45:257-263.

29. Craft PP. Charles Drew: dispelling the myth. South Med J 1992;85:1236-1240, 1246.

30. Ayanian JZ, Cleary PD, Weissman JS, Epstein AM. The effect of patients' preferences on racial differences in access to renal transplantation. N Engl J Med 1999;341: 1661-1669.

31. Roberts KY. Black American attitudes toward organ donation and transplantation. J Natl Med Assoc 1988;80:1121, 1123-1124, 1126.

32. Siminoff LA, Arnold R. Increasing organ donation in the African-American community: altruism in the face of an untrustworthy system. Ann Intern Med 1999;130:607-609.

33. American community to provide organs for transplantation. Mt Sinai J Med 1999;66:273-276.

34. Arnason WB. Directed donation. The relevance of race. Hastings Cent Rep 1991 Nov-Dec;21:13-19.

35. Friedman EA. Advanced glycsoylated end products and hyperglycemia in the pathogenesis of diabetic complications. Diabetes Care 1999;22 Supplement 2:B65-B71.

36. Frishberg Y, Feinstein S, Drukker A. Living unrelated (commercial) renal transplantation in children. J Am Soc Nephrol 1998;9:1100-1103.

37. Cohen B, Persijn GG, Vanrenterghem Y. Commerce in transplantation: how does it affect European legislation? Clin Transplant 2000;14:28-31.

38. Orwell George, Animal Farm : A Fairy Story May 1996, 50th Anniversary Edition, Harcourt Brace, Boston.

39. Pageaux GP, Michel J, Coste V, Perney P, Possoz P, Perrigault PF, Navarro F, Fabre JM, Domergue J, Blanc P, Larrey D. Alcoholic cirrhosis is a good indication for liver transplantation, even for cases of recidivism. Gut 1999;45(3):421-426.

40. Fabrega E, Crespo J, Casafont F, De las Heras G, de la Pena J, Pons-Romero F. Alcoholic recidivism after liver transplantation for alcoholic cirrhosis. J Clin Gastroenterol 1998;26:204-206.

41. Glover JJ, Moss AH. Rationing dialysis in the United States: possible implications of capitated systems. Adv Ren Replace Ther 1998;5:341-349.

42. Nilstun T, Ohlsson R.1995 Should health care be rationed by age? Scand J Soc Med; 23:81-84.

43. Hestin D, Frimat L, Hubert J, Renoult E, Huu TC, Kessler M.1994 Renal transplantation in patients over sixty years of age.Clin Nephrol;42(4):232-236.

44. Morris GE, Jamieson NV, Small J, Evans DB, Calne R.1991 Cadaveric renal transplantation in elderly recipients: is it worthwhile? Nephrol Dial Transplant;6:887-892.

45. Lynn J, Teno JM, Phillips RS, Wu AW, Desbiens N, Harrold J, Claessens MT, Wenger N, Kreling B, Connors AF Jr. Perceptions by family members of the dying experience of older and seriously ill patients. SUPPORT Investigators. Study to Understand Prognoses and Preferences for Outcomes and Risks of Treatments. Ann Intern Med 1997;126:97-106.

46. Wolfe J, Grier HE, Klar N, Levin SB, Ellenbogen JM, Salem-Schatz S, Emanuel EJ, Weeks JC. Symptoms and suffering at the end of life in children with cancer. N Engl J Med 2000;342:326-333.

47. Ventafridda V, Ripamonti C, De Conno F, Tamburini M, Cassileth BR. Symptom prevalence and control during cancer patients' last days of life. J Palliat Care 1990;6:7-11.

48. Lederberg MS. Disentangling ethical and psychological issues--a guide for oncologists. Acta Oncol 1999;38:771-779.

Kolibri 360 GmbH
Ferdinand-Jühlke-Straße 7
99095 Erfurt, Deutschland
produktsicherheit@kolibri360.de